ENDORSEMENTS

Mike Arnold has unfolded in this book often hidden truths that most see, but few dare to say. His writing and perceptions are much like him as a person – honest, clear and forthcoming. You are a better person for having come in contact with this faithful servant of God.

Peter C. Spencer, *executive producer, Return to the Hiding Place*

UPRISING will challenge you to the core. Truth is, it's easier to sit back and watch and wait. It takes a man or woman with conviction and courage to go to battle; a person who knows we win in the end but recognizes that we are in the fight, and desires to be equipped for victory. Mike Arnold is a man who is most definitely in the battle, and his teaching and illustrations will help empower you to join him and countless others in raising the victory flag!

Duke Jonietz, *founder of Transformation: A City Reaching Ministry*

Mike has presented a solid "Way of Life," even unto death and beyond in this solid display of theology (though easy to read and comprehend), more clearly defined as "Practical Theology." I am buying this book to put for sale at our church and recommend this scholarly, practical work to anyone who might think they have all their round pegs in the round holes.

Dr. Bobby W. Leggett, *Senior Pastor, Trinity Lutheran Church*

Mike, I believe your book (and God's word in it) is the key to unlocking the written word. The key to free so many from bondage and hardship. The key to bring churches in alignment with God's vision. The key to unlocking His one true vision. The key that everyone can hold and use. The key that will bring understanding, enlightenment and peace to a world that is searching for its own identity. UPRISING is the key to the gate of God's Kingdom here on earth. Everyone is searching for the answer and wanting to see the light. I believe the search is over; our destiny is awaiting!

Dr. Craig Onstott, *founder of Nikao Wellness*

The message in this book is simple, straightforward, powerful and applicable. It teams with spiritual testosterone and will excite and inspire any man that reads it. Women will be awakened by the warrior within them and their call will crystallize. Young people will be able finally make sense of this "church thing" and advance the Kingdom of God in their generation, perhaps like no generation before them. Read. See. Do. Rejoice!

Charles E. Flowers, *Senior Pastor, Faith Outreach Center Intl.,*
President, The Gathering of Pastor and Leaders,
President, The San Antonio Association of Churches

UPRISING sounds a clarion call for the church to wake-up! Biblically sound and right on time, UPRISING casts a vision that we are responsible for seeing our world transformed – one disciple at a time, to hasten our Lords' return. This book personally motivated me!

Dr. Charles Robinson, *founder, W.I.S.E. Ministries*
Executive coach, CEO, author, and speaker

If the King's children knew who they were, they would engage their world, their culture, their communities, their families and themselves in an entirely new way. This book will help remove the blindness and restore the connection to royal authority that has been stolen.

J. Loren Norris, *author, keynote speaker, executive leadership coach*

I love this book and think it should be mandatory reading! Relevant, uncomplicated, and empowering, Mike has captured the heart of the Lord with a message that resonates across all generations regardless of denomination or upbringing. Clear and concise, presenting biblically-based truths, UPRISING will cause you to look again at your true identity in Christ and call you to action. It is the message of the LORD, and is as relevant today as it was when Christ walked this earth. Love won that day, the day of the cross, and we could all take a pointer or two from that.

Steven Young, *CEO and co-founder, Kingdom Generation Ministries*

UPRISING

Time for Christians to Rise and Shine

Second Edition

Mike Arnold

NP
NIKAO
PRESS

UPRISING: Time for Christians to Rise and Shine
Second Edition

ISBN-13: 978-0-9976318-0-7
ISBN-10: 0-9976318-0-5

The official website for this book is found at www.ChristianUprising.org.

Published by

NIKAO PRESS
1841 Tejas Trail
Blanco, TX 78606

FIRST EDITION (entitled UPRISING: Time for Christians to Stop Waiting and Start Winning)
© 2011 by Mike Arnold

SECOND EDITION
© 2016 by Mike Arnold

To M.K. – a father, forerunner, and pillar in the Kingdom. Thank you for your heroic commitment to calling the Body back to God's original intent.

Those who NIKAO (conquer, carry off the victory) will inherit all things.

Revelation 21:7

CONTENTS

ACKNOWLEDGEMENTS

I could not have written this book without the influence of some very important people in my life. I would like to acknowledge and thank:

John Ofoegbu, my dearly departed friend and spiritual father, for your trust, encouragement and edification. You led me to take this message to an international platform and helped open my eyes to the real-world reality of God's Kingdom come. As a father of the spiritual awakening in Nigeria that is recorded in this book, you lived a humble life that God exalted to change the world.

Dr. Peter Spencer, for your life-changing teaching, absolute trust in me, and ongoing example of selfless service. Your gentle encouragement helped me escape the prison of legalism, and your superior intellect and mind-boggling giftedness – combined with genuine humility – continue to compel me to excellence.

Steven Young, the first man I ever met whom I can rightly call a prophet of God. Your enthusiasm is electric and your prayers deeply felt.

Many friends, including Dr. Craig Onstott, Sandy Ingersoll, Wayne Marcy, Dr. Bobby Leggett, Dennis Bonnet and Rob Wayne, who have blessed me in so many ways.

My beautiful wife and incredible children, for sticking with me during all the ups and downs. It's been one heck of a journey, and I could never have done it without your unflinching love, support and faith. Second only to my relationship with God through Jesus Christ, you are my greatest blessings in this life.

All who have served as sounding boards, crash-test dummies and critics as I've worked to shape and polish this message. Your feedback has sharpened this message and made me a better man.

Finally, my late grandmother Mary Peters, for introducing me to a real relationship with the Living God, and demonstrating for me how to finish strong and emerge victorious over even the greatest tribulation.

INTRODUCTION

Looking back at my lifetime as a Christian, I'm amazed at how much of the Bible I used to skip over. I never did this intentionally, mind you, but when a passage didn't fit into my little box of theological understanding, I would think *well, I guess I don't understand that one…* and move on.

This was especially true for all the decades I was a die-hard member of a tradition-bound denomination. I trusted that the long-ago founder of that order, and its modern professional pastors, knew all there was to know about God and His Word, and if they didn't teach me a passage or principle, then it was either over my head, irrelevant, or intended only for Christians who lived 2000 years ago. They were the designated Holy Men, after all, to whom I'd outsourced my burden of spiritual understanding.

Many things blew right past me. Things like *we are more than conquerors* and *the gates of hell will not prevail against (us)* were somewhat inspirational but utterly impractical.

Jesus saying, "My sheep know My voice," was metaphorical – you know, like all those parables He used to tell about seeds and grapes and such.

Doing greater works than Jesus and *having faith to move mountains* were long-dead promises, along with all that stuff about miracles, healings and having authority over demons.

It sure would have been cool to live back in those days, I'd think. *Too bad none of that stuff happens today.*

Looking back, this selective listening of Scripture stunted me spiritually in many ways. Because all that "cool stuff" stopped happening so long ago, I had no basis for relating to the characters in the Bible. How *could* I relate to them? I mean, they actually heard God's voice, were used by Him to do amazing things, and got to see His power on display. What foreign concepts today!

Skipping over all the juicy stuff also subconsciously enabled me to skip over all the hard stuff, too. Like *trust in the Lord with all your heart; don't store up for yourself treasures on earth; don't worry about you will eat, drink or wear; it's more blessed to give than to receive;* and so on. You know how our minds work; I never really said it, but underlying my approach to faith was the thought that *if God doesn't do all that extreme stuff anymore, why should I?*

I'd marvel at the pastor's stories of sharing Christ with the person on the airplane or in the grocery store. To me that was as impossibly heroic as hitting a grand slam in the Major Leagues. *Good thing I'm supporting this guy's work,* I'd think, *because there's no way I could ever do that!*

I'm going to stop here and ask you a question. Now, you don't have to tell anyone your answer, but I do want you to think about it for a bit, and be honest ....

Do you relate to this?

My suspicion is, if you're like most Christians today, you probably do. Don't feel bad, you have to start somewhere. At least you're engaging the Word of God and thinking about it, and you haven't given up yet!

If you do relate to this, you most likely also relate to what I always felt deep inside: *There's got to be more to it than this!*

I believe this is the case with the majority of Christians around the world. We see people of other religions, which we know in our hearts are false faiths, blowing themselves up for what they believe in. We hear about Christians in some parts of the world willingly facing death to advance the cause of Christ. We hear rumors of *real miracles* still happening, and we may know of folks who are "on fire for the Lord." *And we want more! We want all that God has to offer!* But it always seems just out of reach.

My dear reader, I pray that is all about to change for you.

The good news is, whether or not their meaning has been unlocked to you yet, those "skipped over" passages and principles are still there, just waiting to burst out and bring new energy to your life and faith.

The Bible says people perish for lack of vision,[1] and that's exactly what's happened. Christians today have lost sight of God's vision for mankind, and we – and the world – are perishing as a result.

Thank God the flip-side can also be said: With proper vision people flourish! Truth brings life, freedom and power.

Jesus came to share and demonstrate a clear and specific vision with mankind: *It is our calling and destiny to bring God's Kingdom to earth as it is in Heaven, in a final uprising of His sons and daughters, and the end won't come till we are done.*

This is God's vision. In it we find our true identity, purpose and destiny. Embracing it gives hope to the hopeless, meaning to the downcast and purpose to the adrift. It is the one vision that will unite us as a Body and draw the world to Christ.

In sharing this vision and setting the work in motion, Jesus sparked a movement that transformed the world. Yet over the millennia since He walked the earth, His true vision has all but vanished. As it has, so has the zeal of His people and

---

[1] Proverbs 29:18

their impact on the world.

The Apostle Paul said our life experience is like a race. Imagine runners gathering at the starting line, hearing *ready...set...go!...* and then taking off full-speed, headlong down the track. If they are clueless as to the intended course and finish line, what's the use? Each can run as fast as he can and yet accomplish ... what? In the same way, as Christians have lost sight of our God-intended course and finish line, we've become less and less impactful and relevant in the world, and we've lost our determination to win.

It is my purpose in this book to re-establish the vision that Jesus Christ passionately proclaimed at every opportunity, that Paul and the other original apostles taught and worked towards, and that drove and empowered the early church.

I am calling for a shift in the paradigm of Christian identity, purpose and destiny, back to the vision of empowerment and victory Christ so clearly imparted: *God eagerly desires to pour His full power through us – even today! – when we cease from our own works and allow Him to fully guide our steps. We are not weak in the face of the enemy! Our victory is certain! We need to stop waiting and start winning! It's time to rise and shine!*

This book will establish the pre-eminence of this vision throughout Scripture; it is indeed God's original intent for this world and all mankind. It will look at possible reasons we have lost it. It will further spell out how we can reclaim it, and what that will mean for us and the world when we do. Finally, it will outline the practical paradigm for delivering final victory that was modeled by Jesus and the first apostles.

This message has been right there in God's Word, crystal clear, under our noses, from the first day Adam walked the earth, and yet for many reasons in modern times we've failed to see it.

For me to "get it," the Lord has had to reveal it to me piece by piece, over many years, through my own studies and many wise teachers. You may not have to leave a stodgy denomination to see it, but I did. It has, in many ways, been a hard and narrow path.

And it's been well worth it! God has allowed my faith to grow beyond my comprehension. I've seen and experienced things I had thought stopped 2000 years ago. My relationship with my Father has grown deep and vibrant, and He's used me to advance His Kingdom in ways I would have never thought possible. I have found peace that surpasses understanding, and abiding joy in the face of some very difficult circumstances. I can say with first-hand certainty: *Our God is who He says He is, and all His promises are true, even today!*

In recent years, I've been blessed with many opportunities to present this vision publicly to quite a few people, and have seen it stir up remarkable, universal enthusiasm and impact. From unchurched teenage boys to established pastors, and from successful American businessmen and celebrities to Third World "commoners," it's obvious to me that *God made mankind with an inborn hunger for His original vision, and we know it when we finally see it.*

This is a message that unites and inspires, calling believers to action, excellence and bold outreach. It brings new clarity to Scripture and breathes life into key portions of the Bible frequently skipped over. It calls out the deepest, inborn, spiritual elements of mankind, while unlocking the mystery of life's purpose and kindling faith, hope and passion.

This is a long-lost message, and we need it now more than ever. *God delivering total victory through His sons and daughters is the original – and ongoing – intent of our loving Father.*

As I have applied this vision in my own ministry, I have seen nothing short of genuine revival result. I believe that, as you dig into this book and do your own research, you will experience the same results.

Because this vision restores light to the Word of God – such that even the most familiar Sunday School stories take on vibrant, deeper meaning – I am challenged to map out a simple, straightforward presentation that does not veer into all sorts of meaningful but distracting rabbit trails. So there are many important topics I will touch on only enough to make the point. It is my hope that, after reading this, you will explore those rabbit trails on your own, equipped with this new, clear, illuminating lens.

Please note that when you fully grasp this vision, you may find it stands in sharp contrast to many habits and teachings we have come to embrace. If you're like me, when this happens you'll want to do your own research. Please, don't "just trust me" on all this![2] Pray for the Spirit of God to confirm or refute it. Search your heart and see if it resonates with the deepest intuition of your spirit-man. I'm not asking you to join me on some fantastic exercise in constructing a Frankenstein theology, with a bit here and a bit there, and a bit of "way too complicated" thrown in.

Instead, I'm asking you to take the Word of God at face

---

[2] I am not setting out here to write an academic theological textbook. My purpose instead is to present God's vision with simplicity and clarity, for the "common man," as Christ did. I include more than 400 footnotes along the way for all you skeptical/intellectual types, like me, who feel led to dig deeper.

value. God *really does* love us enough to make His message perfectly clear. It's not that complicated! Jesus, *the Word made flesh*, was a blue collar carpenter, not The Riddler. He said the Kingdom of God belongs to those who approach Him with the sincere teachability of little children. The parables, teachings and examples found over and over again in Scripture are in perfect harmony and all point, with crystal clarity, to one consistent, incredible vision of God's victorious intent for mankind. There's no need to skip over any Bible passage again!

Jesus said the way to life is hard and narrow, and as you awaken to God's true vision, you may face a challenging time. Because we perish for lack of vision, and satan comes to "kill, steal and destroy," you need to know that our mortal enemy doesn't want you to see it.

Let me encourage you to be strong and courageous – the light at the other end is well worth it! As you dig into and embrace God's vision for your life, those inner stirrings you've felt – *that there's more to being a child and heir of the One, True, Living God than what you're currently experiencing* – are about to be unleashed.

I pray this book is used by God to awaken His sons and daughters so we will once again rise up, embrace our true identity, seize our victorious purpose and boldly pursue the wonderful destiny He intends for us.

Praise God, I feel a new Reformation coming on … a genuine Christian uprising!

A personal note to my "end times" friends

A mentor of mine says, "God loves FAT people!" He uses that as an attention getter before explaining that FAT is an acronym for Faithful, Available and Teachable. He's right; teachability is a key personality trait of everyone who has a passion for pursuing truth.

This book is not anti-anyone. Instead, it is my best effort to present a *positive* statement of what I believe is the original intent of our loving God. It just happens that some elements of modern "end times" teachings sharply conflict with this. The Word tells us, "Whatever you do, work at it with all your heart,"[3] and I simply am doing that here. I have been called to proclaim the biblical vision of victory. Doing so *with all my heart* requires I address head-on these parts of this popular teaching, and pull no punches. I must do this because I believe the way some of these teachings are interpreted and applied by many, it sends a discouraging, defeatist message to the Body of Christ which is irreconcilably contradictory to God's true vision for us. In the one chapter I dedicate to this subject, late in the book, I endeavor to do so with utmost respect and humility. My intent is not to tear down, but to build up the Body of Christ by calling us to healthy dialogue, so together we may "test the spirits."

In my years of discipling teenage boys, I've taught them a real man is quick to use two difficult phrases: "I don't know" and "I was wrong." These phrases are readily spoken by those who are teachable and avoided like plague by those who are not. I openly admit: *There are things I believe that simply aren't true, and things that are true I don't know yet.*

---

[3] Col. 3:23 NIV

Every honest man would admit the same.

Many good men of God, including dear friends whom I look up to and admire, have embraced and invested themselves in the currently popular method of teaching about the "end times." To these men, I must say this book is in no way intended to call into question your contributions to the advancement of God's Kingdom. Honest and faithful people can disagree on fundamental things.

As much as I hate to say it, the message of victory and these defeatist teachings can't both be right, and *I do not see these conflicting interpretations as an area of freedom.* Instead, I view it as parallel to the conflict between the apostles Paul and Peter in the days of the early church.[4] That is an amazing story of reluctant boldness meeting humble teachability. They were amazing men.

Peter must have been a personal hero of Paul's. He was a leader among the original twelve, spent three very close years with the incarnate Christ as one of the inner circle of three, witnessed countless miracles, walked on water, and spent more than a month face-to-face with the resurrected Christ. Moreover, he was the first man to proclaim Jesus was the Messiah, and the first great evangelist after the coming of the Spirit at Pentecost.

In the other corner was Paul. He was a loner, late-comer, former persecutor of Christians, a Pharisee, and had the odd and unpopular task of preaching Christ to unwashed Gentiles in faraway lands.

There came a time when the entire assembly of leaders in Jerusalem believed new Gentile coverts must be

---

[4] Recorded in Acts 15 and Galatians 2.

circumcised. Their arguments were well-founded and forceful, such that even Paul's friend and mentor, Barnabas, agreed with them. The circumcision teaching was embraced by all and widely disseminated. *Yet Paul knew it was wrong.* Try as he might to shake the responsibility, he knew this was not an area of "freedom" – that folks couldn't be free to believe as they chose in this matter – but instead, as this issue spoke to the core identity of Christ and His followers, no error or confusion on the matter could be tolerated. And so the lone, late-coming, marginally-trusted, misunderstood ambassador to the unwashed had to travel to Jerusalem to present his case. He spoke the truth in love, boldly. Praise God the other leaders were FAT! They each presented their cases, then let the Spirit of God settle the matter. When He did, Peter and the other respected, passionate leaders on the other side rejoiced in the truth, with no hard feelings. They were *FAT*, thank God!

As brothers and sisters in Christ who are hungry for truth, I pray we will invite the Spirit of God to settle this matter. I realize I, like Paul, may not have the pop-theology "street creds" of those on the other side. Yet I pray pride, popularity and seminary diplomas don't matter, only the truth as revealed by God. And when He does reveal the truth, we can shake hands, rejoice and advance His Kingdom together in unity.

To see victory only when it is within the ken of the common herd is not the acme of excellence.

Sun Tzu – The Art of War

Chapter 1 – It's about winning

Revelation 3:20 is a verse commonly quoted in church: "Behold, I stand at the door and knock. If anyone hears My voice and opens the door, I will come in to him and dine with him, and he with Me." [5]

It is a powerful verse, summarizing the Good News of a real relationship with Jesus Christ for all who believe. The next verse, tied directly to this one, is even more powerful, wonderful and profound. It is in fact the most breathtaking promise of God to mankind. Yet it is rarely if ever quoted.

Before I quote it here, let me say that the typical English translation drains the power from the verse (which is one reason it's not commonly quoted or understood in its fullness). So I will insert the proper Greek word into the verse and then tell you what it means.[6]

Here it is: "To him who NIKAO I will grant to sit with Me

---

[5] NKJV

[6] All Greek definitions taken from Thayer and Smith Greek Lexicon, unless otherwise noted, as found at www.BibleStudyTools.com, which is a fantastic reference. A glossary of Greek words referenced in this book is included at the end.

on My throne, as I also NIKAO and sat down with My Father on His throne."

Even without knowing the meaning of NIKAO, this verse is stunning. The full weight of it is nearly impossible to comprehend. It says a *possible* outcome of our human experience is not simply to "go to heaven when we die," but instead *to sit on God's throne* – the throne over the universe.[7] It speaks directly to the big-picture purpose of this life, and our identity and destiny as God's children. (More on that later.)

To drive home the importance of this word, Jesus in fact said *seven times in a row*[8] that each element of our eternal inheritance is stored up for *those who NIKAO*. Later it is written outright, in black and white: "he who NIKAO shall inherit *all things*."[9] For followers of Christ who have an eternal hope, what is more important than grasping the meaning of this word?

Understanding NIKAO is the key to fully accessing the promises of God in our lives, fully appreciating the power and amazing grace of Christ's work, fully grasping the message of the Bible and, ultimately, attaining our promised inheritance.

Typically, NIKAO is translated as "overcome," and is taken to mean "endure" or "survive" – as in, "well, I *overcame* that darn sinus infection..." But that's *not* what it means. That is

---

[7] In Ephesians 1:21 (NIV) it says that Christ's throne is "far above all rule and authority, power and dominion, and every title that can be given, not only in the present age but also in the one to come." That's huge!

[8] Revelation Chapters 2-3. I find nothing else in Scripture Jesus repeated *seven times in a row* in one continuous monologue. Seven, of course, is the perfect number of God. "Numerologists" should have a field day with this!

[9] Revelation 21:7 NKJV, with original Greek word inserted in the proper place, *emphasis added*.

a watered-down translation that sucks the life and meaning from the Word.

NIKAO means, "To conquer, to carry off the victory." Properly translated, Revelation 3:21 says, "To him who (conquers, carries off the victory) I will grant to sit with Me on My throne, as I also (conquered, carried off the victory) and sat down with My Father on His throne."[10]

Yes, there is common teaching that the Christian life is a victorious life. But the victory spoken of is *personal* victory over sin, addiction, despair, guilt, shame, doubt, etc. Not to diminish personal victory – praise God for it, it is absolutely a key component of God's power and love towards us – but *that's not what this verse is talking about*. It clearly states our job is to NIKAO in the same way that Jesus did.

How did Jesus NIKAO? The Apostle John, author of the book of Revelation, wrote in 1 John 5: 4-5, "For everyone born of God NIKAO *the world*. This is the victory that has NIKAO *the world*, even our faith. Who is it that NIKAO *the world*? Only he who believes that Jesus is the Son of God."[11]

The message of the Bible, and the meaning of NIKAO, is not just about overcoming obstacles or conquering our personal problems. Rather, it is our assignment, our very destiny, *to conquer the world for God*.

Even as you read this, I bet a small pinprick of light is starting to shine in your mind. As you begin to grasp it, it sort of takes your breath away. Could it be? Could "We are more than conquerors," and "The gates of hell will not prevail against (us),"[12] actually have real meaning for us

---

[10] To make the difference clear between "endure" and "conquer," consider this: The French *endured* World War II; Americans *conquered*! Big difference!
[11] NIV, *Greek insertions and emphasis added*.
[12] Matthew 16:18

today, after all?

The Random House Dictionary has "to gain the victory" as the definition for another English word: to *win*.

Revelation 3:21 is about winning *in the big picture*, about conquering for Christ. It says there is a conflict at hand, an objective to achieve and an opponent to vanquish. It says it is not our job to sit idly by, mark time, tread water, or even "do our best" until God does whatever He's going to do – it is *our job* to carry off the victory, *victory over the world*. It says we were made by God to be winners, with a destiny to rule. It says global victory for the Kingdom of God, in the here and now, is a do-able deal!

And it says God's entire eternal inheritance is stored up for those who carry off this victory.

This changes things a bit, don't you think?

Of course, a little information can be a dangerous thing. Just like Peter hacking off that fellow's ear in the Garden of Gethsemane in an effort to "save" Jesus,[13] well-intentioned Christians have long been trying to do things their way, for God, and that never works. Before we can seize our victorious destiny, there are quite a few things we need to re-learn about who we are in Christ, how He desires to work through us, what victory looks like in God's eyes, and how we are all to function as a Body. Only then can we objectively see what we've been doing and thinking wrong, and embrace the battle plan God has given us for victory.

KEY POINTS: The Bible calls followers of Jesus Christ to conquer the world.

---

[13] John 18:10

Paul told the Ephesian believers that he continually prayed for them to receive the spirit of wisdom and revelation,* so they could comprehend the identity, purpose and destiny that was theirs in Christ. I pray the same for you. If your mind is spinning right now, if you're knitting your brow in skepticism, or if you simply don't know what to think, I encourage you to take some time right now to "be still" and pray the Lord will reveal His truth to you in a new and exciting way.

* Ephesian 1:15-23. I put the entire reference here because it summarizes the point of this book:

"Therefore I also, after I heard of your faith in the Lord Jesus and your love for all the saints, do not cease to give thanks for you, making mention of you in my prayers: that the God of our Lord Jesus Christ, the Father of glory, may give to you the spirit of wisdom and revelation in the knowledge of Him, the eyes of your understanding being enlightened; *that you may know what is the hope of His calling, what are the riches of the glory of His inheritance in the saints, and what is the exceeding greatness of His power toward us who believe, according to the working of His mighty power which He worked in Christ when He raised Him from the dead and seated Him at His right hand in the heavenly places, far above all principality and power and might and dominion, and every name that is named, not only in this age but also in that which is to come. And He put all things under His feet, and gave Him to be head over all things to the church, which is His body, the fullness of Him who fills all in all."* (NKJV, emphasis added.)

Winning is not a sometime thing, it's an all time thing. You don't win once in a while, you don't do things right once in a while, you do them right all the time. Winning is habit. Unfortunately, so is losing.

Vince Lombardi

Chapter 2 – What does it mean to win?

I wish I didn't have to include this chapter, but I do. In my years of working with young people, I've found many lack fundamental understanding of what it means *to win*. I don't know if this is epidemic in our culture, but there certainly is reason to believe it is. If a person lacks an understanding of *winning* then the whole point of this book – and, I would submit, the main point of *The Book* – will blow right past him.

Try it yourself. Ask a young person today what it means to be "a winner." Odds are he'll tell you that if you *try your hardest* and are *a good person*, then you're a *winner*. Seriously, that's what our culture tells them – and pounds into their heads with sports leagues that don't keep score, politically-correct rules that every player has to play in every game – no more benchwarmers! – and grading systems that reward effort over achievement.[14] (And we wonder why there are so many losers today?) The only one who benefits from this delusional definition of "winning" is our enemy.

Don't get me wrong. Trying hard and being good are fantastic character traits. But these qualities have nothing to do with *winning*.

It's not rocket science: A winner is *someone who wins*. What does it mean to win? It means to accomplish the objectives of the competition or conflict first or better than your opponent. It means *to gain the victory*.[15] A winner is someone who NIKAOs. Period, end of definition.

What winning means specifically in a given competition is tied to the objectives of the endeavor. In a race, winning means crossing the finish line first. In football it means scoring more points than the other team. In an election it's getting more votes than the other guy. Good people who try hard sometimes win and sometimes lose. Those qualities are irrelevant to the fundamental definition of *winner*.

And – hold on to your hat – if you don't accomplish the objective of a competition or conflict first or better than your opponent – if you don't NIKAO – you are ... a *loser*.[16] This is

---

[14] I'm just being real here. Please don't read too much into what I'm saying. I absolutely agree there is evil in the current "win at all costs" mindset that too often many coaches and parents pound into kids in sports programs that do keep score. And I know programs such as UpWards Sports, that don't keep score, do a lot of good and impact youth in a positive way. I do believe, however, it is not good in the end if we swing the pendulum too far back away from the "winning is the only thing" mindset. We need to be careful not to replace one extreme with the other, because while rightly throwing out the ego-centric hyper-competitiveness, we've also deleted the definition of winning from the minds of too many young people. As with most things, the proper course is a narrow path.

[15] Dictionary.com Unabridged. Random House, Inc.

[16] Random House Dictionary, definition 2b: LOSER – "a person who has failed at a particular activity."

not an insult or a value judgment; it is a fact.

Board game instructions generally get straight to the point. What's always the first heading? OBJECTIVE OF THE GAME (or something similar). The instructions for Monopoly don't beat around the bush. The makers of that game have more than 75 years' experience communicating how to play. They start with this: "HOW DO I WIN?"[17] That's as to-the-point as it gets. For any competition, for any endeavor where there's an opponent, that's the first thing one must know: *How do I win?* Without this, no other instruction – nothing else about the game – makes any sense.

Broadening the discussion a bit, there are some key factors involved in winning. I discern three: natural giftedness, determination and chance. To win most competitions all three must come together in some combination.[18]

Natural giftedness is vital. I don't care how determined or lucky I am, I am not going to beat Michael Phelps in a swim meet. Sports doctors say his body is uniquely designed, almost freakishly so, for speed in the pool. Michael Jordan was made for basketball, Lance Armstrong for cycling, Warren Buffet for business and George Patton for combat command. There is a sense of purpose or destiny at play here.

These people, who were seemingly designed by their Creator for excellence in their particular field, would likely have never accomplished as much in life had they not found *where they belonged*. What if Michael Phelps' mom had never

---

[17] MONOPOLY is a trademark of Hasbro, Pawtucket, RI 02862
[18] Of course there are exceptions to this. There are games of chance, like dice or roulette, and there are games where chance is eliminated, like chess. But if you think about it, the end result of most competitions is decided by all three of these factors in some combination.

let him go swimming, and instead forced him into gymnastics or piano? We likely would have never heard his name. He may have been moderately successful due to the force of his determination, but he wouldn't be the best in the world. Finding where you belong, what you were made for, is vital. The world is no doubt full of undiscovered talent. What if God's gift to baseball (or music, or law ... fill in the blank here) lives in a Third World village and never hears of it, and instead languishes in poverty? That is true tragedy – and once again, the enemy wins.

Natural giftedness (and, accordingly, finding where you belong), however, is not enough. We all know sad stories of people who were naturally gifted at something but simply didn't apply themselves to it. I am reminded of the childhood story of the Tortoise and the Hare. In that fabled race, the rabbit had all the giftedness, yet through his arrogance and laziness – and his opponent's determination – the naturally un-gifted tortoise won the race.

Compared to the hare, the tortoise had only a miniscule amount of natural giftedness: he had four functional legs and could propel himself forward, and that was about it. What he had in abundance was *determination*. When a matter is determined, it is settled, it is done. Determination is the resolute fixing of our will upon a given outcome. It is embracing victory as destiny.

A determined man never *tries*. He *trains* and he *does*. Attempts that come short are considered lessons to build upon towards ultimate success. As a wise man once said, "Do or do not, there is no *try*."[19] What does "try" mean,

---

[19] Actually that was Yoda in the film *The Empire Strikes Back*, but it's definitely a wise saying.

anyway? It is a pre-set excuse for failure. It is an easy way out. It is saying, "well, gee, I'm going to apply marginal effort, and I will accept failure if what I do isn't good enough." *Trying* is resignation. When we *try* against a determined enemy, the enemy always prevails.

One important component of determination is often overlooked: *Winners know how to win.* Their determination is properly focused on the true purpose of the endeavor. Winners discern the meaningful objectives from all possible distractions, they know how to achieve them, they fix their will on those objectives, and they are masters of the tools available for this purpose. This may sound like a given but it's far from it. Take chess for example. It's been many years since I lost a face-to-face chess game. I am naturally gifted in analytical skills and dead set on victory, and there is no "chance" in the game. But that's not enough. I also know what the game is all about: *It is about killing the other player's king,* period. My opponents – including some gifted players – almost always seem to get caught up in other agendas: taking this piece, protecting that one. Their determination is misguided. I have spent considerable time learning the movements of each chess piece and how it can kill the king, alone or in combination with any other piece. At the chess board I am single-minded and focused – not on the "game," not on any lesser piece, not on the other player, only on winning; on the ultimate goal of killing my opponent's king. That is the true purpose of a chess player.

A determined competitor is always hopeful. Regardless of how much the chips are down he sees a path to victory. Vince Lombardy famously said, "Winners never quit and quitters never win." I remember watching the great quarterback Roger Staubach captain the Dallas Cowboys when I was a boy. What I remember most clearly is this: No matter how far Dallas was down, and no matter how little time was left on the clock, it seemed Staubach could always find a way to pull it off. The Cowboys would make one heroic march down the field in just a few quick plays, score, do an onside kick to compel a fumble, recover it, and score again. Basketball is famous for bringing out the last-minute best in a winning team. The late San Antonio, Texas, sportscaster Dan Cook famously quipped, "The opera ain't over till the fat lady sings." It is this reality that keeps sports fans on the edge of their seats waiting till the final buzzer. Winners never give up!

One who is determined embraces the *identity* of Winner, and will do whatever is required to manifest that identity. She will train with passion and focus, eagerly accept teaching and correction, enter competition fully prepared, accept a failure as a lesson learned yet just a temporary setback and, ultimately, *win*. One who is determined has courage, focus and iron will. In a match of equally gifted competitors, where chance is not a significant factor, victory will go to the one who wants it the most, the one who is most determined.

A champion knows he is a champion. A winner *wins* and will not accept losing. Determination combined with natural giftedness, where identity meets destiny, is an unstoppable force. In my opinion, the opening soliloquy of the classic movie Patton, as the great general seeks to impart his spirit to his men in preparation for combat duty, is the perfect expression of the heart, intensity and single-mindedness of a true winner:

> Now, I want you to remember that no bastard
> ever won a war by dying for his country. He won
> it by making the other poor dumb bastard die for
> his country. Men, all this stuff you've heard about

America not wanting to fight, wanting to stay out of the war, is a lot of horse dung. Americans traditionally love to fight. All <u>real</u> Americans love the sting of battle. When you were kids, you all admired the champion marble shooter, the fastest runner, the big league ball player, the toughest boxer. Americans love a winner and will not tolerate a loser. Americans play to win all the time. I wouldn't give a hoot in hell for a man who lost, and laughed. That's why Americans have never lost and will never lose a war. Because the very thought of losing is hateful to Americans.

Now, an Army is a team. It lives, eats, sleeps, fights as a team. This individuality stuff is a bunch of crap. The bilious bastards who wrote that stuff about individuality for the Saturday Evening Post don't know anything more about real battle than they do about fornicating.

We have the finest food and equipment, the best spirit and the best men in the world. You know, by God I actually pity those poor bastards we're going up against. By God, I do. We're not just going to shoot the bastards, we're going to cut out their living guts and use them to grease the treads of our tanks. We're going to murder those lousy Hun bastards by the bushel.

Now, some of you boys, I know, are wondering whether or not you'll chicken out under fire. Don't worry about it. I can assure you that you will all do your duty. The Nazis are the enemy. Wade into them. Spill *their* blood. Shoot *them* in the belly. When you put your hand into a bunch of goo that a moment before was your best friend's face, you'll know what to do.

Now there's another thing I want you to remember. I don't want to get any messages saying that we are holding our position. We're not holding anything. Let the Hun do that. We are advancing constantly and we're not interested in holding onto anything except the enemy. We're going to hold onto him by the nose and we're going to kick him in the ass. We're going to kick the hell out of him all the time and we're gonna go through him like crap through a goose.

There's one thing that you men will be able to say when you get back home. And you may thank God for it. Thirty years from now when you're sitting around your fireside with your grandson on your knee and he asks you what did you do in the great World War II, you won't have to say, "Well, I shoveled shit in Louisiana."

Alright now, you sons-of-bitches, you know how I feel. Oh, and I will be proud to lead you wonderful guys into battle – anytime, anywhere.

That's all. [20]

Within Patton was a fierce combination of natural giftedness with determination. His role as commanding general was not a job title, it was his identity, and he knew it early in life, with crystal clarity. He knew that annihilating the enemy was his purpose, and that total conquest was not an

[20] Taken from the movie *Patton*, produced in 1970 by Frank McCarthy, screenplay by Francis Ford Coppola and Edmund H. North. Note that this text is not a verbatim transcript of an actual Patton speech, but an abridged (and less vulgar!) version, faithfully condensed by the script writers.

assignment, it was his destiny. *And he delivered victory.* Thank God he was on the right side!

I would be slacking if I didn't at least mention the role that chance plays in winning, even though as you will see it has no bearing on the big-picture message of this book. Of course there are instances where a ball makes a bad hop, the dice don't cooperate, or the weather isn't right, and these things can certainly affect the score at the end of a game. No doubt the most naturally gifted, determined champion can lose an occasional match by random back luck. But in the end, as the impact of chance averages out over time, winners will always rise to the top. They may lose a battle but they will never lose the war. You simply can't stop true winners from winning. It is their destiny.

Giftedness, determination and chance. If I had to wager between three competitors who represented extreme examples of these three traits – one who is 100% naturally gifted, one who is 100% determined, and one who is 100% lucky – I'd lay it all down for the one with determination. In my studied opinion, that is the most important for us to possess. Without it, the other two traits are virtually worthless. The tortoise with a winner's heart will beat the lazy and prideful hare every time. More than anything else, this is what we, as a Body, must reclaim.

--

When we embrace God's true vision for mankind, we understand that our identity is His offspring and heirs, our purpose is to conquer the world for His Kingdom, and our destiny is to rule with Him for eternity as His victorious sons and daughters.

Embracing this vision is the key to unlocking the full

potential of our God-given gifts and truly unifying the Body. When we do, our hearts will once again beat with determination, and nothing – not even the gates of hell – will stand in our way.

KEY POINTS: Winning requires 1) Knowing the objective of the competition at hand (our purpose), 2) Having natural giftedness for the endeavor (akin to a sense of destiny), and 3) Being determined (embracing the identity of Winner).

As we dig into God's original vision for mankind, understanding the definition of winning is vital, because it is the destiny God has for us – not just that we "try hard" and are "good guys." He made us to be winners, and to accomplish a specific and amazing objective.

You can't hit a target you cannot see, and you cannot see a target you do not have.

Zig Ziglar

Chapter 3 - What is the objective?

A major, overarching theme of the Bible is ongoing competition or warfare. Good versus evil. Right versus wrong. Light versus darkness. Starting with satan's rebellion and ending with the ultimate victory of Christ – with all of the Bible, creation and *time itself* in between – if we miss this most fundamental point, we are oblivious indeed. We are at war.[21]

As the previous chapter made clear, it is foolish to engage in any competitive endeavor without a clear understanding of the objective of the competition. Who cares how fast you run a race if you're clueless about the course or the finish line?

Since we find ourselves in the midst of an overarching, life-or-death competition, and since every competition has an

---

[21] If this statement causes you any trouble, I encourage you to pause here, skip ahead and read Chapter 7 before continuing. Also it is vital to note that God is not "at war." Christ's victory is complete in the eternal realm. As I explain in coming chapters, He has allowed this conflict to continue on earth for our good, and to accomplish His eternal purposes. Again, *we* are at war, God is far above that. Our assignment is to manifest God's eternal victory on earth as it is in Heaven.

objective, what is it? What are we playing for? What is at stake? How do we win? When is it "game over"?

If we take Scripture as a God-given guidebook for understanding such things, what does *it* have to say?

I think the clearest and simplest way to answer this is to let Christ Himself do so. He understood the objective, worked towards it, and it was where He directed His prayers. If you don't think so – that is, if you think He was merely a curious historical figure with no real insight into the mind of God – then you may as well close the book now, because I base what I say here squarely on the words of Jesus Christ.

If you accept Christ's divinity, then turn with me to Matthew 6: 9-10, where He modeled how we should focus our prayers. He said, "This, then, is how you should pray: Our Father in heaven, hallowed be your name, *your Kingdom come, your will be done, on earth as it is in heaven.*"[22]

Jesus was never one for empty words or feel-good platitudes. It was not in His nature to communicate to us a meaningless objective with no chance of success. Jesus had insight into the Big Picture; all His words were strategic, specific and calculated. He wasn't chanting these words as part of some liturgy. When Jesus prayed, He set the gears of Heaven in motion!

I learned to recite "The Lord's Prayer" as a child and I can mindlessly rattle it off, and did so for most of my life with no real clue as to its meaning. This is unfortunate, because in its meaning we find a key to understanding Scripture, the Big Picture of God's original intent, and our own identity and eternal destiny. Get this and meaning will start to jump off the pages of your Bible as never before.

---

[22] NIV, *emphasis added.*

Here it is: Jesus prayed for, and set in motion, the coming of God's Kingdom to earth, as fully and completely it is in Heaven – one hundred percent!

Coming from "the end is near" mentality that seems prevalent in much of Christianity today, this is a dramatic paradigm shift, and I hope you're catching it. It is even more dramatic when we understanding the meaning of the Greek word we translate as "Kingdom." The word is BASILEIA, and it means the "royal power, kingship, dominion and rule" of God. *Jesus was praying for the royal power, kingship, dominion and rule of God to be established fully and completely over all of Creation.*

By praying *for* it, He also was implying that this was not yet a done deal; the full manifestation of God's Kingdom on earth is something that must still be accomplished. He was clearly stating that this is His, God's and – if we choose to align ourselves with them – *our* objective.

Here we come to an important juncture. Jesus is one who NIKAOd; a winner. He is not a quitter. If we do not believe that His stated objective will be accomplished, we are calling Him a quitter, a loser. I, for one, am not prepared to do that. I believe God's Kingdom *will* be established on earth as it is in Heaven – fully and completely. It is determined.

Of course I'm not basing all this on one Bible verse. (Remember, we're not building a Franken-theology here. I'm not asking you to "just trust me" because the theology is so "complex.") I simply chose to use Christ's own words as a familiar, common-ground starting point. I intend to show you that *the full establishment of God's Kingdom on earth* is indeed the primary, overarching message of the Bible.

Let's look at the facts. The word BASILEIA (*royal power,*

kingship, dominion and rule) of God or of Heaven appears 120 times in the Gospels.[23] By contrast, the phrase "born again" appears only once, when Jesus was talking in private to the Pharisee Nicodemas, when He said, "I tell you the truth, no one can see the Kingdom of God unless he is born again."[24] A few verses later He said, "I tell you the truth, no one can enter the Kingdom of God unless he is born of water and the Spirit." God's objective is clearly not just to get people "born again," *it's to get them to live under His royal power, kingship, dominion and rule.* These are indeed very different objectives.

Look in your Bible and you'll find that virtually every parable Jesus spoke of was about the Kingdom. In the parable of the four soils – which is pretty much the foundation of all outreach ministry – what is the seed Jesus spoke of? *The word of the Kingdom.*[25] Later in that same chapter, in the parable of the wheat and the tares, what is the seed? *Sons and daughters of the Kingdom.*[26]

What did Jesus say will be taught in every tribe and nation before the end comes? *The royal power, kingship, dominion and rule of God* – not just the message of salvation.[27] They are not the same message; salvation is but a subset of the full message of God's Kingdom, it is merely the entry point.

In the "Sermon on the Mount," which is the most comprehensive set of Jesus' nuts-and-bolts instructions to us recorded in Scripture, the heart of it says, "Seek first the BASILEIA of God and His righteousness."[28] Can it be clearer? The establishment of His Kingdom *is our primary*

---

[23] The first four books of the New Testament.
[24] John 3:3 NIV
[25] Matthew 13:19
[26] Matthew 13:38
[27] Matthew 24:14
[28] Matt 6:33

purpose; it's what we're supposed to seek as our Number One objective. In this passage, Jesus goes to the extent of saying that *we're supposed to focus so intently on advancing God's Kingdom that we don't worry about anything else, not even what we're going to eat, drink or wear.* In fact, God's promise to provide for our needs is tied directly to our seeking first His Kingdom – if we don't single-mindedly seek His royal power, kingship, dominion and rule, *then He's not obligated to provide for our needs*; if we do, He must.

The *first* paragraph of Acts says that before Jesus ascended – His last chance to impart to His apostles – He spent 40 days "speaking of the things pertaining to the BASILEIA of God."[29] The *last* paragraph of Acts says that Paul, after finally making it to Rome, spent his last two years "teaching about things pertaining to the BASILEIA of God."

Here's the clincher, if one is still needed: Do you know what Jesus claimed was the specific reason He was sent to earth by the Father? No, not "salvation." He said: "I must preach the BASILEIA of God to the other cities also, because *for this purpose I have been sent.*" Salvation is but a small part of that.

The first thing Jesus asked God for in His model prayer was for God's Kingdom to come, He spoke about it virtually every time He opened His mouth, He said the purpose of being "born again" is simply to *see* it, He claimed it was the purpose He came to earth, and He focused on it exclusively for the last period of time He spent with His apostles before leaving earth.

It's crystal clear and plain to see – no slicing and dicing needed, no seminary degree required: The full establishment of God's *royal power, kingship, dominion and rule* on earth was

---

[29] Acts 1:3 NKVJ, with proper Greek word inserted

the primary message and objective of Christ. *Bringing the Kingdom from Heaven to earth is the reason Christ came – not rescuing people from earth to Heaven!*

This is a fundamental paradigm shift!

KEY POINTS: God's objective is to establish His Kingdom on earth as it is in Heaven – which is one hundred percent. Christ came for this purpose, not to rescue people from earth.

The Bible says truth gives life, freedom and power. Please pray the Spirit of God will enable you to absorb the full truth of His will, even if it means shifting some long-held paradigms.

Ripe vegetables were magic to me. Unharvested, the garden bristled with possibility. I would quicken at the sight of a ripe tomato, sounding its redness from deep amidst the undifferentiated green. To lift a bean plant's hood of heartshaped leaves and discover a clutch of long slender pods hanging underneath could make me catch my breath.

Michael Pollan

Chapter 4 - The Big Picture

In the previous chapter we saw that the full manifestation of God's Kingdom is His ultimate objective on earth. Since it is His desire for everything in the world to bow to Him, why doesn't He just snap His fingers and make it happen? Is it because He is lazy, cruel, distant or incapable of imposing His will on the world? Of course not! If that were the case, this life would be pointless indeed, and He would not be a very loving God. Instead, He is not "just snapping His fingers" because *it is simply not His plan,* and *it would go against the entire purpose of Creation.*

To see this, we must step back even further and look at the whole Bible in context. When we do, this becomes obvious: *God's original intent behind the entirety of creation is to raise up*

sons and daughters with whom to share His domain for eternity.[30]
Understanding this, the father heart of God, is the key to
unlocking meaning in God's Word and finding our identity
and true purpose.

God desires sons and daughters who truly love Him, *so He
gives us free will.* He desires sons and daughters who trust
Him completely, *so He wraps us in blindfolds of flesh and
requires we walk by faith.* He wants sons and daughters who
are hungry for His ways, *so He buries His wisdom so only the
diligent will find it.* He wants sons and daughters who are
fully dedicated, *so He reserves His promises for those who are
all-in.* He wants sons and daughters who are strong, *so He
gives us a formidable enemy to vanquish, tribulation to press
through, and a wild world to conquer.* God wants sons and
daughters who are capable and wise in wielding His power,
so He releases it to us gradually as we mature in His ways. The
Father wants sons and daughters who are passionate for
their eternal inheritance – His Kingdom – *so He gives us the
mandate to seek this first, and assigns us the task of establishing it
on earth as it is in Heaven.* God wants sons and daughters
who are winners, *so He reserves His inheritance for those who
bring the victory!*

That right there, my friends, is a huge download. I wish I
could hit a "pause" button in your reading so you could just
chew on it for a while. I pray you will go back and absorb
that paragraph and not read on till it hits you. I'll endeavor
to unpack all this over the next few chapters, but first please
take time to let the Spirit of God start to expand your vision.
When you grasp this – the original intent of the Father – then

---

[30] The Greek word translated in many Bible versions as "sons" – HUIOS – is often
actually gender-inclusive, meaning both male and female descendants. Ladies,
realize that you too are "sons" of the King!

everything in the Bible, everything around you, and everything you've ever experienced, will begin to take on a whole new meaning.

I know when I began to understand that *those who cling to Jesus Christ are fully embraced as eternal offspring by the Creator and King of the Universe, with a destiny to inherit all that is His and rule over it for eternity*, it kicked my faith and passion for God into overdrive. This truth is mind-boggling. The very thought of it leaves me breathless. How can I, a mere mortal man, a sinner, have such an identity and destiny? God's father heart, the magnitude of His amazing grace, is beyond my comprehension. Yet throughout Scripture this message is crystal clear: It is our Father's good pleasure to give us His royal power, kingship, dominion and rule.[31]

If I believe the Bible, I must believe and embrace this truth: "When the time had fully come, God sent his Son, born of a woman, born under law, to redeem those under law, that we might receive the full rights of sons and daughters. Because you are sons, God sent the Spirit of his Son into our hearts, the Spirit who calls out, 'Abba, Father.' So you are no longer a slave, but a son; and since you are a son, God has made you also an heir."[32]

When I embrace this truth, I see clearly there is no way on earth God will ever override His original intent by directly intervening in the task He has given us, or removing us from the battlefield before *we* emerge victorious. *God has given the task of bringing His royal power, kingship, dominion and rule to earth as a project for His sons and daughters to accomplish – so that we may grow into full maturity, ready to rule with Him for eternity – and He will wait patiently until we do.*

---

[31] Luke 12:32
[32] Galatians 4:4-7 NIV

I believe God gives us our own children in part so that we can gain insight into His father heart. I have a son who just turned fourteen. I want him to be a safe and responsible driver and to understand how a car works so he's equipped to take care of his vehicles in the future. I also want to be able to trust him to drive the family car as needed once he gets his license, and not worry about him so much when he's out late. So my wife and I went out last year and helped him buy an old Toyota 4Runner. The thing is in pretty good shape, and it's all there – *only the whole thing, including the motor, is disassembled*. We've got a project on our hands! Over the next two years, I am looking forward to working with him on this project. I've bought him a shop manual for the thing and he's reading it – but the real education, the real fulfillment of my fatherly goals, will come in the work that lies ahead. Yes, I have the power to take it to a mechanic and have him do it, and I have the ability to do it all myself. But if I did that, my son would not gain the benefit I intend for him. I will definitely work alongside him, and I won't let him fail, but most of my involvement will be coaching, not turning wrenches. I want him to do it – not because I'm lazy, distant or incapable – *but because I love Him*. From my perspective I can see well into his future, and this is for his greatest good.

Creation is filled with beautiful pictures of this concept. For example, if you help a butterfly out of its chrysalis, or a chick out of its egg, it will likely die. Its struggle gives it strength to fulfill its destiny. Similarly, it is the dense growth rings in a tree that give wood strength, and these are the ones that grow during the dry season. The strongest trees grow in the toughest environments, and precious gems form where pressure is greatest. A muscle must work hard to grow strong. These things didn't happen by random chance; our

Creator programmed His essence into the world so we can know Him better, so those who dig for wisdom will find it.[33]

This same theme we see in butterflies and diamonds is an underlying theme of the Bible. To help all this settle into your existing base of biblical knowledge, allow me to briefly walk you through The Book from a "Kingdom Victory" perspective:

When God created Adam and Eve, He proclaimed, *"Let them rule."*[34] He gave Adam dominion over everything in the garden. In doing so, *God constrained Himself to doing His work on this earth through His sons and daughters.* He established us as His image bearers and His dominion bearers, created to rule and reign with Him for time and eternity. This is a concept I will refer to as "the agency of man;" we are God's agents and ambassadors on earth. This is our rightful and God-given identity.[35]

In the Garden of Eden, God walked with Adam in the cool of the day; not as a Master with His groveling slave, but as a Father and son – like a Father who had just left the family business to His favored son and was dropping in for a visit to offer some constructive advice and encouragement. Like me walking through our garage, looking at all the auto parts and saying to my son, "Man, your truck is going to be nice! Where do you think we should get started?" The Father

---

[33] In Hebrews 5:8-9 NIV, it says of Jesus, "Although He was a Son, *he learned obedience from what he suffered* and, *once made perfect*, He became the source of eternal salvation for all who obey him." (Emphasis added.) Yes, Jesus was eternal, He was the Word made flesh, and it was through Him all things were made. He lived a perfect life and died an innocent death. Still, *He learned obedience* and *was made perfect* through His experience here on earth. God has engineered "the earth experience" to teach His sons – even Jesus – lessons that will stay with us for eternity. It's part of His master plan.

[34] Genesis 1:26 NIV

[35] More on this in the next chapter.

gave Adam the Kingdom mandate: Establish dominion and subdue the earth. *God commissioned Adam to plant the flag of His Kingdom in all things, to bring the earth into His order.*

Then satan was thrown by God into the Garden *and played the role God intended.* (Or did you think the defeated serpent actually "pulled one over" on our omnipotent God? He wouldn't be much of a God if that were the case!) Think about it: satan was in place in the garden – cast there by God – when the Father specifically gave us dominion over everything there. When we embrace our God-given identity, we realize we have dominion over the enemy, *just as the words of Jesus, Paul and John have been trying to tell us!*

You know, as I think about it, that disassembled truck has some serious "gremlins" in it, too. For example, the guy who sold it to us pointed out that there are a few bolts broken off in the clutch assembly. That's going to be a tough one for my boy. I've conquered those before, and it will be a frustrating job for him at first. I will help and encourage, but fact is, I want him to overcome that one himself. I want him to learn to conquer life's challenges! It will seem impossible to him – how do you remove a bolt when the head has broken off? – but it's not, not with the right knowledge and tools. To gain the victory, he will need to connect with people who know how (me, for one), he may need to try and fail a few times using wrong tools, and he will *learn and grow through it.* Think I'm a cruel father? Maybe by modern standards! No, I want the best for my son and believe this will bring it out.[36]

To continue our Big Picture journey through the Bible, satan knew all about the limitations of our God-designed flesh

---

[36] Not only does God give us parental instincts so we can learn more about Him, He also reveals to us His own paternal instincts so that we can apply them and thus be better parents, too.

blindfolds and how to use them against us. Through deception, he tricked us into abandoning the dominion authority God gave us, and then he gladly stepped into our rightful place (until Christ knocked him out of it once and for all). He himself did not truly possess what he offered, and Adam and Eve did not truly lack what he told them they were lacking. Yet, like Jacob in the tent with Isaac, by playing on their blindness, he stole their birthright.

One could say that satan's crime against mankind was the original identity theft. He stole their identity as victorious sons and daughters and heirs of the King who have been entrusted with His authority and given dominion over the earth. *It's the voice of the enemy, the deceiver, that tells us we can't do it, that we're passive agents, that he's stronger than us, that we need to be afraid and hope for the end to come soon.*

The New Testament says Jesus came as the Last Adam[37] to reclaim that which was lost in the garden by the First Adam. What was it that Adam lost? In addition to our identity and dominion, Adam also lost the experience of walking with his Father in the cool of the day; that is, his personal relationship with the Father. Jesus came to give back our identity of victorious, responsible sons and daughters who have a mandate to establish God's Kingdom on earth. He came to give us back the keys to the Kingdom we forfeited to satan, and to bring us back into a right relationship with our Father.

In the garden, all authority was given to Adam and he was tricked out of it. When Jesus came, He said all authority was given to Him – *and then He gave it to His followers.* This can be seen clearly when He sent out the 70: He delegated to them God's full, supernatural power to do all the things they had

---

[37] 1 Corinthians 15:45

seen Him doing.[38] When they took and used it, Jesus said He saw satan fall to the ground like lightning![39] In the wilderness, satan tried to rob Jesus' identity like he did Adam's – I can just hear his snarling voice as he repeatedly taunted Jesus, "if you *really are* the son of God...." – and Jesus defeated him once and for all.[40] Now we are invited and empowered to participate in bringing that victory to full fruition.

Relationship with God, a victorious identity, a victorious purpose and a victorious destiny. It's what Genesis starts with, it's what Jesus was all about, and it's what the Revelation ends with – God's sons and daughters walking in a real relationship with Him and bringing victory over the world. From start to finish, and all points in between, it's what the Bible is all about: *relationship with God and victory over the world.*

Jesus gave all this to us and then He left, telling us we'd do even greater works that He did.[41] ("I got that main bolt out for you, showed you how it's done, and gave you the tools and confidence you'll need to get this truck running.") Now, the Bible says <u>seven times</u>, *Jesus is seated at the right hand of*

---

[38] God doesn't give his sons a job to do and then leave them ill equipped to succeed. On the contrary, when you study the original Greek text of the New Testament and see the full magnitude of the power He gives us, it's breathtaking. In Luke 10:19, Jesus told His followers, "Behold, I give you EXOUSIA (mastery, superhuman strength, jurisdiction, delegated influence – from Strong's Concordance) to trample on serpents and scorpions, and over all the DUNAMIS (ability, miraculous power, strength) of the enemy." Yes the enemy has great power, but here Jesus says that, in Him, our firepower is superior to it: we have superhuman mastery – full jurisdiction, backed by the delegated influence of God Himself – over satan and his legions.

[39] Luke 10:1-24

[40] Matthew 4:1-11

[41] John 14:12 NKJV

the Father, waiting for His enemies to be made His footstool.[42] If the Father is seated on His throne, and Jesus is seated at His right hand, who will defeat His enemies on earth and drag them under His feet? We will! And no, Jesus will not get tired of waiting, get up and come do it for us. He said Himself, *His* work is finished.[43]

The Bible goes on to make perfectly clear that Jesus will return again only after the Body of believers rises up and embodies the fullness of Him, growing up in maturity into Christ who is our Head.[44] Jesus said, *"This gospel of the Kingdom (BASILEIA – God's royal power, kingship, dominion and rule) will be preached in all the world as a witness to all the nations, and then the end will come."*[45] In the Book of Revelation, it says the wedding feast will occur *after the Bride has made herself ready.*[46] Jesus said that just as the flood came after Noah entered the ark, so shall the end come and wash away the wicked.[47] Noah entered the ark when he was finished building it. What is that foreshadowing? What are we building? The Kingdom! *The end will come only after we finish building this new and eternal ark.*

The completion of God's Kingdom objective will trigger the

---

[42] Originally prophesied by David in Psalm 110:1, this verse is repeated in Matthew 22:44, Mark 12:36, Luke 20:41-43, Acts 2:34-35, and Hebrews 1:13. When God repeats Himself, we best listen! Then in Hebrews 10:12-14, He drives the point home: "But when this priest (Jesus) had offered for all time one sacrifice for sins, *He sat down at the right hand of God. Since that time He waits for His enemies to be made His footstool*, because by one sacrifice He has made perfect forever those who are being made holy." So all told, it's in the Bible SEVEN TIMES. This is a key! NIV, *parenthetical information and emphasis added.*

[43] John 19:30. Instead, of doing it *for* us, He wants to do it *through* us!

[44] Hebrews 4:11-13

[45] Matthew 24:14 NKJV, *Greek definition and emphasis added.*

[46] Revelation 19:7. Of course "the Bride" is another term for "the church" or "the Body of Christ" on earth.

[47] This is found in Matthew 24, Luke 17, and 1 Peter 3.

end of time. *When we are done, Christ will return, and not a moment before.* If the earth is the game board, with the sons and daughters of God on one side and satan on the other, what we are playing for is nothing short of complete domination.[48] Our God is not a loser, and neither are those made in His image. Satan is! When God's Kingdom comes it's "Game Over," and He will say to each victorious son and daughter, "Well done, good and faithful servant! You have been faithful with a few things; I will put you in charge of many things. Come and share your master's happiness!"[49]

It is often quoted that "no one knows the day or the hour" when Christ will return. The reason for this is simple: No one knows the day or the hour because He has delegated the task of bringing His Kingdom on earth to us, and we have free will. It's like asking, "When will Jacob (my son) ever finish building that truck? He's sure been at it a long time!" Well guess what – it's up to my son![50] Thankfully, the Bible says repeatedly that God is patient with His sons and daughters, because we've sure missed this one. It's about time we got on with it, don't you think?

The Gospel (good news) of the Kingdom Jesus taught, and Paul and the other original apostles expounded upon, *is the good news of victory* – and it is the central message of the Bible. Sadly, some Christians are hunkered in pews, so glad that while everything else may fall apart, at least those gates of hell won't prevail against us,[51] believing that we'll be beaten and crushed, then Jesus will have to come, yank us

---

[48] God is far above the "game board;" Christ's victory is complete. He is waiting now for His sons to rise up and manifest that victory in creation.

[49] Matthew 25:21 and 23 NIV

[50] Trying to "read the tea leaves," study the shop manual for hidden clues, or come up with some magical mathematical formula to predict it would be foolish.

[51] Matthew 16:18

out of here, and finish the job for us. Guess what? Gates
don't march – we do! They won't prevail against us because
we're more than conquerors,[52] and we're going to kick them
down! Jesus didn't come to console a losing team and send
them out to just "try their best" and be "the good guys"
while the enemy whoops 'em. Instead, He planted the
incorruptible seed of global NIKAO into the hearts of His
people, and sent them out to conquer the world.

He's not coming back to rescue a bunch of losers, He's
coming back to rule with a Body of winners! We're not going
to flee, we're going to set the nations free! We're not going to
fly, we're going to occupy! We're not going to run, we're
going to reign! We shouldn't run from the beast, we should
run to the feast![53]

Now *that's* Good News!

Embracing this message is vital to living victoriously and
seizing the eternal inheritance stored up exclusively for
those who conquer.

I've heard this metaphor in ministry (maybe you've heard it
too): People are in the water, drowning in sin. Sharing the
message of salvation is like throwing them a life preserver
and pulling them onto the beach. Fantastic, truly. *Now let me
continue this metaphor in light of the complete Gospel message
that Jesus was sent to preach...* Lots of congregations and
denominations seem to stop there, pitch a tent and have a
party. (I call them "Beach Party Christians.") Combined with
modern "end times" teachings – that say we are passive
participants in the ultimate establishment of the Kingdom,

---

[52] Romans 8:37
[53] I must tip my hat to my good friend and teacher Mitch Kersh for these colorful
one-liners.

and "the end is near" – this is a dangerous place to leave a newborn spiritual infant! At the very least they are going to have a tough time, and they may well be killed. *Because the beach we're pulling them onto is Normandy, and it's D-Day.* Not a place for a beach party! We're a conquering army, and the enemy is shooting at us with everything he's got. We have a job to do! It doesn't stop there – because when we are able to hook up a communication link to our Commander, find the path He marked out for us, and access the spiritual reinforcements that are ours for the asking, we will make it through the battle, over the cliffs and trounce the enemy. Victory is our destiny! Then, after we bring the victory, we'll find a palace prepared for the victors, where the King is waiting to lavish us with His splendor and make us co-rulers over His whole dominion.

Give folks the Gospel truth – the *good news of the Kingdom*, the seed that Jesus told us to plant! – and you're recruiting an army for the Lord; soldiers who are ready for battle, sons and daughters of the Kingdom who embrace their victorious identity and destiny.

KEY POINTS: God is waiting for His sons and daughters to embrace their true identity and rise up in their purpose to establish His dominion over the earth. This mandate was given to Adam, re-established by Christ, reinforced in the Revelation, and continually repeated throughout Scripture. He has chosen to do this through us so that in the process, we may develop the character and maturity necessary to rule with Him for eternity.

Just to make sure that I'm not leaving the wrong impression here, the point is not that God is limited by us. Instead, it is that we are unlimited in Him! We must fundamentally shift how we perceive our identity in Christ. Sons and daughters of the Living God, made in His image, are not designed by Him to be passive plankton, swept around in currents we cannot control. While this is perfectly clear in the Bible, it is a 180-degree turnaround from much of today's pop theology. Keep praying for eyes to see, ears to hear, and a mind to absorb the paradigm-shifting truth of God.

You have to learn the rules of the game. And then you have to play better than anyone else.

Albert Einstein

Chapter 5 – The rules

The conflict between the Kingdom of God and the kingdom of darkness is not an all-out free-for-all. If that were the case there'd be no conflict to begin with – God would have simply done away with satan and his demons the moment they rebelled, and that would be that. Or do you think satan has any power that threatens God's?[54] *Satan is a defeated, cast-down, created being.* On the other hand, Christ, *through whom all things were created*, is seated "far above all rule and authority, power and dominion, and every title that can be given, not only in the present age but also in the one to come."[55] The only reason satan is still in existence is that *God is keeping him around to advance His divine purpose of raising up sons and daughters.*

In the previous chapter I showed how God has constrained Himself on this earth so His original intent can be fulfilled.

---

[54] Satan himself is the only one who ever claimed to have anything to offer anyone – to the first Adam (and Eve) in the Garden, and to the Last Adam (Jesus) in the wilderness. I've heard pastors present as truth that satan has power over the world – when In fact they're relying on the words of satan himself. Last I checked, he's a liar!

[55] Ephesians 1:21 NIV

God has similarly constrained satan and imprisoned him on earth for the same reason. These constraints, as they apply to us, boil down to what you might call "rules of engagement" that govern our experience here on earth. We must learn these rules so we may understand what's going on, and ultimately carry off the victory. Ignorance of them can lead to defeat and death.[56]

So that I may keep this in simple terms, go back with me to the idea of board game instructions. We've already covered the first and most important point, and that is, "How do I win?" The next thing we need to know is how the board is laid out.

In this metaphor, the "game board" is creation. The reason creation exists is simple: *God made what we call creation for the sole purpose of raising up sons and daughters with whom to share eternity.* In many parables Jesus repeatedly compared creation to a field, garden or vineyard for the growing of sons and daughters, and said that when they reach maturity, God will harvest them, and that will be the end of it.[57] *All of creation is an incubator in which God is growing mature sons and daughters to share His Kingdom for eternity.*

To put this "game board" in context we need to look at what is beyond it; that is, the eternal realm of God. Just calling that "Heaven" is not entirely accurate. [58] (I don't want to get too technical here, but it is important to go into this briefly

---

[56] This topic is one of those incredible rabbit trails that I encourage you to explore. To maintain the focus and flow of this book I am constraining myself to giving only a brief overview here.

[57] See Matthew chapters 13, 20 and 21, Mark chapters 4 and 12, and Luke chapters 13 and 20.

[58] When an ancient Greek used the word we translate as heaven, OURANOS, he could have meant three different realms, which I – following Paul's lead – will refer to as the three levels of heaven.

so the rules make sense.) To be precise, Paul talked about "Third Heaven" as being the realm of God.[59] Third Heaven is the broader setting into which all creation fits. If that's a bit too much to grasp, let me put it this way: If creation is a game board, Third Heaven is God's living room, and all of creation sits on a card table in front of Him.

In the broadest sense, you could define creation – the game board – as what theoretical physicists call "the time/space continuum." You need to grasp this: God not only created the three-dimensional space we call the universe and all the matter, natural laws, etc., in it, *He also created the linear progression of events we call "time,"* and space/time together make up the realm in which we function. This created realm includes the earth as well as the first and second heavens.

God created linear time for us to live in, and He Himself is not bound by it – He sits above it and can move about it freely.[60] Seeing it this way, we can understand that eternity is not merely "a long, long time," it is instead *the absence of time.* Note that Paul told both Timothy and Titus that God put IIis plans in place "before the beginning of time."[61] Also, we must realize Third Heaven is not "far far away" in outer space; instead, our domain lies fully within it, in another "dimension" if you will. (This is not a concept we can fully grasp with our limited human mental capacities, and a deeper exploration of it is beyond the scope of this book.)

Understanding that Third Heaven, the domain of God, is the realm beyond time and space, we can now see the first two

---

[59] 2 Corinthians 12:2
[60] From God's perspective, Christ was crucified and resurrected before time began, and has been the victorious Lord all along. That is how Old Testament believers could be saved – Jesus had already paid the price for their sins. His was an *eternal* sacrifice, not merely temporal.
[61] 2 Timothy 1:9, Titus 1:2

levels of heaven in context. The first heaven is the visible creation that lies above the surface of the earth, including the atmosphere, sky, sun, moon and stars. These are "the heavens" that we can perceive with our senses.

Second heaven is the invisible spirit realm that occupies the same time/space continuum but is invisible to our senses. It has the same footprint, we just can't see it with our flesh-eyes. This is the realm in which angels and demons (fallen angels loyal to satan) primarily function. It is just as real and current as anything you can see, hear or touch. It, too, is a component of creation – it is part of the game board – and *our God-given dominion, authority and destiny to conquer includes not only visible creation, but also second heaven and all that is in it.*

God cast satan and the other rebellious angels down from Third Heaven before the beginning of time; second heaven is their temporary prison until final judgment, when they will be thrown into eternal torment (after God has used them to accomplish His original intent of training His offspring).

It is also important to note that creation itself was placed by God on a crash course with destiny. The universe is winding down, and the only hope for creation is the coming of God's Kingdom, when it will be "liberated from its bondage to decay" by the sons and daughters of God.[62] Like in a poker tournament where they continually raise the ante to force out stragglers, God has orchestrated the gradual decay of

---

[62] Romans 8:18-21 NIV "I consider that our present sufferings are not worth comparing with the glory that will be revealed in us. The creation waits in eager expectation for the sons of God to be revealed. For the creation was subjected to frustration, not by its own choice, but by the will of the one who subjected it, in hope that the creation itself will be liberated from its bondage to decay and brought into the glorious freedom of the children of God." Also discussed in Hebrews 1:10-12.

creation so His victorious sons and daughters must eventually rise to the top.

--

Okay, so that was a bit about the game board; the setting in which our conflict takes place. I hope all that wasn't too deep, but I had to touch on it so the "rules" make sense. Now let's look at some of those rules. [63] Remember God is the one who established these constraints and He voluntarily follows them.[64] Satan, on the other hand, has no choice in the matter – they are terms of his incarceration. The only power satan has lies within these constraints, and God has not given him license to cheat. They are established so that God's purposes are fulfilled; *satan has nothing to gain from this world other than temporary reprieve from his eternal punishment.*

The first rule we need to understand is that the Kingdom of God and the kingdom of darkness only advance through human activity. I will refer to this as "the agency of man." This principle sat right under my nose for most of my life and I never picked up on it. You'll find this to be consistent throughout Scripture. The "agency of man" was first established when God gave Adam dominion over the world. Now, two people can't be in charge of the same thing; "you

---

[63] Each of these rules is quite profound and worthy of significantly more ink that I am giving them here. My purpose is to establish a framework for the message of victory, and I don't want to make this too deep or complex. I encourage you to study further. If I were to list all the Biblical references to back this up, the footnotes alone would fill volumes! I believe that as you dig into Scripture yourself, you will find virtually every writer of the Book understood these rules and communicated them in one way or another.

[64] Job 1:7 shows just how pathetic satan's existence really is: "The LORD said to satan, 'Where have you come from?' Satan answered the LORD, 'From roaming through the earth and going back and forth in it.'" NIV There's nothing else satan *can* do but roam back and forth on the earth; he is cast out of eternity!

can't serve two masters" is a principle Jesus talked about, and neither can creation serve two masters. When God made Adam the master of creation, He was specifically constraining Himself not to directly intervene without the partnership of a human. This fully makes sense only when we accept our identity as His sons and daughters, and our destiny to bring His Kingdom. Of course He holds ultimate dominion, but on earth He has chosen to exercise that dominion through us.

When God partners with us it can take many forms, with our part including physical labor, spoken words, laying on of hands, administration of "sacraments," resisting the enemy and directed prayer. When we do these things in obedience to God's direction, God is able to work in and through them to unleash His divine power. God tells us to do something, we do it, and then He gives His power to our words and efforts. This is clearly demonstrated in the Book of Exodus: after Moses spoke to Pharaoh the words God had given him, it says that then *"the LORD did according to the word of Moses."*[65] Revelation Chapter 8 similarly describes how the prayers of the saints on earth are taken up to God in a golden container. An angel then takes that container, fills it with fire from the altar and hurls it back down to earth with significant impact. This paints a beautifully clear picture of the power of prayer – we offer it up to God and He returns it to earth full of His power.

Look at the facts: When God wanted to save a remnant from the flood, who built the ark? God gave Noah the instructions and *Noah did the work.* When God worked the plagues and miracles that set the Israelites free from Egypt, each one

---

[65] Exodus 8:13 and again in 8:31, NKJV (emphasis added)

followed this pattern: God told Moses what to do or say, Moses was obedient, and *God worked through Moses' obedience* to bring about these supernatural occurrences. *The Lord did according to the word of Moses!* Same when Joshua conquered the Promised Land, David defeated his enemies, and on and on. David understood this principle clearly when He said, after a victorious battle, "God has broken through my enemies *by my hand.*"[66]

And guess what? Satan is forced by God to obey this rule. He didn't even have power to introduce sin to the world directly – he needed to partner with a man! The Bible says in Romans 5:12 that *sin entered the world through Adam.* That same chapter goes on to say that salvation came the same way – through a man. *God had to come in the form of a fully-human Christ in order to deliver salvation to mankind.*

There is a big difference, however, between how God and satan apply this rule. God desires that we love Him, and love requires conscious choice, so He doesn't force Himself on us. Satan doesn't care if we love him or not   he just wants to delay the coming of the Kingdom. So satan *will* force himself on us if we let him, and he doesn't care if we serve him intentionally or not.

Indeed, our enemy most often works in the shadows, through trickery and deception. For one, he tries to rob our identity by tempting us to embrace feelings of guilt, shame, doubt, worry and pride that are incompatible with our identity as God's sons and daughters. He also tempts us to operate in anger, hate or selfishness, and to pursue temporary pleasures over the joy of righteousness. He lures us into submission and ties us in knots by telling us that Christianity is merely a religion – that we should get

---

[66] 1 Chronicles 14:11 NKJV (emphasis added)

personal fulfillment merely from its regulations and rituals – and a real relationship with God is not possible. *He also uses us as often as he can to hurt other people and interfere with their relationship with God.* There are many more ways satan uses this rule (this alone warrants an entire course of study), but the bottom line comes to this: *When we give in to the enemy's tricks and temptations, we are serving as agents of his purposes, and he can use even the smallest foothold in our heart or mind to cause terrible damage to God's work on earth.*[67]

The way God has set it up, humans are the link between the eternal and the temporal. God establishes His plans and purposes in the eternal and He communicates them to us through His angels, the Holy Spirit, occasional dreams, obedient people and His Word. *Our job, our purpose, is to take what has already been established in the eternal realm and bring it fully into the created realm.* Satan is already defeated and cast out from the eternal. "It is finished!"[68] Yet it is our job to bring that eternal reality into what we call "reality." I see our job here somewhat like the Lewis and Clark expedition. America already owned the Louisiana Purchase. That was settled. But the inhabitants didn't necessarily know that! Lewis and Clark went, in part, to establish the American BASALEIA over the territory, and while they met frequent resistance, victory was a foregone conclusion.

According to the rules He established, *God won't bring His Kingdom to earth without us.* When you realize this, you can begin to see the cross from God's perspective. Jesus came to

---

[67] Note that in the original language, there is no reference to demonic "possession" – the word used is "demonized." A person's agreement with a demon's tricks and deception can be so deep that he appears to be owned by the devil, but the fact is, that person was bought and paid for by Jesus Christ, and so they are His rightful property!

[68] John 19:30

be an open door, so that man once again can have a personal relationship with God. *From our perspective the cross is a means of* salvation. *From God's perspective, it is a means of* invasion. God, too, now has an open door to men, through Christ, to expand His Kingdom army here on earth!

Of course to every rule there are exceptions, but I can't find very many exceptions to this one. After the act of creation itself,[69] I can only see one clear example of God bending this rule in the Bible, and that was at the request of satan – and He did it just to further humiliate His foe! In the Book of Job, satan was so jealous of Job that he went to God and asked for permission to attack Job directly, circumventing the agency of man. God granted him this permission, and satan's plans still failed![70]

--

The next rule we need to understand is that, for the fulfillment of His purposes, God has put us in what I call "blindfolds of flesh." Let me use a pop culture reference to explain why. In the movie Star Wars, when young Luke Skywalker first gets his lightsaber, there's a scene in which Obi Wan Kenobi is training him. Luke is blindfolded, and this little orb is hovering around him zapping him with a laser. Luke is learning to "use the force" to block it. Our training on this earth is similar. To build us up our Father has blindfolded us, requiring us to learn to be led by His Spirit. We are blindfolded by flesh. Our flesh-eyes can't see everything that exists around us, our flesh-ears can't hear

---

[69] Which, in fact, John 1:1-3 says even this was done through Christ, the Word made flesh. So the case could be made the even creation literally was created by God working through a flesh-and-blood man.

[70] Contrary to what I've heard taught, I believe that satan needs God's permission only to break the rules. He has free license to attack us within the constraints God has set up, without specific permission from God.

and our flesh-mind can't understand. There is more to our reality than meets the eye! There is a spirit realm we live in our flesh cannot perceive. This is by God's grand design and fulfills His purposes in many ways. For one, He is glorified by the fact that His "power is made perfect in (our) weakness,"[71] because when people see His majesty held in our frail, cracked, "jars of clay," there's no choice but to glorify God.

God is working to raise sons and daughters who have faith, who are latched onto eternal things. If mankind could see God directly, faith would not be necessary. We can see His handiwork, discern His intelligent design, even prove instances of His miraculous power. But He has ordained that we can't find tangible "proof" of His existence, and we never will – outside of our personal experiences with Him – as He requires that "we live by faith and not by sight."[72]

One reason for this is so God's sons and daughters will not feel fully at home here in this world. The part of us that is dying, our flesh, can only perceive that which is dying, and that is *creation*. The eternal in us, our spirit, can only latch onto that which is eternal, which is God and His Kingdom. As a result, we are compelled to "set (our) minds on things above, not on earthly things,"[73] so that, ultimately, "we make it our goal to please Him."[74]

---

[71] 2 Corinthians 12:9

[72] 2 Corinthians 5:6-10 (NIV) "Therefore we are always confident and know that as long as we are at home in the body we are away from the Lord. We live by faith, not by sight. We are confident, I say, and would prefer to be away from the body and at home with the Lord. So we make it our goal to please him, whether we are at home in the body or away from it. For we must all appear before the judgment seat of Christ, that each one may receive what is due him for the things done while in the body, whether good or bad."

[73] Colossians 3:2 NIV

[74] See Corinthians reference above.

Satan knows all about our blindfold and uses it against us at
every opportunity. While every earthly, flesh-based pleasure
quickly turns sour, and everything that pulls us away from
God leads to despair, his deception and temptations can be
quite powerful. He now has thousands of years' experience
outfoxing men. No wonder that in the New Testament alone,
the word we translate as "beware"[75] is used 24 times. Looks
can be deceptive! Our thoughts can betray us!

There are a few rare examples of exceptions to this rule in
Scripture, where God made Himself visible or audible to the
senses of our flesh. Moses spoke with God at the burning
bush. The Israelites were given a continual glimpse into the
"supernatural" with the pillar of fire and cloud that led them
through the wilderness. Elijah saw a portal between the
second and third heavens, which he described as a golden
ladder. Those around Jesus when He was baptized heard the
audible voice of God. Peter, James and John were taken by
Christ to the Mount of Transfiguration, and Paul
encountered Christ on the road to Damascus. There are not
many other examples I can find.

Thank God that in Christ we have a different set of senses
available to us. The Bible talks about "the eyes of our heart"
and speaks of people perceiving things "in the Spirit." I will
discuss this more in future chapters. For now it is important
to point out that we *do* have the ability to see and hear God
quite clearly – but it is a spiritual gift and not flesh-based
perception.

The "blindfold rule" has a few corollaries, one of which is
this: *Our first battle is internal, it is flesh versus spirit.* There is a
battle raging inside us, and the first place we must establish
God's BASILEIA (Kingdom; *royal power, kingship, dominion*

[75]Greek PROSECHO

and rule) is in our own heart and mind. The Bible refers to
our flesh as our "self," "old self" or even the "old Adam"
that lives in us, with the "new self" being our spirit-identity
of *victorious son of the King.* According to this corollary rule,
self-indulgence and self-serving are bad, and self-control is
good, because the enemy uses our "self" – our flesh – against
us. This is an ongoing battle, as satan and God each want to
use us for their purposes, and neither will give up without a
fight. This is a fight to the death: The Bible says we are to die
to self; that we are to allow the Spirit to crucify our flesh
with Christ, so that we can identify and relate to His
resurrection. To avoid getting too far down this rabbit trail,
let me leave it with this: It is vital to know that our flesh is
not our friend![76]

Here's another corollary to the "blindfold" rule: Our
external battle is *not* against flesh and blood.[77] I don't care
how much someone hurts you, they are a victim. Now I'm
not some bleeding heart, saying they should not be held
accountable in this world for what they do in the flesh; the

---

[76] There are a bunch of great scripture references that make this distinction
clear. Here are a few (all NIV): Colossians 3:9-10, "… you have taken off your old
self with its practices and have put on the new self, which is being renewed in
knowledge in the image of its Creator." 1 Corinthians 15:49-50, "And just as we
have borne the likeness of the earthly man, so shall we bear the likeness of the
man from heaven. I declare to you, brothers, that flesh and blood cannot inherit
the Kingdom of God, nor does the perishable inherit the imperishable."
Philippians 3:3, "For it is we … who worship by the Spirit of God, who glory in
Christ Jesus, and who put no confidence in the flesh…." Ephesians 4:21-23,
"Surely you heard of Him and were taught in Him in accordance with the truth
that is in Jesus. You were taught, with regard to your former way of life, to put
off your old self, which is being corrupted by its deceitful desires; to be made
new in the attitude of your minds; and to put on the new self, created to be like
God in true righteousness and holiness."
[77] Ephesians 6:12 (NIV) "For our struggle is not against flesh and blood, but
against the rulers, against the authorities, against the powers of this dark world
and against the spiritual forces of evil in the heavenly realms."

rule of law is important. What I am saying is that, in the battle to bring the Kingdom of God to earth, our real enemy is spiritual, and the only effective weapons are spiritual. [78]

When someone hurts me they are agents of the enemy, whether they realize it or not, and the long-term implications are much worse for them than they are for me. Even if someone murders me and takes everything I own, the worst case scenario is that I go to be with God. Best case scenario for them, if they do not accept Christ, they will live a miserable life separated from God and eventually must answer to Him for their actions. *The love of God requires us to see others this way, as Christ sees them.* Our fight is *for* people, for their hearts and minds – not *against* people. It is our job, each one of us, together with the Holy Spirit, to crucify our own flesh. And despite what seems to be popular practice today, we must embrace the fact *it is not our job to help our brothers crucify their flesh.* Instead, it is our job to appeal to the deep, eternal, seed of Christ that is in them. When we do that, the rest is between them and God.[79]

One final corollary to the "blindfold" rule is this: Contentment cannot be found outside the will of God. God did not leave us hanging when He blindfolded us in flesh. *God is love,* and He knows what's best for us, even when we don't. He gave each man a compass, so to speak, that always points to Him – in fact the darker our surroundings, the stronger the signal. In each of our hearts, He put a deep

---

[78] Some so-called "Christian" leaders today question the existence of the devil. Poor, blind, foolish men – you can't fight what you deny exists; you have already forfeited the battle for your heart and mind.

[79] I grew up in a denomination that taught the mechanism for evangelism is "show them their sin, then show them their Savior." For years I thought this was the right way, and I wondered why I was never effective! Now I "show them their Savior, then continue to show them their Savior." He deals with their sin much better than I could!

craving only fellowship with Him can satisfy. I am not going out on a limb to say this: *Everything that everyone in the history of the world has ever searched for, longed for, or pursued can only be found one place, and that is in the middle of the will of God.* I don't care whether they've been chasing sex, drugs, rock and roll, or anything else under the sun – *God wants them to find what they're looking for*, because what they're really looking for is the fruit of the Spirit. True love, deep joy, peace that surpasses understanding, patience in affliction, kindness to all, authentic goodness, faithfulness, gentleness and self-control[80] – these are the fruit of the Holy Spirit living in us, and we can only find them when we walk in the will of God.

Satan is very good at counterfeiting every good thing of God, but his counterfeits never fully satisfy. When we buy into satan's definition of "love" or "faith" or anything else, it's like licking our lips on a windy day – it may feel better momentarily, but before you know it it's worse than before. Nothing can satisfy our dying flesh. The further we get from the will of God, the more miserable we will be in this life, and the deeper we get into His will, the more contentment we'll find. This is not to punish us; on the contrary, it is because God loves us and He wants us to find Him! In this life there is always a path back to Him, and when we follow the true desires of our heart, we will always find Him.[81] Wherever we are, whatever we've done, if we draw near to God, He will eagerly draw near to us;[82] there is no sin so great that Christ hasn't already paid for it, and redemption is ours for the asking. When we understand this, it helps us

---

[80] Galatians 5:22-23

[81] Repentance actually means to return to the path of God, it does not mean to say "I'm sorry." This is what John the Baptist was calling people to when he said, "Repent, for the Kingdom of Heaven is near" in Matthew 3:2.

[82] James 4:8

have more compassion for our fellow men, as we realize how much they have been victimized by the deception of the enemy.

--

I've already included a bit about the fact that we have the freedom of choice. This is a fundamental rule God has established, which He chooses to abide by and satan must follow. He wants sons and daughters who love him, and because true love cannot be forced, this purpose can only be accomplished by giving us freedom. To flesh this out a bit more, it is important to point out *we must actively choose the path of God – there is no passive acceptance of Christ, and there is no neutral ground.*

Jesus said, "Enter through the narrow gate. For wide is the gate and broad is the road that leads to destruction, and many enter through it. But small is the gate and narrow the road that leads to life, and only a few find it."[83] The pathway to fellowship with God is narrow and difficult, and we must search for it – like salmon swimming upstream. On the other hand, if we choose an easy, go-with-the-flow approach to life, we'll get washed downstream with all the garbage. God wants sons and daughters who are not at the mercy of their surroundings like spiritual plankton, but instead who rise above circumstance to deliver victory.

Throughout the Bible, God makes it perfectly clear that if we choose Him, we must be all-in; we can't hedge our bets. Jesus said, "He who is not with me is against me, and he who does not gather with me scatters."[84] He also said, "No one can serve two masters. Either he will hate the one and

---

[83] Matthew 7:13-14
[84] Matthew 12:30 and Luke 11:23 NIV

love the other, or he will be devoted to the one and despise the other."[85] There is no spiritual equivalent of Switzerland, the famous "neutral" country that endeavors to stay out of every conflict. *If you think you're on the sidelines, you're really behind enemy lines.* In a later chapter I'll elaborate more on what it means to be "all in," and all the things God ties to that. It is a key to victory, a key to the Kingdom.

There is one facet of the "choice" rule that I'd like to flesh out a bit here: *It takes dedication because it's not easy.* While the offer of being born again "to see the Kingdom" is free to us, everything else costs dearly.

Matthew, Mark and Luke all recount the story of the rich young ruler who came to Christ and asked Him the way to inherit eternal life. This story is quite illuminating. Here's a man who had earthly authority and yet called Jesus "master." We know Jesus drew crowds while in public, so this man must have forcibly pressed in to get close enough to ask his question. And when asked by Jesus, the man said he was exceedingly faithful to the rites and rules of their religion. As it's frequently taught today, this is all that is necessary to be a "Christian" – press in on Christ, call Him master, ask Him for eternal life, and faithfully practice our religion. If this were the truth Jesus came to establish, here He had the world's easiest softball pitched at Him, and He knew the words He spoke would be recorded for all time. What was Jesus' answer? "Sell everything you have and give to the poor, and you will have treasure in heaven. Then come, follow me."[86] It says the man went away dejected because he couldn't do this. I believe too many teachers water down this message because they perceive it as "too

---

[85] Matthew 6:24 NIV
[86] This story is told in Matthew 19:16-22, Mark 10:17-22 and Luke 18:18-25

hard." That is not my intention here, but I do need to say that I don't think Jesus' specific instruction to "sell everything you have and give it to the poor" applies to all of us. Rather, the message even more profound: *If you choose to follow Christ, you must go all in and hold nothing back – the price is high, it's not easy, and not everyone can do it.*[87]

Related to this, it's also clear in the Bible that only the most diligent and dedicated followers of Christ will be able to latch onto all He has to offer us in this world. God wants sons and daughters who are passionate and persistent, so He hides things from those who are not. A friend of mine says, "God doesn't hide things *from* us, He hides them *for* us." Proverbs 25:2 says, "It is the glory of God to conceal a matter; to search out a matter is the glory of kings." And Proverbs 2:1-5 says, "My son, if you accept my words and store up my commands within you, turning your ear to wisdom and applying your heart to understanding, and if you call out for insight and cry aloud for understanding, and if you look for it as for silver and search for it as for hidden treasure, then you will understand the fear of the LORD and find the knowledge of God." Hebrews 11:6 says God "is a rewarder of those who diligently seek Him."[88] Our choice to follow Christ involves a lot of hard work! Of course it is not our work that makes us righteous in God's sight, *but it is indeed our tested and proven obedience and commitment that makes us mature and trustworthy in His sight.*

Moreover, it is very clear in the Bible that God is patient in raising *trustworthy* sons and daughters, who are in it for the

---

[87] Beware of teachings that water this down any further than that! Jesus also said, "The man who loves his life will lose it, while the man who hates his life in this world will keep it for eternal life." John 12:25 (NIV). It's not as easy as you may have been taught. This point is very clear in Scripture if you choose to see it.
[88] All verses in this paragraph are NIV except the last one, which is NKJV.

long run. He doesn't just unleash His full power and resources through an "infant" believer, no matter how sincere or committed. Instead, He is growing His sons and daughters to be "oaks of righteousness"[89] Oaks grow slowly. If you cut down a tree and look at its growth rings, they alternate between lighter-colored thick rings, and darker thin ones. The darker, denser rings are the ones that give a tree its greatest strength, and *they are the ones that grow in the dry season.* God established this example in nature for a reason – it's how He raises His sons and daughters. He purifies us with fire[90] and builds our character through trials.[91] He will entrust us with smaller amounts of provision, power and responsibility, and when we are faithful with them, He'll give us more.[92] Let me share an example from my own fatherhood that makes this point clear. My youngest son, Stephen, is eager to go hunting with me and the older boys, but he just turned four and simply isn't old enough. I long to give him a deer rifle and turn him loose in the woods, but it'd be foolish. Stephen knows the principles of gun safety and has never been unsafe with a gun, yet he hasn't been *seasoned* in his safe habits. For now he has a BB gun with no BBs. Next year I'll let him have BBs. After that we may work up to a pellet gun, then a .22 and, as he grows into it, he'll get his deer rifle. God relates to us the same way. *Choosing to follow Him requires long-term commitment and endurance.*

--

There's one more "rule" I'd like to bring up at this point: All this only makes sense when you live life in light of eternity.

---

[89] Isaiah 61:3
[90] Malachi 3:3
[91] James 1:2-4
[92] The "Parable of the Talents" in Matthew 25 clearly illustrates this principle.

As I've pointed out, the "rules of engagement" require hard work, continual sacrifice and long-term commitment – and all this for things we cannot see, hear or understand with our "flesh blindfolds." At the same time, we must choose a difficult path that requires us to turn away from all the "best" the world has to offer us. Instead of following the easy way, we're supposed to listen to a voice nobody else can hear, do things we can't understand and follow a path that may even lead us into physical pain. It doesn't make any sense at all from the time/space perspective, and our friends and family may indeed think we're insane! As Paul wrote, "The man without the Spirit does not accept the things that come from the Spirit of God, for they are foolishness to him, and he cannot understand them, because they are spiritually discerned."[93]

The only way any of these choices makes sense is if you trust God and view your life on earth from the perspective of eternity. Jesus said if we seek treasure or recognition for our labor now, then we are robbing our eternal inheritance.[94] We must believe without any doubt that none of our acts of service or sacrifice will go unrewarded in eternity, *if we choose to defer our rewards until then.* Yes, if we seek God we will find Him, and in addition to the fruit of the Spirit and an eternal inheritance (which is all we need for truly joyful and contented living) God may indeed choose to provide us with material blessings here on earth. However, if material blessings are what we seek first in this world, we may well find them – but that is all we can expect ever to receive, and they will burn up at the end of time.

---

[93] 1 Corinthians 2:14

[94] Matthew 6:19-24 is one verse that states this clearly. I did a keyword search on "reward" in the New Testament, and found so many Scriptures that back this up, it's too many to list ... some points are so clear they don't need references!

--

When you understand the "game board" and "rules of engagement" in which we operate, you will have a new appreciation for the victory Jesus Christ won, and to which He calls us. It's really no big deal in the big picture that the King of Kings and Lord of Lords defeated a created, fallen angel – that's less dramatic than an elephant stepping on a doodle bug. What *is* a big deal is that Jesus defeated satan while walking the earth as a full-blooded human being, *bound by the exact same limitations and rules that apply to us.* While He could have broken the rules, He willingly chose to follow them – to model for us what *a man* can do.[95] He did not live a super-human life, just human. The trail He blazed is not impossible for us to follow, and the victory He won is not beyond our grasp.

KEY POINTS: God has constrained Himself (and our enemy) to working through people. There is no neutral ground – we are either working for God or against Him. The choice is ours, and it's a hard one.

---

[95] What Jesus said in Matthew 26:53-54, when the armed mob came to arrest him, speaks to this point quite powerfully: *"Do you think I cannot call on my Father, and He will at once put at my disposal more than twelve legions of angels? But how then would the Scriptures be fulfilled that say it must happen in this way?"* (NIV)

"Therefore, since we are surrounded by such a great cloud of witnesses, let us throw off everything that hinders and the sin that so easily entangles, and let us run with perseverance the race marked out for us. Let us fix our eyes on Jesus, the author and perfecter of our faith, who for the joy set before him endured the cross, scorning its shame, and sat down at the right hand of the throne of God. Consider him who endured such opposition from sinful men, so that you will not grow weary and lose heart."
(Hebrews 12:1, NIV)

The most pathetic person in the world is someone who
has sight, but has no vision.

Helen Keller

Chapter 6 – A vision of victory

The enemy knows his fate is settled; at the end of days he
will enter eternal torment. His only reprieve is in the
continuation of days. The longer he can prevent the Body of
Christ from achieving victory, the better it is for him and his
demonic horde. It is opposite for us: our reward is stored up
in eternity, while our days are constant struggle. When
Christians finally come to a unified understanding of this,
and realize that *final victory is ours to achieve and within our
grasp*, I believe it will not take us long to finish the job to
which He has called us.

Let me say those last words again: I believe it will not take
us long to finish the job to which He has called us.

Even as I write this it hits me like a ton of bricks. Finish the
job. *Finish bringing God's royal power, kingship, dominion and
rule to earth as fully as it is in Heaven.* As we've allowed
ourselves to be conditioned in this day and age, I must say –
those are hard words to think, speak or even type. The
thought of it makes my heart beat faster!

The very possibility of us *winning*, of Christ's prayer for
God's Kingdom to come *on earth as it is in Heaven* actually

being answered, of the Body of Christ actually growing up and crossing the finish line – *in the here and now* – of the Bride of Christ *making herself ready*,[96] is nothing I have personally ever heard from a pulpit,[97] and flies in the face of the bulk of "pop Christianity" today. But this is the inescapable culmination of God's original intent as clearly communicated in Scripture, and the work that Christ set in motion. In Christ, winning is our identity, purpose and destiny. Some generation, someday, will get this – we'll stop playing church and start playing to win – *and then it will all be over*. Why not us?

There's a wise old saying, "If you don't know where you're going, you're never going to get there." We need to understand exactly what God intends so we can know what we're working towards. In this chapter, I want to paint a picture of what it will look like *as we bring God's Kingdom to earth as it is in heaven*.[98] There are examples of this in Scripture. And believe it or not, there are also contemporary examples, as God's Kingdom is starting to break out in places around the world.

--

Before we dive into that, it is important to address some *wrong* paradigms. History shows when we pursue our own vision of God's Kingdom, instead of His original intent, the results are disastrous. Because if we, like the Jewish leaders

---

[96] Revelation 19:7

[97] I am in no way claiming to be the only person who knows this stuff! The fact remains, however, that this information is "news" to virtually every Christian I've shared it with, which is quite a few.

[98] By necessity, I will use a broad brush, and the painting will be somewhat impressionistic. While I will flesh it out a bit more in remaining chapters, were I to fully spell it out, as the Apostle John said, "Even the whole world would not have room for the books that would be written." (John 21:25 NIV)

of Jesus' day, have a wrong expectation for the manifestation of the Kingdom of God then we, too, will reject the best He has to offer us – and we will continue to languish.

The Jewish leaders of the day rejected Jesus because they expected the Messiah to be a political figure, leading them to throw off the shackles of Roman oppression and re-establish the nation of Israel – and they crucified Him because they thought He was blasphemous in claiming otherwise. "Church" leaders in the Dark Ages burned "heretics" (including many great Reformers) at the stake because they thought they were protecting God's One True Church. The crusaders brutally hacked up countless thousands of people because they thought they were advancing the cause of Christendom.

Today, many people still follow these age-old patterns. I remember the big ordeal in my old denomination when we switched to a more up-to-date hymnal, for Heaven's sake. It was a nasty fight, and while I'm sure everyone thought they were doing the Lord's work, I can tell you first-hand, He was anything but glorified in the whole mess. Very often we think the advancement of our own preferences, denomination or organization is the answer, and we work aggressively toward that end. While we may boost attendance or the number of "church" buildings, generally the thing we're really advancing is a man-made system and, ultimately, division.

I spent many years very active in politics, and at some small level was considered a leader in the "Religious Right." With all the best intentions, and for all the "right" goals, I eventually came to view my candidates or causes as "God's will" – and those people on the other side as "the enemy." That's how politics is played, and it sure seems to simplify things! And so I would fight against flesh and blood, using carnal weapons, thinking I was advancing the Kingdom of God – when all I was doing, at best, was putting a Band-Aid on the open wound of sin in our society, and at worst, I was actually driving people away from God, *in His name.*

Now understand, I'm not judging anyone's heart – not the Jewish leaders, Dark Ages inquisitors, bloody crusaders, or even today's church leaders or political activists. Indeed, I sympathize and relate. When we live in the world, and it's all we can perceive with our senses, it's hard not to take our cues from the world. Even the great apostle Peter, after walking with Christ for three years, pulled out his sword and hacked off the ear of the high priest's servant who came with the mob to arrest Christ.[99] Just like the Apostle Paul when he was the great Pharisee Saul – who thought he was advancing God's purposes by killing Christians – I have personally, passionately pursued the wrong things for the right reasons for much of my life. It is only a personal encounter with Jesus Christ that can lead us to fix our eyes on things above and to understand that our battle is not against flesh and blood,[100] and our weapons are not carnal.[101]

Yes, the coming of God's Kingdom will be accompanied by sweeping political, institutional, cultural and societal changes. It is not wrong to deeply desire these things. Yet these are just like any other reward this world has to offer – if you seek "it" first, you may get "it" but you won't ever

---

[99] John 18:10

[100] Ephesians 6:12, "Our struggle is not against flesh and blood, but against the rulers, against the authorities, against the powers of this dark world and against the spiritual forces of evil in the heavenly realms." NIV

[101] 2 Corinthians 10:4 "For the weapons of our warfare are not carnal but mighty in God ..." NKJV (Carnal means pertaining to the flesh – things we can perceive with our senses and understanding.)

find what you're *really* looking for. What we really want is God's *royal power, kingship, dominion and rule* to come! Sure we have free will, and can pursue political change, or build another "church" building, for example, that we think will glorify God, and we may achieve some measure of earthly "success" – but the Kingdom won't come through that effort.[102] Instead, like everything else, *when we seek first the Kingdom of God and His righteousness,* then all the things we desire will be added to us as well.[103]

When the Kingdom of God comes on the earth, the government will be on Jesus' shoulders.[104] But establishing a theocracy is not the means to accomplish that. There is an old truism that says, "a man convinced against his will is of the same opinion still."[105] Under penalty of earthly law, people may be physically obedient to the Ten Commandments and still be far from God. Pornography may be outlawed, but people still commit adultery in their hearts, which Jesus said was just as bad.[106] Illegal drugs may be wiped from the face of the earth, and people still seek to "get high" on something other than the Holy Spirit. People may flock to our church services because we have the best praise team around, our parking ministry is super-convenient, our facilities are state-of-the-art and our pastor can deliver a real humdinger – and we can sell them into embracing all sorts of outward signs of obedience – and the

---

[102] This is not to say God doesn't call people to be active in politics. He can and does do that. Just like He calls some people to be extremely wealthy. But there are certainly many, many more people pursuing those "callings" than are truly called.

[103] Matt 6:33 paraphrase

[104] Isaiah 9:6

[105] I've seen this attributed to Sir Walter Raleigh, Benjamin Franklin and others. I don't think anyone really knows the original source.

[106] Matthew 5:28

lives of every single one still be completely empty. We can do all sorts of things "in Jesus name," and on the last day He could still tell us, with sadness in His heart, "I never knew you...."[107]

God's Kingdom is spiritual, not physical. Its establishment will be fully reflected by the physical, but it cannot start there. Our man-made structures, organizations and governments will willingly come under His authority when we allow Him to establish His BASILEIA through us, as men cast their crowns before the King of Kings. No guns, marketing, peer pressure or electoral majority can do it; instead, people must freely opt-in to His Kingdom, because if they are forced or "sold," then it is not built on love.

--

From beginning to end, and all points in between, the Kingdom of God, and our work to advance it, is all about a personal relationship with the Father through Jesus Christ. It is about each of us walking in this relationship, and all of us working together to help others, one at a time, enter into this relationship as well.

I've come to see it this way: In the final analysis, seeking first God's Kingdom and walking the walk as a Christian really boils down to just three things: First, cultivate the seed of Christ in us such that He's the only one people see when they look at us. Second, help others accomplish the same thing. And third, connect it all together in a community of love. *When we finally do this, God's Kingdom will shine over the face of the earth.*

Paul said in Romans 14:17, "The Kingdom of God is not a matter of eating and drinking, but of righteousness, peace

---

[107] Matthew 7:21-23

and joy in the Holy Spirit."[108] Stated another way, since God is love, then the BASILEIA of God is the *royal power, kingship, dominion and rule* of LOVE. The Gospel of the Kingdom is all about first knowing our identity as fully-empowered sons and daughters of the King, and then taking His authority and dominion into every aspect of life, in every corner of the world. It's not about establishing theocracy, or forcing court cases to legalize prayer in schools, or voting for the "right" candidates. *It's about washing over everything in an unstoppable tsunami of God's love, righteousness, truth, grace, mercy and glory.* Yes, the unstoppable tidal wave of the Kingdom of God will certainly cover all governments and institutions made by man, but it's not about earthly power – it's about God's love conquering all.

Our battle is *for* people; for their hearts and minds. It is *against* the spiritual forces that deceive them and hold them in bondage. By staying connected to the Father through the Son and living from that reality in all areas of our lives; by personal relationships, love, service, and genuine care for others; by standing up for and speaking the truth in love in every situation; by exuding deep, abiding peace and joy in all circumstances; and by waging *spiritual* warfare against the *spiritual* powers of this dark age,[109] we will win hearts, one at a time, and lead them to experience fellowship with the Father, Son and Holy Spirit as we ourselves experience it, and into the community of believers who live the same way.

As we do this, one person at a time, we will be expanding the territory of the Kingdom of God and diminishing the territory – of human hearts – available to the enemy. Victory

---

[108] NIV
[109] More on spiritual warfare in coming chapters.

will be achieved when there is no quarter left for the devil and his ilk; no one left for him to influence, no way left for him to hold off the unveiling of the perfect Bride of Christ. *This* is what we are fighting for. *This* is what God intends, the job He has given us to do, and the inevitability Jesus set in motion *for us to accomplish.*[110]

--

Embracing our God-given purpose of achieving Kingdom victory should compel us to look more strategically at how best to tackle the problems facing our world. When we do this, we see that for each of the enemy's cultural strongholds, there is both a supply side and a demand side. There are people who produce pornography and people who purchase it, people who sell illegal drugs and people who use them, people who govern poorly and people who vote them into office, and so on.

Our human nature is to look for shortcuts – the perceived path of least resistance – and also to seek recognition for our endeavors. This nature generally leads us to attack the *supply side* of a stronghold – it just seems to be the logical way to bring it down, and we can certainly make a big splash by doing so. As a result we picket abortion clinics, organize electoral campaigns, wage war against drug cartels, seek to outlaw pornography, and the like.

---

[110] Do I believe every human being at this time will be saved? Certainly not. The Parable of the Wheat and the Tares in Matthew 13 makes it perfectly clear that, just as there are sons of the Kingdom, there are also sons of the wicked one. What will the proportion be? I don't know – but if I had to guess I would say that two-thirds for God, one third for the devil (the same proportion as the fallen angels) may be a good starting point. I'm not setting out here to predict the future, only get us focused properly in the present. Whatever it is, I know for sure that before the end, God's people will be operating in unprecedented practical influence and spiritual authority.

Now, we each need to do as the Lord leads, and there's nothing wrong with any of these activities. If the Lord calls you personally to focus on the supply side of a stronghold, then you should do it with all your strength. However, if we as a body embrace these tactics as our sole strategy for pulling down strongholds, *victory is impossible*. How can I say this? It's a simple lesson in Economics 101: *For any given demand, limiting the supply simply drives up the price.* For example, attack the supply chain for illegal drugs without addressing the demand, and you've only hiked the street value – and as a result, you're driving addicts to do even more extreme things to get them!

Want to tear down the stronghold of illegal drugs? Just like every other cultural stronghold, *attacking the demand is the winning strategy*. When former drug addicts would rather "get drunk on the Holy Spirit"[111] than high on dope, the illicit drug trade will disappear! Instead, we've spent oceans of money and manpower fighting the supply ... and how's it working for us?

When men hunger and thirst for righteousness more than for the desires of the flesh, the pornography industry will collapse. Attack the supply – whether it be through shutting down pornographers or simply putting "porn blockers" on computers – and allow the demand to linger – and men will still commit adultery in their hearts. No victory there!

When our elected leaders are storing up treasures in Heaven instead of pursuing earthly riches, corruption will vanish. When the hearts of the electorate are turned towards righteousness, and they vote accordingly, the righteous will once again rule. Connect gang members to real, loving,

---

[111] Ephesians 5:18

edifying relationships and street violence will stop. When the truth of God's love is known by all, then all religions and sects based on legalism, division or hate will fail.

Attack the supply side of any of these, and you may get some temporary relief, but it's no better than putting a Band-Aid on an infection. It may look fine on the surface for a time, but the real problem is still there, only getting worse.

When you get to the heart of these issues, you realize the ultimate supply of all our cultural ills is the deception of the enemy. Even those people who are agents of the "supply side" are, in their hearts, simply demanding gratification from something other than God, and they have believed the lie that they can find what they're looking for through sin.

We must remember that our battle is *for* people and not *against* them! Any perceived shortcut is really a dead-end street. God's Kingdom will come when we personally connect with the hearts and minds of individual people, one at a time, and turn them towards Christ. Victory will not be accomplished through blunt force, but instead through loving kindness. Put two and two together –"The meek shall inherit the earth" [112] and "He who (conquers, carries off the victory) will inherit all things"[113] —and it becomes clear that we will conquer through *meekness*. There is no other way.

--

As God's Kingdom comes, we will correctly identify our true foe and fight accordingly. We will realize that people who work against us in this holy endeavor *are victims of our enemy*; they themselves are not our enemy. Of course men

---

[112] Psalm 37:11, repeated by Jesus in Matthew 5:5.
[113] Revelation 21:7

will stand in our way. They may even persecute and martyr many of us like they did Jesus and most of the original apostles. But, like Jesus, we'll be able to see them through eyes of love and say, "Father, forgive them, for they do not know what they are doing."[114]

Moral purity is a hallmark of the Kingdom of God. Paul wrote, "For of this you can be sure: No immoral, impure or greedy person—such a man is an idolater—has any inheritance in the Kingdom of Christ and of God."[115] And, "Do you not know that the wicked will not inherit the Kingdom of God? Do not be deceived: Neither the sexually immoral nor idolaters nor adulterers nor male prostitutes nor homosexual offenders nor thieves nor the greedy nor drunkards nor slanderers nor swindlers will inherit the Kingdom of God."[116] The manifestation of this purity will be the reflection of our love of God, not legalism.

The root problem of every societal ill comes from sin and its ripple effects. One of the great Founding Fathers of America, James Madison, recognized this when he said, "If men were angels, no government would be necessary."[117] The criminal justice system, welfare, the military … orphanages, retirement homes, health insurance … even locks on doors and computer anti-virus programs … all spring from the fact sin has free reign over people in our world, and we prefer to outsource our biblical responsibility of taking care of others.

Imagine a community where the *royal power, kingship, dominion and rule* of our loving God has come in fullness. Where *true* religion is practiced – that is, everyone pitches in

---

[114] Luke 23:34 (NIV)
[115] Ephesians 5:5 (NIV)
[116] 1 Corinthians 6: 9-10 (NIV)
[117] The Federalist Papers, No. 51

personally to take care of widows and orphans and those in need.[118] Where no one lacks anything because all is freely shared.[119] A community where crime is non-existent, families stay together through thick and thin, leaders serve the common good, everything in the media is clean and pure, and where God is worshipped in spirit and in truth.

A community of unity, where group decisions are made by reaching consensus through consultation with the Spirit and no political conflict or factions exist – with no bureaucratic red tape and no one left out of the process. Where people work out their differences according Jesus' instructions – one on one, in love – and lies, gossip and slander are abolished. Where brothers and sisters in Christ help each other grow instead of hammering them down when they stumble. Where humble servant-leaders are respected for their wisdom and fairness, such that they continually grow in influence in the world at large.

A community where gatherings center on Christ and are joyful, vibrant and universally uplifting. Where signs and wonders are commonplace, miraculous healings are routine, and the presence of the Holy Spirit is tangible. Where people from far and wide come to be delivered and healed of all sorts of ills. Where all other faiths and creeds are shown to be false – not by argument or attack, but simply in light of a living manifestation of the real thing – and so adherents gladly discard their idols and holy books as they embrace

---

[118] James 1:27 (NIV) "Religion that God our Father accepts as pure and faultless is this: to look after orphans and widows in their distress and to keep oneself from being polluted by the world."

[119] Do this by force and it fails miserably. It's called socialism! Done willingly and in love, and it's the model that Christ established. Just read the books of Acts and Paul's epistles and you'll agree.

the Kingdom of God.

A community like this is infectious. Led by the *real* enemy, those with hard hearts certainly seek to disrupt or attack it, but it still thrives – and is ever-expanding.

--

Think I'm daydreaming? It could never happen? Facts say otherwise. Not only are communities like this showcased in the Bible as examples of the coming of God's Kingdom, they are popping up in the world even today.

The Book of Acts records the lifestyle of early Christians, who were led by men personally tutored in the ways of the Kingdom by Christ Himself. Here's how thousands of Christ followers lived in Jerusalem: "They devoted themselves to the apostles' teaching and to the fellowship, to the breaking of bread and to prayer. Everyone was filled with awe, and many wonders and miraculous signs were done by the apostles. All the believers were together and had everything in common. Selling their possessions and goods, they gave to anyone as he had need. Every day they continued to meet together in the temple courts. They broke bread in their homes and ate together with glad and sincere hearts, praising God and enjoying the favor of all the people. And the Lord added to their number daily those who were being saved."[120] This wasn't la-la land or some hippy commune. Founded under and lead by the headship of Christ, it was a manifestation of His Kingdom come.

It was from this core community that missionaries were sent to cultivate similar communities elsewhere.[121] One early

---

[120] Acts 2:42-47 (NIV)
[121] Like Amish Friendship Bread starter – a living culture of yeast and nutrients, which women in America often pass around – the living leaven of the Kingdom (a term Jesus used in Matthew 13:33 and Luke 13:20) is similarly spread.

branch was in Antioch, and it was from there that Paul and Barnabas were sent all over the known world. They weren't *evangelists*, as we define it today; instead, they were *community builders*, establishing outposts under God's *royal power, kingship, dominion and rule* wherever they went. They called it *the Way* because that's what it was: the way of living that Christ established. Paul's epistles, which make up a huge portion of the New Testament, were written to the brethren in these outlying regions to help them better reflect the Kingdom of God – Christ's way – in their communities.

Ephesus was one such community. Look in Acts 19 to see all that happened there. Here's just a quick rundown: Paul went to Ephesus and, as was his custom, started teaching at the local Jewish synagogue. When the Jews rejected his teaching, he went to a non-descript location called the School of Tyrannus and started building a Kingdom community. From this one old man, modeling and teaching the way of God's Kingdom, here's a few highlights of what happened within two years:

- Everyone in Asia heard about Jesus,

- Miraculous signs and wonders were common,

- Many who followed pagan practices willingly brought their books together (of exceedingly great value) and burned them,

- The trade of silver shrines for the pagan goddess Diana was upended, such that there was a massive riot of silversmiths who complained that Paul was running them out of business (even though it says Paul never "blasphemed" Diana[122] – instead, people were willingly abandoning that false

---

[122] Acts 19:37

religion when they learned the truth about Christ).

This is life under the *royal power, kingship, dominion and rule* of God! The Greek word for this – BASALEIA (Kingdom) – is used 120 times in the first four books of the New Testament. The rest of the New Testament is all about the Kingdom coming on earth as it is in Heaven. Like Christ, this was what the first apostles lived and died for. *The full establishment of this kind of community across the globe is our job, birthright and destiny.*

--

I've heard Christian leaders rationalize away the fact that they don't personally see miracles today by simply saying "those things don't happen anymore." They believe our current legalistic, ritualistic, Sunday-only "church" system is the best we can ever hope for, and the very concept of the Kingdom of God coming to earth *today* as it is in Heaven is as far-fetched as Santa Claus sliding down their chimney on Christmas eve. This is worse than tragic, because when they communicate this defeatism to their followers, it lowers their expectations, diminishes the validity of God's promises, robs them of their victorious identity, purpose and destiny and, ultimately, guts their faith. The reason those leaders – and most of the "church" in the industrialized world today – don't encounter God's miraculous power today is the same reason that Jesus Himself couldn't do many miracles in His hometown: because the people lack faith![123]

Reality is, everything that happened in Jerusalem, Ephesus and the other outposts of the early church is happening today; I have seen it firsthand. In my own work in the United States, I have seen the power of the Kingdom

---

[123] Mark 6:5

transform lives, families and groups. I have personally witnessed miraculous wonders, healings and dramatic deliverance from demonic oppression.[124] No doubt in the industrialized world today these manifestations of God's Kingdom are few and far between, but they do still occur.

Where they are happening on a large scale is in the Third World. I started writing this book while on a mission trip in the town of Owerri in Nigeria. I had carried the message of victory for quite some time before that, but seeing what I saw there was the clincher. Owerri today is a remarkable, modern parallel to what is recorded about Ephesus in Paul's time.

Rationalizing nay-sayers claim stories of miracles still happen today in Third World countries because "the people there have such a simple faith." I must tell it like it is: This is not only untrue, it is ignorant, arrogant and insulting. The Christians I spent time with in Owerri have *anything but* a simple faith! The people are highly literate, educated and exceptionally knowledgeable of the Bible – on the whole, much more so than any community of believers I've seen in America. Every single Bible I saw was well worn, marked up and highlighted, and carried with respect. Everywhere I went in the community (with a population of approximately 500,000), I saw open, joyful expressions of faith. Driving around town you see countless simple, hand-written banners praising God, carefully painted praises on the backs of a multitude of three-wheeled taxis, stores named to give glory to God, obituary posters proclaiming the parting of a loved one into their glorious inheritance, billboards

---

[124] I spent 30 of my 40 years on this earth very active in a very stodgy denomination. I don't say these things lightly!

proclaiming "Imo State is in God's Hands," and such. None of it came across as trite or commercialized. Even through a car window it was touching.

The most powerful impressions came from personal encounters with the people. I was blessed to visit about a dozen local congregations, and each one blew me away with their joy and generosity. I saw one pastor of a relatively large congregation – in a ramshackle building in a poor neighborhood – take the morning's offering and hand it to a young single mother who had lost her job. I saw an old woman lead a goat to the pulpit as her offering; it was the very best she could give. I saw prison ministries, hands-on service to the sick and hungry, and all forms of outreach – carried out by loving neighbors as part of their daily lives. I heard voices raised with such an outpouring of joy I was moved to tears (which, as my wife of 17 years will tell you, simply doesn't happen to me!). I saw a little old lady, bent over like an upside-down L from osteoporosis, hobble into a prayer gathering with a cane – who after being prayed for and healed, threw down her cane and danced around, fully upright and nimble, while being high-fived by her friends. They reacted like it was certainly cool, but not anything they hadn't seen before. I had personal conversations with numerous people – male and female, young and old, from all stations in life – and was blown away by their studied knowledge, probing insight and spiritual maturity. "A simple faith?" No sir ... a genuine, tested, *true* faith!

In the city center, we drove by a modern, three-story building that looked as if it had been bombed. My host told me it had been the headquarters for a big-time Nigerian internet scammer, and when the people found out about it, they descended on the place, tore it down, and ran the fellow out of town. He also told me that a few years before, the governor of the state had tried to appoint a Muslim to a high-ranking position. The people stood up and stopped him. Not only did a Christian get the job, but that governor was voted out and replaced by a Christian!

I could go on and on, but I'm afraid my words aren't doing justice to the manifestation of the Kingdom that I saw first-hand in Owerri. I felt as if I were standing in the mountains on a clear night after a lifetime in the city. Sure, in the city you can look up at the night sky, see a few stars and think there are a lot – but in the mountains, away from the light pollution we take for granted, the clarity takes your breath away. I thought I'd seen miracles, praise, worship and expressions of faith in America. And to be sure, I've seen a bit. But when I went to a place that has been freed from so much of the spiritual pollution we're used to, I was floored.

It wasn't always that way in Owerri. My host told me that just 18 years ago, when his group started ministry there, they were literally beaten, stoned, and threatened with imprisonment and death. Yet like Paul in the School of Tyrannus, they kept at it – praying, teaching and modeling the Way. As a result, today their community not only reflects God's Kingdom like a modern Ephesus, it is in fact rolling back the tide of Islam in the nation of Nigeria and sending missionaries out to other towns and nations.[125]

This is the start of the Kingdom come, the BASILEIA, the *royal power, kingship, dominion and rule* of God, being manifest on earth as it is in Heaven. *This* is the purpose Jesus was

---

[125] I am informed of communities across the globe, even here in America, where the Kingdom is being manifest. You won't hear about it in "mainstream media," or even in "Christian" media from groups skeptical of such things. I encourage you to talk to people you trust who have traveled and confirm this for yourself. For credibility's sake, I will only report on the one I have experienced in person.

sent, what He prayed for, and what His work set in motion. *This* is what the first apostles lived and died for. *This* is what we were created to establish. *It is our purpose and destiny – and the end won't come till we've achieved this victory globally.* It could be this generation or another, but one thing is certain: It is inevitable. The Kingdom is coming, whether or not we "sophisticated" Christians choose to join in!

KEY POINTS: When the Kingdom of God is fully manifest on earth as it is in Heaven, there will be no more room for the enemy. All of God's children will live in a community of absolute love, peace and joy as modeled by the early church in Acts. God's miraculous power will be an integral part of our daily lives. Jesus Christ will be exalted as the King of all nations.

"For to us a child is born, to us a son is given, and the government will be on his shoulders. And he will be called Wonderful Counselor, Mighty God, Everlasting Father, Prince of Peace. Of the increase of his government and peace there will be no end. He will reign on David's throne and over his Kingdom, establishing and upholding it with justice and righteousness from that time on and forever. The zeal of the LORD Almighty will accomplish this." *(Isaiah 9:6-7 NIV)*

Nobody ever defended anything successfully — there
is only attack and attack and attack some more.
Gen. George S. Patton, Jr.

Chapter 7: War

There are many today who seem to view Jesus as a bearded,
robe-wearing, ancient-times version of Mr. Rogers. Like the
old children's television show host who was always warm
and fuzzy, soft-spoken and seemingly couldn't harm a fly,
they picture Jesus as nothing more than a sweet, passive,
peaceful little lamb, who just wants everyone to hold hands
and skip happily down a primrose path while singing
Kumbaya.

Nothing could be further from the truth. Yes, He is the
Prince of Peace,[126] and He proclaimed, "Blessed are the
peacemakers."[127] But the peace Jesus pursued and, yes,
fought for, was not the kind of false "peace" that comes
about through tolerance of evil and appeasement of the
enemy. He was about true, eternal peace – the kind that can
only result from the total triumph of the Kingdom of God
and the absolute destruction of the kingdom of darkness.
Jesus knew *peace* and *victory* are one in the same, and it can
only come about through all-out, take-no-prisoners, no-
holds-barred, winner-take-all warfare.

---

[126] Isaiah 9:6
[127] Matthew 5:9

When you consider Jesus' career as a carpenter – hewing workable slabs of wood from giant timbers, hauling heavy construction materials, swinging hammers and axes, working primitive saws and other hand tools – there is no way to conclude He was anything but a brawny, callous-handed man's man. Some of the toughest working men of the day – the net-hauling, seafaring fishermen – were quite willing to lay down their nets and follow Him. Even the battle-hardened, Roman-military-trained Centurion paid Him the highest respect.[128] Jesus was no wimp.

Jesus was fiery and fierce when circumstances required. When Jesus saw the money changers in the temple, He took time to fashion a whip and carefully choose His words, and then – strategically, intentionally, consumed by zeal yet under full control of His emotions – He exploded into a table-kicking, butt-whipping rage.[129] There is no doubt this was a terrifying and intimidating display of raw human strength and outrage. He was no soft, slight, whisper-voiced weenie flying off the handle in a tizzy, as some would have us think.

The Old Testament prophets knew this about Jesus. In Exodus 15:3, Moses wrote, "The LORD is a warrior; the LORD is His name."[130] Isaiah said, "The LORD shall go forth like a mighty man. He shall stir up his zeal like a man of war. He shall cry out, yes, shout aloud; He shall prevail against His enemies."[131] And John, the apostle who was personally closest to Jesus, and through whom God chose to download the Book of Revelation (and four other New Testament books), wrote, "The reason the Son of God

---

[128] Matthew 8:8
[129] John 2:13-17
[130] NKVJ
[131] Isaiah 42:13 (NKVJ)

appeared was *to destroy the devil's work."*[132] Jesus Himself said, "Do not suppose that I have come to bring peace to the earth. I did not come to bring peace, but a sword."[133] He later said that folks who are "lukewarm" make Him want to vomit.[134] Hardly sounds like a passive pansy to me! And you know what? The Bible is perfectly clear that we are to emulate Jesus; *He is the firstborn of many brothers,*[135] *and we were created in His image.*[136] Jesus is a man of war, and we are to be also.

The Apostle Paul was a mighty warrior as well. While outwardly he was no doubt a bit more genteel than Jesus (as a tutored, thoroughbred Pharisee) and certainly rather decrepit physically in his later years, until his dying breath he waged intense warfare and trained others to do the same. Here's something he wrote to the brothers in Corinth: "For though we walk in the flesh, we do not war according to the flesh. For the weapons of our warfare are not carnal but mighty in God for pulling down strongholds, casting down arguments and every high thing that exalts itself against the knowledge of God, bringing every thought into captivity to the obedience of Christ, and being ready to punish all disobedience when your obedience is fulfilled."[137] That is the language of a seasoned, fighting man!

Paul exhorted his spiritual son Timothy to "fight the good

---

[132] 1 John 3:8 NIV, emphasis added
[133] Matthew 10: 34 NIV. It continues (v. 35-36) "For I have come to turn 'a man against his father, a daughter against her mother, a daughter-in-law against her mother-in-law—a man's enemies will be the members of his own household.'"
[134] Revelation 3:16 NKJV
[135] Romans 8:29
[136] Genesis 1:26 NIV, "Let us make mankind in our image, in our likeness, so that they may rule..."
[137] 1 Corinthians 10:3-6 NKJV

fight of faith,"[138] and as his own days drew to an end, he wrote him again saying he himself had "fought the good fight."[139] The old apostle wrote in great detail about the battle armor of God,[140] as one who had mastered its use in bloody spiritual combat. The book of Acts tells how he was such a fierce spiritual warrior he'd even developed an intimidating reputation in the spirit realm.[141] As the story goes, when Paul was ministering in Ephesus, some Jewish leaders went out and tried to emulate his success by attempting to drive out a demon using the name of Jesus. While these seven sons of Sceva had the words right, they clearly didn't have any spiritual warfare "street creds." As a result, the demon possessing the man beat the tar out of the brothers, saying "Jesus I know, and Paul I know, but who are you?" Old, frail, proper Paul was indeed a mighty man.

As followers of Christ, we best become similarly seasoned in spiritual fighting. The enemy comes to steal, kill and destroy[142] and we are exhorted to stay sharp because he "prowls around like a roaring lion looking for someone to devour."[143] The only one who wins when we are seeking "peace" through passivity is the enemy. In the Kingdom, if you think you're on the sidelines, you're really behind enemy lines, and satan is winning in your life.[144] The rightful place for a son of the King is on the front lines, fighting for victory.

--

[138] 1 Timothy 6:12 NIV
[139] 2 Timothy 4:7
[140] Ephesians 6:10-17
[141] Acts 19:13-16
[142] John 10:10
[143] 1 Peter 5:8 NKJV
[144] In Matthew 12:30 and again in Luke 11:23, Jesus said, ""Whoever is not with me is against me, and whoever does not gather with me scatters." NIV

Jesus and the early church leaders did not just model a warrior nature; they displayed a keen understanding of the strategy of warfare. It is no coincidence that Jesus came at the peak of the greatest empire on earth. The people of the day understood the concept of BASILEIA, and understood what He meant when He used that word over and over again. Rome was an expansive, militaristic empire. When they conquered a territory they instituted a regime change, introducing and enforcing a new way of doing things. They cut the head off the old system and inserted the Roman BASILEIA in its place. It was a complete cultural makeover from the top-down, starting with the displacement of the old regime's rulers, and including a ruling council to model and carry out the ways of Rome.[145]

In a spiritual sense, the Kingdom of God advances in the same way as the Roman Empire. Spiritual powers over given areas (geographic, cultural or personal) are pulled down and replaced with the headship of Jesus Christ, ushering in a complete cultural makeover. God's people then gather in fellowship *as a spiritual ruling council* to model and carry out the Way of God's *royal power, kingship, dominion and rule.* [146] This was fully understood and modeled by the early church leaders. It's what happened in Ephesus and Owerri, Nigeria – and will happen across the entire world when the Body of Christ finally grows up.

Jesus and the early church leaders understood that spiritual warfare directed at spiritual regime change is the key. The words of Jesus reflect this in a very specific way. The phrase, "The Kingdom of God is near," is used many times in the

---

[145] In Greek, the term for such a ruling council is EKKLESIA – a word we translate today as "church."
[146] This is what God thinks when He says the word EKKLESIA, or "church." We've sure missed that one, haven't we?

Gospels, most often in the context of a healing or other miraculous sign. Yet only one time does Jesus say, "The Kingdom of God has come upon you," and that is when He said, "If I drive out demons by the Spirit of God, then the Kingdom of God has come upon you."[147] When the power of God is observed in the natural realm, it means His Kingdom is close. *When the power of God displaces the enemy, His Kingdom has come.*

Paul told his apprentice Timothy, "You must therefore endure hardship as a good soldier of Jesus Christ. No one engaged in warfare entangles himself with the affairs of this life, that he may please Him who enlists him as a soldier."[148]

Warfare is not just our nature, it is our calling.

--

The wisdom of God is deep and multi-faceted. Fact is, Jesus *is* the Prince of Peace. Proverbs says of Wisdom that "all her paths are peace."[149] And the great warrior-apostle Paul wrote, "If it is possible, as far as it depends on you, live at peace with everyone."[150]

Jesus, the man of war, said, "But I tell you, do not resist an evil person. If anyone slaps you on the right cheek, turn to them the other cheek also."[151] He hung out with "sinners and tax collectors,"[152] was gentle with the adulteress and the sinful woman at the well,[153] received the thief on the cross into salvation, and told his followers to "give to Caesar what

---

[147] Matthew 12:28 and Luke 11:20, NIV
[148] 2 Timothy 2:3-4 NKJV
[149] Proverbs 3:17
[150] Romans 12:18 NIV
[151] Matthew 5:39 NIV
[152] The Jewish leaders of the day frequently criticized Jesus for this.
[153] John 8:3-11 and John 4:1-26

is Caesars."[154] When they came to crucify Him, He went willingly, like a lamb to the slaughter.[155] There certainly were key times when our great Warrior Savior was as meek and mild as ... well, as a bearded, robe-wearing, ancient-times version of Mr. Rogers.

And yet He went ballistic in the temple against the money changers, occasionally rebuked His disciples in no uncertain terms, and was frequently downright surly to the established, respected Jewish leaders of the day.[156]

And then He forgave them, even as He hung on the cross.

So what's going on here?

If you don't see things from the same perspective that Jesus saw them, His words and actions can seem random and conflicting. If you don't understand the purpose He was sent – to proclaim the Kingdom of God and set in motion the total conquest of the world by His follower-brothers – then Jesus is an enigmatic figure indeed. And so when we fail to see the Big Picture, original intent of God, we can be drawn into doing all sorts of "good" things *in His name* – and actually be working against His master plan. *"Where there is no vision, the people perish."*[157]

There is no disputing we are at war and our divine design is to be men of war, just like Jesus. We have a God-given fighting nature within us, bursting to come out. Just step into the average church council meeting when they're debating the color of carpet or what to name the upcoming Vacation Bible School and you'll see what I mean!

---

[154] Matthew 22:21, Mark 12:17, Luke 20:25
[155] Acts 8:32
[156] Check out Matthew 23. Them's fightin' words!
[157] Proverbs 29:18, KJV

And therein lies the problem. You get a bunch of natural-born fighters together, *deprive them of the proper understanding of their identity, purpose and destiny,* and you'll get what we have today – a generally aimless, divided, ineffective army that can be "tossed to and fro and carried about with every wind of doctrine, by the trickery of men, in the cunning craftiness of deceitful plotting."[158]

Jesus said, "The eye is the lamp of the body,"[159] meaning our vision permeates our very being. On the whole, our corporate vision has become warped and watered-down. Instead of working together to bring total victory over the planet for the Kingdom of God, we are seeking to build more buildings, achieve more "prosperity," and generally make the most of our time here while we wait for some random day when God mercifully decides it's time for this whole thing to be over.

As a result, we don't understand what made Jesus tick. We fight each other over the stupidest things, and yet we look the other way when there is blatant sin in our midst, our "church" leaders lower the bar and water down God's message, our Lord is blasphemed in public, our faith is increasingly marginalized, and, in many places, "the house of God has become a den of thieves." We often scorn the very "sinners" we are called to love and serve, and consider those who view things differently as "the enemy" – and all the while, the real enemy has free reign to steal, kill and destroy in our midst.

The Apostle Paul, before his road to Damascus experience, was a fierce fighter *for* God. Yet because he was caught in a religious system that had lost God's Big Picture, his warfare

---

[158] Ephesians 4:14, NKJV
[159] Matthew 6:22 and Luke 11:34

was misdirected towards tracking down and killing followers of the Way – for all the "right" reasons! After meeting Christ face-to-face and spending years in the wilderness being trained in the ways of the Kingdom, Paul's vision was clarified – and he finally knew who, how and when to fight.

To unlock the strengths of our inborn, God-given identity of warrior-sons and daughters, we need to understand and embrace God's original vision for mankind, His purpose for Creation, His deepest desires for us. We need to grow in spiritual maturity and discernment, so that our aggression is properly directed – so we know when to fight or turn the other cheek, fashion a whip or warmly embrace. Until we do, the Body of Christ will continue to languish, and victory will be nothing but a distant dream.

KEY POINTS: The Bible says the LORD is a warrior, and we are made in His image. We must learn to focus our inborn aggression towards our real enemy, the devil, and not our fellow man.

The best executive is the one who has sense enough to pick good men to do what he wants done, and self-restraint enough to keep from meddling with them while they do it.

Theodore Roosevelt

Chapter 8: Our Commander in Chief

Allow me to take you to back long ago, to the rustic home of a renowned prophet in a remote village. Elisha had been receiving messages from the Lord regarding the enemies of Israel and passing the information along to his king. Enraged at being continually undone by this divine intelligence, the hostile king of Aram sent an army to surround the village where Elisha lived and strike down the man of God. The next morning, Elisha's servant stepped out and saw their home surrounded by a strong force of chariots and enemy soldiers. Alarmed, he ran to his master and exclaimed, "Oh no, my lord! What shall we do?"

At this point in this book, this is where you may be. If you've followed along, dug in and pondered the biblical truths presented, perhaps you've come to a point where you now believe that total victory over the kingdom of darkness is our destiny – *and our job*. If you feel like I did as this paradigm shifted, it may all be a bit overwhelming. I mean, really. Here we are, wrapped in blindfolds of flesh, facing down a fierce, fallen archangel leading a full one-third of the angelic host who followed him into rebellion. They've had thousands of years' experience outfoxing men, they know precisely what's at stake, and they're quite entrenched. We, on the other hand, are immersed in the deceitfulness of riches, overwhelmed by a toxic culture and encased by long-established structures and systems and industries that are favorable to our enemy. The world itself and our very flesh are in league against us. Everywhere we look are powers, principalities and strongholds of the kingdom of darkness, dug in, strongly defended ... and growing. And look at our side! We're by and large fragmented, confused, conflicted and complacent. Many of us don't even believe we're at war, and most have no clue that *we* are the army who must deliver victory. How on earth can *we* do *this*? Elisha's servant expressed his hopeless perception quite well: *Oh no, my Lord, what shall we do?*

Oh, for a prophet like Elisha to rise to prominence today and lead us the way he led his servant! Here's what he said to that fearful, frantic man: "Don't be afraid. Those who are with us are more than those who are with them." Then he prayed, "Open his eyes, LORD, so that he may see." At that, the Lord opened the servant's eyes, and he looked and saw the hills full of horses and chariots of fire all around. The great prophet then simply asked God to strike the enemy forces blind, and he led them like lost puppies straight to the doorstep of his king.[160]

Had Elisha reacted with alarm and ran out with a sword to defend himself and his property, there is no doubt he'd have been cut down. He had every right and reason to do that. They were enemies of God's chosen people. He had an important and influential ministry to protect. He *had* to

---

[160] This story and these quotes are taken from 2 Kings 6:8-23 NIV

defend his home, his property, his very life....

Yet Elisha had *eyes to see* and *ears to hear*. He understood God's Big Picture plan, the role he played in it, and how to wage war God's way. Today our situation seems just as dire, the odds similarly insurmountable – especially in light of the reality that our job is not to merely *endure* but to *conquer*. Thankfully, the forces arrayed on our side are just like Elisha had, too. All we need to do is see things from God's perspective and play the role He intends us to play – and the results will be the same! *We can and will lead the enemy – as fearsome as he is – right under the feet of our King.* Elisha wasn't an anomaly, he was an example.

--

In his letter to the brothers in Ephesus, who had witnessed first-hand the manifest coming of God's Kingdom through his faithful work in their town, Paul gives us a perfect picture of what it will look like when the church grows to maturity: We will "grow up in all things into Him who is the head – Christ."[161] This is not just some meaningless word picture. On the contrary, it is a precise blueprint for the way God intends for His Kingdom to come, and we would be well advised to dig into it.

In a body, all senses are processed in the head, all understanding is in the head, all nourishment is received through the head and all the signals that control the body originate in the head. The head is in real-time, absolute control of every single function of the entire body.

This is exactly the role Christ must play in our lives – and in the fellowship of believers – for us to finally grow into the victorious sons and daughters God is longing for. When we

---

[161] Ephesians 4:15 NIV

do grow up into Christ who is the Head, we will see and hear things as He sees and hears them, receive all our provision through Him, and He will call the shots for every single thing we do – individually and as a body. Victory is impossible any other way.

When we finally wake up and get it, I believe victory will come "like a bolt of lightning from the east to the west."[162] The enemy simply cannot stand in the presence of the mature Body of Christ, fully connected to the Head. Not for one minute! Yet, as Paul said, *until* we grow up into Christ who is the Head, we will continue to "be children, tossed to and fro and carried about with every wind of doctrine, by the trickery of men, in the cunning craftiness of deceitful plotting."[163] It's simple: With Christ as our Head, victory is a done deal. Without Christ as our Head, we are going nowhere.

--

It's one thing to wax philosophical on the lofty theological principle of "the headship of Christ." It's quite another to walk it out. If you haven't gathered by now, I'm not much for lofty theological philosophizing. Talk is cheap. I want to know what it means to me, right here and right now, so I can *live it* and not just talk about it. Thankfully, living with Christ as our head is not complicated or difficult at all. Jesus told us *His burden is light,*[164] and we are invited to *enter into His rest.*[165] Living with Christ as our head is not some

---

[162] Matthew 24:27. I don't say this lightly. In *Chapter 15 - Endgame* I show very practically how this can happen.
[163] Ephesians 4:14 NKJV
[164] Matthew 11:30
[165] Hebrews 4 talks about this, and says that embracing the Good News IS entering His rest. Fact is, our victory is finished in eternity, God is just waiting for us to get in line with it in the here and now.

sophisticated thing we must aspire to after years of studying and ritualistic observance. It is not the top rung of the ladder of religion. Instead, the opposite is true: it is how we should *start* our walk with the Lord, how our lifetime relationship with Him must be founded. As Christ said, "Truly I tell you, unless you change and become like little children, you will never enter the Kingdom of Heaven."[166] Indeed, the *hardest* thing in the world is to continue to do everything our own way, under our own strength, using our own understanding. Continuing to do things that way is the very definition of foolishness, because it is impossible to establish God's Kingdom on our own, and because His promises of guidance and complete provision are reserved for those fully submitted to the headship of Christ.

Are you searching for God's will in something? Romans 12:2 says, "Do not conform to the pattern of this world, but be transformed by the renewing of your mind. Then you will be able to test and approve what God's will is—His good, pleasing and perfect will."[167]

Do you want to know what your next step should be? Proverbs 3:5-6 says, "Trust in the LORD with all your heart, and lean not on your own understanding. In all your ways acknowledge Him, and He shall direct your paths."[168]

Are you concerned you don't know what to do in a given situation? Jesus told us not to worry, because "the Advocate, the Holy Spirit, whom the Father will send in my name, will teach you all things and will remind you of everything I have said to you."[169] He said this is not some broad, vague,

---

[166] Matthew 18:3 NIV
[167] NIV
[168] NKJV
[169] John 14:26 NIV

good feeling of "inspiration," but rather specific, step-by-step instructions – to the extent that, when you are called to give account for your faith, you should "just say whatever is given you at the time, for it is not you speaking, but the Holy Spirit."[170]

Paul prayed fervently for the brothers in Ephesus to live this way so they could continue to expand the Kingdom of God: "I keep asking that the God of our Lord Jesus Christ, the glorious Father, may give you *the Spirit of wisdom and revelation*, so that you may know Him better. I pray that the eyes of your heart may be enlightened in order that you may know the hope to which He has called you, the riches of His glorious inheritance in His holy people, and His incomparably great power for us who believe."[171] In his letter to the Corinthians, Paul went so far as to say *"we have the mind of Christ."*[172]

Jesus Himself lived this way. Our example, our friend, the firstborn of many brothers, said, "I love the Father and do exactly what my Father has commanded me."[173] He didn't call the shots in His own life; instead, He said, "Very truly I tell you, the Son can do nothing by himself; He can do only what He sees His Father doing."[174]

God deeply desires to serve as our ever-present Commander-in-Chief, allowing us to perceive things with His senses, guiding every word and action, and giving us full access to His omniscient strategies and insights. "I will instruct you and teach you in the way you should go," He says. "I will

---

[170] Mark 13:11 NIV, restated in Luke 12:12
[171] Ephesians 1:17-18 NIV, *emphasis added.*
[172] 1 Corinthians 2:16 NIV, *emphasis added.*
[173] John 14:31
[174] John 5:19 NIV

guide you with My eye."[175] Indeed, the mind of Christ is promised and fully available to us, and it is our Father's heart's desire for us to put it to good use.

In addition to this, God promises to provide *everything we need* to fully carry out His instructions. In what we call the "Sermon on the Mount,"[176] Jesus made this point clear. After telling us that we cannot store up for ourselves both treasure on earth and treasure in Heaven, He specifically instructs us not to worry about or pursue provision for our physical needs, or even worry about tomorrow at all. Instead, He says, "Seek first His Kingdom and His righteousness, and all these things will be given to you as well."[177] If we occupy ourselves, fully and without any other concern, in pursuing His original intent – the establishment of His *royal power, kingship, dominion and rule* on earth as it is in Heaven (which He prayed just a few sentences before) – and do it according to the steps He gives us, then He *promises* to give us everything we need, every day.

These are very meaningful words to me. Some time ago, when the Lord called me into full-time ministry, this was one verse my family and I literally lived on for many years. Before jumping in with both feet, I remember specifically pondering this promise of God. I had sat in a pew most of my life, sincerely gone through the motions, believed every

---

[175] Psalm 32:8 NKJV

[176] It is recorded in both Matthew and Luke. Of course, everything Jesus said is of vital importance, but when you look at this teaching in the context of the entirety of the Gospels, it takes on even greater weight. The vast majority of the words that are in red ink in my Bible (meaning Jesus spoke them), are either parables about the Kingdom, rebuke of the Pharisees, explaining His historical context, casting out demons, or interacting with people. He actually gave very little by way of step-by-step instructions for daily living, and most of it is found in this portion of Scripture. So if we're going to "walk the walk," it's important to really grab onto what He's saying here.

[177] Matthew 6:33 NIV

word in the Bible was true, and trusted God with my death (what have you got to lose, anyway?) – but I'd never really gone all-in and trusted Him with my life. With a stay-at-home wife and growing family, I was feeling called to leave a well-paying job for the unknown work of pioneering a new ministry. And here in front of me were these words in red ink: Seek first His Kingdom and righteousness, every day – and don't worry about what you're going to eat, drink or wear – and Jesus promises God will provide everything we need. My wife and I decided: *It's about time we find out if all this stuff is true or not.* I mean, if this one promise isn't true, then none of it can be true. And if it's not true, why are we wasting our time with all these religious regulations and stuff? If it's *not* true, let's live it up! But if it *is* true… well, we'd be fools not to take Him up on this offer.

So we jumped all-in. I had a lot to learn, and God was very patient in teaching me. Over the next five years combined, our family income added up to less than it was my last year in the business world. We didn't have a lot in savings or other assets and these were soon gone. Yet we never worried, despite being tempted sometimes. Instead, we focused on seeking first His Kingdom and righteousness. And you know what? We never once went without food, clothing, transportation, medicine, or anything we needed. A forensic accountant couldn't tell you how we did it. Many, many months in a row when bills were due, we'd sign the checks, stick them in the envelopes and set them by the front door. And pray. Every time – every single time, for many years – what we needed would fall in our laps, often to the very penny, at the very last moment. We never got behind on our mortgage or failed to pay any of our bills. Our average bank account for these years was about nine dollars – no exaggeration. And yet we never went without. I could tell you story after story of God's miraculous provision, but that'd be a whole book of its own![178] Let me just tell you this, because I know it first-hand: God *is* who He says He is, and His promises *are* true. Take Him up on it, and you'll see for yourself![179]

--

On our own small scale, my family's experience has paralleled many of the stories recounted in the Bible. God gave Noah precise plans for the ark, and Noah rescued the human race through simple obedience.[180] When Moses at the burning bush told God he wouldn't know what to say to Pharaoh, God replied, "Who gave human beings their mouths? Who makes them deaf or mute? Who gives them sight or makes them blind? Is it not I, the LORD? Now go; I will help you speak and will teach you what to say."[181] Almost every aspect of the Israelites' wilderness experience supports this point: God told them what to do, step by step. When they did it, it worked, and when they didn't, it didn't work. And He gave them fresh manna every day to keep them on the right path.

In fact, do you remember why Moses couldn't enter the Promised Land? God gave him a simple instruction – speak to the rock to make water come out – and Moses did it his own way instead; he struck it with his staff. For this, he had to die before seeing the culmination of his life's work.[182] God

---

[178] Stay tuned – maybe I'll write it someday. We'll see how this one does!

[179] Please don't read this and think that just because God called me to quit my job and go into full-time, faith-based ministry, that I'm suggesting this path for anyone else. That's missing the point entirely. The point is to follow the specific, personal, unique steps He lays out for you, wherever they may lead.

[180] Genesis 6

[181] Exodus 4:11-12 NIV

[182] Numbers 20

is serious about His role as Commander-in-Chief!

After stepping into Moses' place of leadership, Joshua led the Israelites to conquer the Promised Land.[183] Despite the seemingly impossible task of leading a band of desert-dwelling nomads to conquer a race of giants and other warring tribes and drive them out of heavily fortified, walled cities, when you read the details of Joshua's job it actually seems quite simple. He just followed God's step-by-step instructions! Some of them, like parading around Jericho,[184] didn't make any sense at all. Others were pretty straightforward. Whatever the instructions, when the people obeyed, they succeeded, and when they didn't obey, they failed.

This is really a simple concept and a continual theme throughout the whole Bible, but it eluded me most of my life. When I viewed the Bible merely as a holy book of long-ago stories, regulations for righteous living and the means of going to a better placed when I die, I failed to pick up on this concept. But when I took that leap of faith – trusting God with my life, and not just my death – I grew to realize the Bible is simply a partial transcript of God's interaction with man over time. Everything that happened in the Bible still happens today, and God still longs to relate to us the same way He did to the people we read about in Scripture. Then it all started to click into place. All we need to do is live with Christ as our Head – seeing and hearing with His eyes and ears, understanding with His mind, following His lead and banking on His provision. When we do, even when the tasks

---

[183] The conquest of the Promised Land is a clear Old Testament "type" (a historical scale model, intentionally given by God, to foreshadow a New Testament occurrence) of how God's people will bring His Kingdom to earth at the end of time.

[184] Joshua 5-6

He gives us seem impossible by the world's standards, it truly is a light load!

--

That brings us to the big question: What *is* required for us to grow into Christ who is our Head? How *do* we walk in His continual guidance and provision? The answer to this is clearly spelled out in the verses I quoted earlier in this chapter. Throughout the Bible, promises like this follow a consistent pattern: They are if/then conditional statements, meaning *if* we do our part, *then* God is obligated to do His.

And what are the *ifs*? To fully connect to Christ the Head, we must trust in Him will all our heart, not lean on our own understanding and acknowledge Him in all our ways.[185] We must stop conforming to the patterns of this world and let Him totally renew the way we think about things.[186] We must not worry about our material wellbeing and not pursue treasures in this world; instead, we must seek His *royal power, kingship, dominion, rule* and righteousness at every step.[187] There are many other similar promises, and all of them have these same things tied to them. In short, we must live exactly as Jesus said He Himself did: "I love the Father and do exactly what my Father has commanded me."[188] Step by step.[189]

Bottom line, we must do what Jesus told the rich young ruler: We must go all-in.[190] We must stop merely trusting

---

[185] Proverbs 3:5-6
[186] Romans 12:2
[187] Matthew 6:33
[188] John 14:31
[189] Each of these if/then promises is worthy of deep meditation and study, but that is beyond the scope of this book. I encourage you to take the time to really dig into these things. I have found this to be a powerful exercise.
[190] See the story recounted in Matthew 19, Mark 10 and Luke 18.

Him with our death; we must instead trust Him with our life, and everything in it. We must stop doing things our own way, relying on our own senses and understanding and worrying about the things of this world. We cannot hold anything back. *Only then, when we go all in, is God obligated to guide our steps and provide for our needs.*

I used to passionately pray, begging for God's guidance and provision. Finally I came to realize this was like standing in front of a soda vending machine and begging it for a soda. The mechanism for getting a soda is crystal clear and spelled out – put the money in, push the button and get your drink. Same with God's divine guidance and provision. His fulfillment of His promises is automatic and reliable. When you do your part, He'll do His, every time. If you do anything less, He is not obligated to guide or provide. God wants sons and daughters who trust Him fully and hold nothing back!

Before I understood this, I used to be overcome with fear at Jesus' statement, "Not everyone who says to me, 'Lord, Lord,' will enter the Kingdom of heaven, but only the one who does the will of my Father who is in heaven. Many will say to me on that day, 'Lord, Lord, did we not prophesy in your name and in your name drive out demons and in your name perform many miracles?' Then I will tell them plainly, 'I never knew you. Away from me, you evildoers!'"[191]

I was doing *my* very best to do all kinds of things *I* thought were advancing the Kingdom, and yet there was this lingering fear I might be rejected this way in eternity. And you know what? Looking back now, that's exactly what would have happened. I was doing things according to my own understanding, leaning on my own perception of the

---

[191] Matthew 7:21-23 NIV

world around me. Sure I was putting a lot on the line, but I was not *all-in*; instead, I was seeking first to provide for my physical needs (and desires) and giving God what was left over.

Jesus said, "No one is good—except God alone,"[192] and the Prophet Isaiah said, "All our righteous acts are like filthy rags."[193] When we do things our way – even "great" things "for" God – this is how He sees them. No man acting on his own can do anything in the world that pleases God – whether guided by the best intentions, traditions, strategy, human counsel, education, or anything but God Himself. It's not what I can do *for* Him that matters; instead, it's what I allow Him to do *through* me. This is a key point to understand: God does not work *for* us, and He will not help *us* with *our* work. Rather, we are to work for Him, and our job is to help *Him* with *His* work.

Yes, it is our task to NIKAO (*conquer, carry off the victory*). Yet God's role is anything but hands-off and passive. Instead, He is the Commander in Chief of His army of sons and daughters. In a war, the Commander in Chief does not pick up arms and never sets foot on the battlefield. His role is more important than that! All plans, orders, resources, weapons and authority originate with Him. They are fully available to those who serve obediently under Him, and entirely unavailable to anyone who operates outside His chain of command.

---

[192] Mark 7:18 NIV

[193] Isaiah 64:6. The Hebrew here is even more graphic, showing just how filthy our works really our in God's sight. Literally translated, our best works are "as rags of menstruation." These were considered by Hebrew law to be one of the most unclean things. Any person coming in contact with them was also considered unclean, and to be cleaned required remaining separate from the community for a time, and then offering specific sacrifices to God.)

When we are connected to Christ the Head, the task of wiping out the kingdom of darkness is not a heavy burden! We are each – and all – implored to stop *trying*, stop *doing* and start *becoming* the victorious sons and daughters He longs for us to be. All direction, provision, power and authority we need to conquer the world flow freely from a place of absolute devotion and simple obedience. Everything we are looking for, everything we need and desire, is found only one place, and that is right in the center of His will.

KEY POINTS: While it is our calling to establish the Kingdom of God on the earth, God is by no means a passive observer. On the contrary, He promises to give us step-by-step instructions and everything else we need to do the job. Victory will come only when we allow Him to call the shots and live a life of full submission to His will.

"Be still, and know that I am God; I will be exalted among the nations, I will be exalted in the earth." (Psalm 46:10, NIV)

Never forget that the most powerful force on earth is love.

Nelson Rockefeller

Chapter 9 – Firepower

A good deal of military training involves learning to employ the weapons of warfare. What good is an army with no firepower, and what good are soldiers who don't know how to use it? Thankfully, in our mission to implement a regime change against the kingdom of darkness – the fiercest and most important war of all time – we are given access to the most awesome force in the universe: the very power of God Himself. The enemy's weapons are no match against what is available to us. When we learn to access and properly employ God's promised firepower, nothing can stand in our way.

The Bible says God's people have power to accomplish mighty deeds. Jesus said, "These signs will accompany those who believe: In my name they will drive out demons; they will speak in new tongues; they will pick up snakes with their hands; and when they drink deadly poison, it will not hurt them at all; they will place their hands on sick people, and they will get well."[194] He Himself performed incredible demonstrations of God's power – healing the sick, casting out demons, calming storms, commanding the weather,

---

[194] Mark 16:17-18 NIV

raising the dead, etc. – and then He said, "Very truly I tell you, whoever believes in me will do the works I have been doing, and they will do even greater things than these."[195] Paul said that we have power to pull down spiritual strongholds, cast down arguments and every high thing that exalts itself against the knowledge of God and bring every thought into captivity to the obedience of Christ,[196] and that we are more than conquerors.[197]

If we believe the Bible we must believe these things. But fact is the vast majority of Christians don't see many demonstrations of this power today, and even fewer actually walk in this power. When we hear reports of God's power on display, my experience is that much of the Body greets these reports with extreme skepticism, and even derision.[198]

I've actually had a pastor, a dear friend and a fine man, tell me point blank he believes, and his denomination teaches, that the acts in Acts don't happen anymore. "There was a burst of spiritual energy back then because Jesus was around," he said. "But it's fizzled out over time." That poor, poor man. By his own admission – that he believes God doesn't give us His power anymore – he is trying to lead a group of believers *on his own strength*. And he wonders why his congregation is dysfunctional, fragmented and lacking any real community impact.

On the other end of the spectrum, we have teachers who

---

[195] John 14:12 NIV

[196] 2 Corinthians 10

[197] Romans 8:37

[198] There are certainly enough hucksters out there to warrant a healthy degree of skepticism. Unfortunately, the skepticism I've seen through the years is mainly the *unhealthy* variety, as many folks seem to start with the fundamental assumption that any report of modern miracles is a fraud.

take these power promises and flippantly apply them to selfish, material things. The so-called "name it and claim it" crowd teaches that if you want a Ferrari, all you have to do is "speak it" and it'll show up in your driveway. Of course, they often tie this in with false teachings that this "favor" is predicated on your giving money to them, so the Ferraris only show up in their own driveways ("see folks, it works!") while the poor followers tend only to get poorer.

Of course a good father wouldn't turn loose an immature son with a loaded .357 Magnum, and God is the same way. He releases His power to us gradually, as we mature. As a result, the propagators of this "name it and claim it" teaching don't have many real demonstrations of God's power to exhibit. The resulting fruit? (Other than their own "prosperity?") Their students are misled, and the rest of us just grow more and more skeptical.

There is no denying it: The vast majority of the Body of Christ today, for myriad reasons, are not employing the overwhelming, miraculous power of God that is repeatedly promised to us. Because of this, there's no wonder most Christians don't see or embrace God's original intent vision of victory. For weak, powerless human beings to conquer the kingdom of darkness, we'll need some mind-boggling firepower. Since we don't understand or access that power, the thought of us displacing our ferocious and powerful enemy from the world is not even on our radar screens. If we *could* be winning, we *would* be winning, right? No! God is waiting for us to grow up and get this. When we do, *then* victory will be ours.

If God's miraculous power is promised to us, why have most Christians today never really seen or felt it? That's simple. Just as with the word NIKAO, in large part it comes down to a bad translation/interpretation of a crucial, lynchpin word in Scripture. Understand this word and its use in Scripture and you'll hold the key to unlocking the promised power of God in your life.

A bit of a warning here: I'm going to get a little academic for a few pages. At first blush, you may wonder what a Greek lesson is doing in a chapter about God's firepower. Stick with me and you'll see. Moreover, if you do, I believe this study may even inspire a significant paradigm shift and lead to genuine revival in your life. I know it has for me and quite a few people with whom I've shared this information. Rest easy – it's not a mystery, it's not a new pop theology, it's not an odd mountaintop revelation from some mystic, and I'm not asking you to "just trust me" – it's simply Greek, and it's been there all along, lost in translation.

The word we're going to briefly dig into here is just that: The English word "word." Bible translators slap this four-letter word on top of several Greek words with vast differences in meaning. Much more than simple nuance is lost. Rather, a vital, foundational principle of the Christian faith has for generations been virtually erased from the Bible by this translational shortcut.

For years I've asked Christians what they think of when they read or hear the phrase "the Word of God." Every single person I've asked has the same answer: The Bible. That's all there is to it: The Word of God is the Bible, and the Bible is the Word of God. Period, end of subject.

So when they hear, "In the beginning was the Word, and the Word was with God, and the Word was God,"[199] they picture a Bible floating in space. When they hear, "Man shall

---

[199] John 1:1 NIV

not live by bread alone, but by every word that proceeds from the mouth of God," "Faith comes by hearing, and hearing by the word of God," or "Take ... the sword of the Spirit, which is the word of God,"[200] their minds insert "Bible" and come up with this: We live by the Bible, have faith by hearing the Bible, and fight the devil with the Bible.

I must ask you to pause for a moment before you read on. Please ask God to open your heart to His truth. It's hard for me even to type this, because I know most readers who (as I do) revere the Bible more than life itself may initially take this statement as shocking blasphemy, but the fact is this: *Inserting the word Bible into these great verses is wrong, sucks meaning out of them, drains them of power, and robs us of possibly the most precious promise of God in this life.*

There, I said it.

I hope you're still with me (and still breathing normally!), and that seeking God's truth is more important to you than holding onto long-standing, traditional paradigms that simply aren't working. Once again I ask you, if you have difficulty with anything I am presenting here, please dig into it! Get a Strong's Concordance or other Biblical Greek dictionary and see for yourself.[201]

Ok, back to it. As I said, there are numerous Greek words, expressing widely divergent meanings, which most English-language translators simply lump under our word, "Word." These include LOGOS, GRAPHE and RHEMA. [202]

---

[200] Matthew 4:4, Romans 10:17, Ephesians 6:17 NKJV
[201] There are many fantastic, free internet resources for this kind of research. I frequently use www.biblestudytools.com.
[202] There are multiple words for "word," in both Greek and Hebrew, but I'm going to only go into three of them here, to avoid going down too many rabbit trails. I hope you'll study this further on your own.

As I dig into the definitions for these, allow me to couch them in a metaphor so they make more sense. Think of God as an architect and us as His laborers. He wants us to complete a building project and is seeking to guide our steps as we do it. He has a crystal clear vision for the structure, including every detail, and He must communicate this to us so we can build it according to His demanding specifications.

At its essence, *communication* is the effort to transfer a thought from one mind to another. There are lots of ways to do this – through writing, speech, pictures, demonstration and much more. When you look at all the Bible words we translate as "word," you begin to see that *God employs all of these means* to transfer to us His vision and guide our steps. Yes, the static, printed words of the Bible are a vital and incredible source of divine communication, but they are just a small fraction of what He offers "those who have ears to hear."[203] As long as we remain stuck in man-made tradition, and continue to view the Bible as the sum total of God's "Word," we will never be able to complete our Kingdom building project.

Before the dawn of time, God had a vision for His Kingdom, His sons and daughters, and this world. This original, founding vision is best expressed in Greek by the word LOGOS. It is "a decree, mandate or order; what is declared, a thought, declaration, aphorism, a weighty saying, a dictum, a maxim." This word is used 316 times in the Greek New Testament. It says, "In the beginning was LOGOS, the LOGOS was with God, and the LOGOS was God,"[204] and

---

[203] This is one of the most repeated phrases of Christ in all of Scripture.
[204] John 1:1, NKJV with proper Greek word inserted.

that Jesus was LOGOS made flesh.[205] Before the dawn of time, there were not little scrolls or books floating around in Heaven; instead God had a vision, a plan, a Big Picture. And Jesus was not a talking Bible with arms and legs! Instead, He was the physical incarnation of God's original intent. (Is it starting to make a little more sense?)

An architect must start with a clearly defined vision. This is the source of all other forms of communication related to the building project. All other methods of attempting to transfer this vision from his mind to others' – including scale models,[206] drawings, etc. – are derived from this original vision. It is important to understand that nothing less than the finished building itself fully expresses the architect's vision. *Every other form of expression, while accurate, is incomplete.*

Once the architect has the vision complete in his mind, next he drafts a set of blueprints. These are printed sketches, descriptions and instructions intended to guide the steps of the builders. The Gospel writers used the word GRAPHE for this concept. It means, "written word, scripture," and is used 51 times in the New Testament. The printed pages of the Bible are GRAPHE. Interestingly, this is always translated as "scripture" in the standard King James Version – and so while this is never called "word" in the Bible, it is the one thing people think of when they talk about the "Word" of God!

Our traditions have led many of us to take the Architect's blueprints and then just run along with the assumption that they fully and completely express His divine purpose, plan and will. But as anyone who works in construction can tell

---

[205] John 1:14
[206] In this metaphor, Biblical "types" are akin to the Architect's scale models.

you, if you simply take blueprints and hand them out to
your work crews – with no hands-on, step-by-step
supervision from the architect or a general contractor – the
building will never take the precise form intended by the
architect. *A building may come together, but it will be
plagued by quirks as the different subcontractors interpreted
things their own ways, and the look, feel and functionality
will differ from what the architect intended. As hired hands
for God's Kingdom construction, we need more than
blueprints!*[207]

Let me step out of this metaphor for a moment. You deserve
more than human reasoning to accept this point so let me
spell it out straight from the Bible. At what we call the Last
Supper, Jesus told His disciples that His time on earth was
coming to an end, and there was of course much more
information they needed to know in order to continue with
His work.[208] "I have much more to say to you," He said.
"More than you can now bear."[209] But He couldn't because
His time was up. He told them not to worry, however,
because "the Advocate, the Holy Spirit, whom the Father
will send in my name, will teach you all things and will
remind you of everything I have said to you."[210]

Right here, in Jesus' own words, He clearly said there is
much more to the Architect's vision than He could
communicate to His disciples, even after spending three
years in their close company; that all the words He spoke
and demonstrated to His disciples were but a fraction of the

---

[207] Try putting together a complicated toy with the instructions only (which these
days are usually translated from Chinese!), without looking at the picture on the
box!
[208] This incredible monologue is contained in John 14-16.
[209] John 16:12, NIV
[210] John 14:26 NIV

entirety of God's LOGOS. Then, just a few chapters later in John, the great apostle concludes his book by saying, "Jesus did many other things as well. If every one of them were written down, I suppose that even the whole world would not have room for the books that would be written."[211] And so my point here is confirmed by the words of Christ and the personal admission of one of the Bible's primary and most prolific writers:[212] The GRAPHE (written word) – what most Christians assume is the entirety of God's Word – *is but a fraction of a fraction of all that God desires to communicate to us.*

Of course Jesus didn't leave us hanging. As He said, in reference to the Holy Spirit, "When He, the Spirit of truth, comes, He will guide you into all the truth. He will not speak on His own; He will speak only what He hears, and He will tell you what is yet to come. He will glorify me because it is from me that He will receive what He will make known to you. All that belongs to the Father is mine. That is why I said the Spirit will receive from me what He will make known to you."[213]

Back on the metaphor, Jesus is saying here that the Architect isn't going to leave us hanging with just a set of blueprints; instead, He will send a jobsite foreman (in the form of the Holy Spirit) to fully and completely communicate His vision to us, every step of the way. This brings us to what I believe is the most important Greek word for "word" of them all: RHEMA. This word means, "that which is or has been uttered by the living voice, thing spoken; word any sound

---

[211] John 21:25 NIV. While it's debatable, some scholars believe that the Gospel of John may be, in chronological order of writing, the last book of the Bible, so this may in fact be the last statement given to us by God in all of the written Word!
[212] John wrote five books of the New Testament: The Gospel of John; 1, 2 and 3 John and The Revelation.
[213] John 16:13-15 NIV

produced by the voice and having definite meaning." It is used 67 times in the New Testament, in some very key places.

RHEMA is the personal, conversational, relevant, relationship Word of God. It is God's voice for each of us, like it was for Samuel as a youth when God called out to him in the middle of the night, saying, "Samuel! Samuel!"[214] Interestingly, in this story it says, "In those days, the word of the LORD was rare."[215] There weren't fewer scrolls in the temple than before. Instead, because of the high priest's disobedient household, *the personal, spoken word of God is what was rare.* This story also says the great prophet-to-be didn't recognize that voice because "Samuel did not yet know the LORD: The word of the LORD had not yet been revealed to him."[216] By this time in his life, he had been fully inculcated into the religious structure, he obviously believed in God, and he had been exposed to the Scriptures. But he still didn't *know* God, in the true sense, because he hadn't yet been introduced to God's RHEMA word. Personal communication is the basis of every real relationship. Jesus said, "My sheep hear My voice, and I know them, and they follow."[217] Prior to hearing and following His RHEMA, Samuel wasn't in the flock. But then God's living voice came to him and he responded – and that changed everything.

Let's go back to some of those key verses I mentioned earlier and insert the proper Greek word. I believe this will make them come alive for you in a new and exciting way. In

---

[214] 1 Samuel 3 recounts this story. The Hebrew word here is DABAR, which Jesus in his own words bridged directly to the Greek word RHEMA (Matthew 4:4 and Luke 4:4).
[215] 1 Samuel 3:1 NIV
[216] 1 Samuel 3:7 NIV
[217] John 10:27 NKJV

Matthew 4:4 Jesus said, "Man doesn't live by bread alone, but by RHEMA." In context this is particularly stunning. If you recall, Jesus spoke this to satan after His first temptation in the wilderness. Satan had come to Him after a 40-day fast and tempted Him to turn rocks into bread and eat them. Now let me ask you, what would have been the sin in that? Where is it written, "Thou shalt not turn rocks into bread and eat them?" It's not! Only a few times in the Bible do we see beyond the veil into the spirit world. No doubt satan dangled temptations in front of Christ over and over again – like when He was walking on water, the enemy must have been screaming, "you're gonna sink!" – but it's simply not recorded for us. If this story were like the others, and we only saw the "natural" side of it, we'd simply think it was another miracle if Jesus had finished fasting, turned rocks into bread, ate them, and moved on. Nobody would look at that and say, "See! He wasn't God after all! He sinned!" – because there was nothing in and of itself "wrong" in the thing He was being tempted to do.

Indeed, our whole human checklist for decision-making was satisfied: Jesus had the power, the right, the freedom – and no doubt the desire and physical need – to do that very thing. So why didn't He do it? Herein lies the vital importance of RHEMA. Jesus said, in effect, "Satan, I acknowledge that I need bread, but what's more important to me is that I follow the step-by-step instructions of God, and He hasn't told me to do this yet." Jesus would have rather starved to death than do anything outside of God's specific, step-by-step, RHEMA-given instructions for His life! He didn't live on bread alone, and not on GRAPHE (the written word – because on that basis alone, the thing tempted would have been just fine!), but on RHEMA.

Here's another key verse: "Faith comes by hearing, and

hearing by the word of God."[218] If you have dedicated your life to evangelism according to our traditional methods this may hurt you in the gut, like it did me, because here's the truth: The "word" in this verse is RHEMA. *Faith comes by hearing RHEMA from God.* Like in the story of young Samuel, a person can be dedicated to God, live in the temple, observe all the proper religious activities, have a trusting knowledge of GRAPHE, *and still not have faith as God defines it.* If we do not, like Jesus, recognize and follow God's personal, present voice in our lives, we simply are not in His flock.

I admit this is a hard word. It was painful for me to accept – because of all the years I tried to serve God without this understanding – and it is painful for me to have to break this to those who've never heard it before. Most denominations don't teach this, but it is the Bible truth, and as such I know that when you accept it, it will give you new life, freedom and power. We can give away cases of Bibles, quote Scripture till we're blue in the face – and the people we are working to reach can believe every word of it – and yet without a real, meaningful, personal relationship with God through Jesus Christ – a relationship with RHEMA at its heart – then it is all a waste of time and energy.[219] This is precisely what Jesus meant when He said, "Many will say to me ..., 'Lord, Lord, did we not prophesy in your name and in your name drive out demons and in your name perform many miracles?' Then I will tell them plainly, 'I never knew

---

[218] Romans 10:17

[219] Please don't get me wrong here. I'm not saying Bible-based outreach or ministry is a waste of time. On the contrary! 2 Timothy 3:17-17 (NIV) says, "All Scripture is God-breathed and is useful for teaching, rebuking, correcting and training in righteousness, so that the servant of God may be thoroughly equipped for every good work." What I *am* saying is that if the Bible is simply taken as nothing more than "religious" information – with no real relationship with God behind it – then it *is* pointless.

you. Away from me, you evildoers!"[220] *He just wants to have a real relationship with us – built on intimate communication – that's all.* Nothing else we can do matters. Nothing else can lead to victory.

Before I present one last key RHEMA verse, I want to make something perfectly clear: I value, honor and revere the Bible more than life itself. I'm old fashioned in that I never let anything sit on top of my Bible – it's always the top of the stack. I believe it is the infallible, inspired GRAPHE of God. Just look below at the footnotes – several hundred in this book – to see how much I reference it and base my entire life and worldview upon it. But fact is, *the written Word, while fully true, is just a portion of what God desires to communicate to us, and mere intellectual acceptance of the Bible as truth does not save us.*[221] Without a real relationship with God through Jesus Christ, based on personal RHEMA, everything else is worthless.

Of course, God often gives RHEMA to me through GRAPHE, but RHEMA is much more than that. He speaks in all the ways He promises: guiding my steps, making sense of things, giving me words to say, and – dare I say it – even telling me what to write. When you realize the believers in the Book of Acts didn't have what we call the Bible – the few scrolls they had were hard to access, especially for the Gentiles – and instead, only had RHEMA, you begin to realize how important it is. Look at what God was able to do

---

[220] Matthew 7:22-24

[221] Look at how Jesus rebuked the Pharisees in this passage: "The Father who sent me has Himself testified concerning me. You have never heard His voice nor seen His form, nor does His Word dwell in you, for you do not believe the one He sent. You diligently study the Scriptures because you think that by them you possess eternal life. These are the Scriptures that testify about me, yet you refuse to come to me to have life." (John 5:37-40 NIV)

through them! They weren't skeptical of God's power – they lived in it! Were I in a situation where I had to choose between RHEMA and GRAPHE, I'd choose RHEMA, 100 percent of the time. Thankfully, we don't have to choose. But sadly, out of tradition and ignorance, most Christians *do* choose – they choose GRAPHE alone, and the results are ... well, the results are what we have today.

Ok, so you may be wondering what all this is doing in a chapter entitled "Firepower." When I present one last key "word" verse from the Bible, you'll understand. In his letter to the believers of Ephesus, who were called out by the Lord and being shepherded by Paul to maintain and expand upon the spiritual regime change that had been won in their community, the great warrior apostle wrote:

Finally, be strong in the Lord and in his mighty power. Put on the full armor of God, so that you can take your stand against the devil's schemes. For our struggle is not against flesh and blood, but against the rulers, against the authorities, against the powers of this dark world and against the spiritual forces of evil in the heavenly realms. Therefore put on the full armor of God, so that when the day of evil comes, you may be able to stand your ground, and after you have done everything, to stand. Stand firm then, with the belt of truth buckled around your waist, with the breastplate of righteousness in place, and with your feet fitted with the readiness that comes from the gospel of peace. In addition to all this, take up the shield of faith, with which you can extinguish all the flaming arrows of the evil one. Take the helmet of salvation and the sword of the Spirit, which is the word of God.[222]

Did you notice – in all of the items Paul lists, *there is but one*

---

[222] Ephesians 6: 10-17 NIV

weapon? One tool we are given with which to tear down every stronghold, demolish every argument that exalts itself against the knowledge of God, and utterly defeat satan and his kingdom of darkness? What is this one, all-powerful weapon? *It is not the written Word.*

The sword of the Spirit is RHEMA.

This has been translated as "word" and interpreted as "Scripture" for too long! You can't beat the devil by quoting the Bible to him – he knows that Book better than any man ever will, and he believes every word of it, because he was there when it all happened! What satan doesn't have access to, which we as followers of Jesus Christ do, is the RHEMA of God – His fresh, relevant, personal word, through which He guides our paths, orders our steps, tells us what to do and when to do it, when to pray and what to pray for, puts the proper words in our mouth, and prompts us at all times in all things to do His will. And when we are in His will, His power flows through us to defeat anything the enemy can throw at us. When we are in His will, the very gates of hell can't stand in our way!

The RHEMA of God proves Christianity as the one true faith. *Only a Living God can utter a living Word*, and no other faith offers this. Practiced without RHEMA, however, Christianity is just a religion, no better than any other. Without RHEMA, our faith is merely a collection of holy writings, a prescribed way of living, a system of worship, a community of like-minded people, belief in a distant and silent deity, an avenue for "prayer," a reason to hope, a basis of ethics and morals, an opportunity for full-time ministers to make a living, and the promise of "heaven" when we die if we play things by the book – *just like virtually every other religion on earth.* Without RHEMA, Christianity is empty, ritualistic, legalistic, and ultimately pointless. Without RHEMA, our religion truly is, as Karl Marx famously wrote, "The opiate of the masses" – a mysterious, superstitious code that keeps the deluded population under control.

Jesus didn't come to start another religion. He came, ultimately, to reconcile us to a real relationship with our Father. All the other things He accomplished – destroying the works of the devil, reclaiming that which was lost in the garden, setting the coming of the Kingdom in motion – all spring from this one thing: We now, through Him, have open access to a personal relationship with the Living God, and all the benefits that come with it.

--

When it comes to understanding and walking in God's power, it's vital to remember what's going on here: God is raising up a Body of sons and daughters whom He can trust to rule His Kingdom in eternity. God doesn't give us supernatural power to build our own kingdoms. He doesn't give us supernatural power to hurt people, or to lord over anyone. We're quite proficient at doing that in our own strength, thank you. Instead, God gives us His power to build His Kingdom, raise up sons and daughters and unite the Body.

The enemy will always try to knock us off track. His very name means "deceiver." He will come "masquerading as an angel of light."[223] We must know what God's power looks like, so when He guides us to employ it we are certain we are hearing from Him. (This is one of the great blessings of Scripture, that we have countless examples to follow.)

God's power brings destruction to the enemy, but the

---

[223] 2 Corinthians 11:14

opposite to people. The power of God, when employed in the natural realm, brings peace, love, grace, mercy, tenderness and kindness. The power of God builds people up even as it tears demons down. Of course, when they are hard-hearted – stubbornly and intentionally standing in the way of God's will – God's power can wipe people out, as it did with Pharoah.[224] When people are aligned with evil, willingly or not, there is no doubt the truth hurts. Jesus minced no words with the Pharisees, for example. *But even His harshest words were spoken in love, and aimed at raising up the son-seed of God that was in each of them.* Jesus, our example, had nothing but compassion and gentle words for repentant sinners. He frequently used God's power to heal; He never once used it to harm a man (only demons), or even to defend Himself. The mighty Lion of Judah Himself told us "the meek … will inherit the earth,"[225] and this is how He lived.[226]

The power of God, the assignments RHEMA will give us, all come down to one thing: Love. Paul wrote, "Love is patient, love is kind. It does not envy, it does not boast, it is not proud. It does not dishonor others, it is not self-seeking, it is not easily angered, it keeps no record of wrongs. Love does not delight in evil but rejoices with the truth. It always protects, always trusts, always hopes, always perseveres. Love never fails."[227] Even when He was kicking over tables and whipping the wicked money changers from the temple, *Jesus was operating out of love.* Confusing? No doubt![228] That's

---

[224] Exodus 8-9

[225] Matthew 5:5

[226] Since the meek will inherit the earth, and all inheritance is stored up for those who conquer, then it stands to reason that meekness is the only way to conquer!

[227] 1 Corinthians 13:4-8 NIV

[228] The moment you think you've got it figured out, then you're leaning on your own understanding, and God is no longer obligated to guide your path. (Proverbs 3:5-6)

why we need God's RHEMA. When you rely on that, it'll all make sense as He guides you step-by-step.

--

Having a set of Kingdom blueprints from God is a great blessing. The even greater blessing, one that we as a body have neglected for too long, is that the Architect Himself sends a jobsite foreman to personally stand beside us and guide every single detail of our construction project! If we "go" and "do" under our own strength, in our own understanding, then that's all we've got to work with: our own strength and understanding. We may be able to accomplish quite a bit in man's eyes this way, and secure plenty of treasure for ourselves, but our works will be meaningless compared to what's possible. We have free will to build that way, but the things we build will never be close to what God intends, or anywhere near as magnificent.

The release of God's full power – *delegated, superhuman, jurisdiction and mastery over the enemy*[229] – in our lives requires that we continually listen, submit and live in simple obedience to Him. When our will, words and actions are conformed perfectly to His, nothing is impossible for us – *not even the absolutele annihilation of the kingdom of darkness as we bring God's Kingdom to earth as it is in Heaven.*

KEY POINTS: The most powerful force in the universe is the living Word of God. It is freely available to us. Things we do in our own strength are meaningless.

---

[229] From Luke 10:19, this is the EXOUSIA power Christ gives His followers. It means *mastery, superhuman strength, jurisdiction, delegated influence. (Definition taken from Strong's Concordance.)*

"For though we walk in the flesh, we do not war according to the flesh. For the weapons of our warfare are not carnal but mighty in God for pulling down strongholds, casting down arguments and every high thing that exalts itself against the knowledge of God, bringing every thought into captivity to the obedience of Christ, and being ready to punish all disobedience when your obedience is fulfilled." (2 Corinthians 10:3-6, NKJV)

Now, an army is a team. It lives, eats, sleeps, fights as a team. This individuality stuff is a bunch of crap.

General George S. Patton

Chapter 10 - Our army

To make possible the fulfillment of His original intent for mankind, that His sons and daughters grow up and deliver victory for His Kingdom, God has built into us the potential to rise up into the most powerful, gifted, disciplined, mighty fighting force in the universe. When this army finally rises up, we will cover the earth with "the measure of the stature of the fullness of Christ,"[230] who is "far above all rule and authority, power and dominion, and every name that is invoked, not only in the present age but also in the one to come."[231] I hope you'll chew on that for a moment; it's a powerful truth, promised by God. When we come to true unity in the faith, not even the gates of hell can stand in the way of our march to total world conquest for Christ. *If we only understood the power of unity....*

Even in our extreme diversity, we are each made in the image of God.[232] From the poet to the diesel mechanic, from the primitive jungle dweller to the president, from the truck driver to the symphony conductor, and everyone else – male

---

[230] Ephesians 4:13 NKJV
[231] Ephesians 1:21 NIV
[232] Genesis 1:26

and female, rich and poor, intellectual and ignorant – we are all bearers of His likeness. We hold this image in jars of clay, each one fragile, cracked and incomplete.[233]

Yet His majesty is greater than any one of us can contain; we can each only bear a miniscule fraction. Like a drop of water, which is indeed completely H2O and has all the properties thereof, the image of God we carry is fully God, but it is not God in full. God is like the ocean, we carry but a drop. Only Jesus Christ was, could be, and is all in all.[234] He came and lived among us to make God manifest; proving that a being that is fully human could fully carry the image of God.

Driving through the countryside in the American South, one can't help but notice the sprawling vine known as kudzu. It's a non-native plant that is taking over, covering literally everything in its path. Left unchecked it will cover forests, trees, farms … anything. What is incredible to think is that, while kudzu is not from the area, everything that constitutes the substance of this aggressive and ubiquitous plant really has been there all along, in the soil, water and sunlight of the South. Nothing is there that wasn't already there. Not one cell, fiber or nutrient was imported into the state. Nothing, that is, but the DNA contained in a seed. That seed, planted into the rich soil, slowly but surely is re-organizing its environment into a living thing that's conquering the region.

The same is true with our world. Remember, Jesus said that all creation is a field for the raising up of sons and daughters to inherit God's Kingdom.[235] Everything we need to grow into victorious, world-conquering sons and daughters is fully available to us.

---

[233] 2 Corinthians 4:6
[234] Colossians 2:9
[235] Matthew 13:24-30

Just like one seed of kudzu can take over a vast territory, it only takes one kernel of wheat to produce a full crop of wheat. Plant it and it will grow into hundreds. Plant those and they will become tens of thousands. Plant them; millions. Plant them … and from one seed you can feed the world. In the same way, Jesus came as the seed of God. He said, "Very truly I tell you, unless a kernel of wheat falls to the ground and dies, it remains only a single seed. But if it dies, it produces many seeds."[236] *We are the many seeds who came from the One.* Our hearts are carrying a seed, which Jesus identified as the LOGOS of the Kingdom.[237] Yet the seed in each of us is but a small part of the whole of God. Yes, it is fully God, like the drop of water is fully water. But the seed in each of us is not the *fullness* of God. The fullness of God can only become manifest on earth through the unified Body of Christ. The first coming was a body of one. I believe the second coming will be the rising up of the Body of many. When the Body (or Bride, as the unified Body is also called in Scripture) *makes herself ready*,[238] He will come again as the Head, to be married to a unified Body of believers,[239] and that will be the end of this age.

The DNA in your fingertip is the same as the DNA in your eyelash. Exactly the same. Leave a fleck of skin off your finger or one eyelash at a crime scene and the authorities will know it came from you, because the DNA is fully you. But it is not you in full. I marvel that even though the information in each cell of our body is identical, each cell is unique. Cut off the very tip of your finger and a fingertip

---

[236] John 12:24 NIV
[237] Matthew 13:19
[238] Revelation 19:7
[239] Ephesians 4:15 NIV says, "we will grow to become in every respect the mature Body of Him who is the head, that is, Christ."

grows back; each cell just slightly different from the other, so that the end of your finger completes itself. Lose an eyelash and an eyelash grows back, just slightly different in form and purpose than the eyelash next to it. How does each cell know where it belongs if the DNA is the same? Only by the design of God.

Just like this, the seed of God in us, the DNA of Christ, is implanted not so each of us can grow into little autonomous Christs, but so each of us can grow into our own unique part of His body, each with a purpose, each with a place, each a little bit different from the next, so that, when we all reach maturity and join in unity, the Body of Christ will be complete, He will come to be joined to it, and that will be the end. Jesus came originally in the form of one man. He will come again, as the head of a body comprised of a vast multitude of unified, unique cells. The complete and mature Body of Christ *is* the Kingdom, and the Kingdom *is* the complete and mature Body of Christ; every seed living under His royal power, kingship, dominion and rule. This is our building project! This is what the enemy fears and is fighting to stop!

Understanding it this way, our purpose in this life becomes clear: Our job as believers is first and foremost to cultivate out the seed of Christ in ourselves, so that He's the only thing people see when they look at us. Then second we are to help plant and cultivate that seed in others, so that He lives fully through them, too. And third, we are to knit each cell of His body together through KOINONIA,[240] which is the deep, intimate, loving, Christ-centered fellowship of believers. That is our mission, and in concept it's really quite simple. Of course, in practice it is also the most difficult

---

[240] Another word we generally translate as "church" today.

thing we can do; it is the grand fight and struggle of this age.

Finding our specific calling means learning who we are in Christ. For me to know who I am is for me to know my specific purpose, where I belong and my destiny. Your unique identity in Christ *is* your calling.

Metaphorically, the Kingdom of God is like kudzu. Starting with the DNA of Christ that was planted in the grave and grew into new life, drawing off of the nutrients that God placed in the earth and in our hearts, and re-organizing everything for His purposes, He will eventually take over all creation. The "kudzu plant" that is Christ is really one vine with many branches – each one of us is a branch, each one unique – and God is the Master Gardener.[241] Looked at even closer, each branch produces fruit, each piece with a seed inside that can continue the process. Piece by piece, each unique part of the plant comprises the wholeness of God.

--

There's a lot more I could say about the Body of Christ, but there's not much I can write that's better than what Paul wrote on this subject. Here's what he wrote to the believers in Rome:

> For by the grace given me I say to every one of you: Do not think of yourself more highly than you ought, but rather think of yourself with sober judgment, in accordance with the faith God has distributed to each of you. For just as each of us has one body with many members, and these members do not all have the same function, so in Christ we, though many, form one Body, and each member belongs to all the others. We have

---

[241] John 15:1-5

different gifts, according to the grace given to each of us. If your gift is prophesying, then prophesy in accordance with your faith; if it is serving, then serve; if it is teaching, then teach; if it is to encourage, then give encouragement; if it is giving, then give generously; if it is to lead, do it diligently; if it is to show mercy, do it cheerfully.[242]

And this is what he wrote to the Corinthian brothers and sisters:

Just as a body, though one, has many parts, but all its many parts form one body, so it is with Christ. For we were all baptized by one Spirit so as to form one Body—whether Jews or Gentiles, slave or free—and we were all given the one Spirit to drink. Even so the Body is not made up of one part but of many.

Now if the foot should say, "Because I am not a hand, I do not belong to the body," it would not for that reason stop being part of the body. And if the ear should say, "Because I am not an eye, I do not belong to the body," it would not for that reason stop being part of the body. If the whole body were an eye, where would the sense of hearing be? If the whole body were an ear, where would the sense of smell be? But in fact God has placed the parts in the Body, every one of them, just as He wanted them to be. If they were all one part, where would the Body be? As it is, there are many parts, but one Body.

The eye cannot say to the hand, "I don't need

---

[242] Romans 12:3-8 NIV

you!" And the head cannot say to the feet, "I don't need you!" On the contrary, those parts of the body that seem to be weaker are indispensable, and the parts that we think are less honorable we treat with special honor. And the parts that are unpresentable are treated with special modesty, while our presentable parts need no special treatment. But God has put the Body together, giving greater honor to the parts that lacked it, so that there should be no division in the Body, but that its parts should have equal concern for each other. If one part suffers, every part suffers with it; if one part is honored, every part rejoices with it.

Now you are the Body of Christ, and each one of you is a part of it.[243]

And to the fellowship in Ephesus:

Speaking the truth in love, we will grow to become in every respect the mature Body of Him who is the Head, that is, Christ. From Him the whole Body, joined and held together by every supporting ligament, grows and builds itself up in love, as each part does its work.[244]

--

One key facet of unity in the Body of Christ is foreign to most Christians, and that is the thought of tearing down the wall between what we call "clergy" and "laymen." The distinction between the "full time ministers" and "all the other Christians" is artificial and manmade, and a sure-fire

---

[243] 1 Corinthians 12:12-27 NIV
[244] Ephesians 4:15-16 NIV

formula for the Body to continue to languish.

Don't get me wrong. Of course there's a place for people to make a living doing full-time ministry work. Even though New Testament examples of full-time vocational "ministers" are sketchy at best, fact is the Body has grown and specialized to an extent that there certainly is a place for men and women to make a living advancing the Kingdom.

What's wrong is the idea that these full-time servants are the only ones rightly equipped to minister, and the rest of us should simply outsource our ministerial responsibilities to these full-timers.

Jesus was a carpenter. Peter was a fisherman. Matthew was a tax collector. Paul was a tentmaker. In Christ there are no divisions between "marketplace" and "ministry" – we are all part of the royal priesthood. [245] Those who hold to the belief that special certification or full-time "religious" employment constitute a higher calling, or make a person especially equipped to do ministry, entirely miss the meaning of the word "ministry." In Greek, the word is DIAKONIA, and it means to serve others, period. We are all called to serve others; it's the "true religion" James wrote about.[246]

Paul spelled out a key principle in his letter to the believers in Ephesus when he said that God is giving some to be apostles, prophets, pastors, evangelists and teachers, *"for the equipping of the saints for works of ministry."*[247] According to this, whose job is it to do the works of ministry? The saints! Who are the saints? Everyone who has faith in Jesus! In fact, this passage makes it clear that our "full time ministers" are

---

[245] 1 Peter 2:9
[246] James 1:27
[247] Ephesians 4:12 NKJV (emphasis added)

not intended by God to be the front-line foot soldiers of His Kingdom army; *instead, they are to equip the average believer to serve that role.*

It's like this: Does a top sports team need a good coach? Of course! But fact is, the coach never touches the ball. He equips the team, and the team goes out on the field and scores all the points.

It's not the job of the pew-sitters to equip their pastor for works of ministry. It's the other way around! He's the coach and the church building is the locker room. The world is the playing field, and everyday Christians are the team. If the team never takes the field, how will we ever win?

I used to think the sum total of my evangelistic responsibility was fulfilled when I invited someone to church or introduced him to my pastor. I bought into the artificial distinction between "clergy" and "layman," and so I sought to outsource my ministry to the "professionals." It was *my* job to equip *them*. That is so wrong!

In the Body, there are no higher or lower callings. Where you are called, the position in the Body that God made you to fill, is your highest calling. If you're called to be a waitress, an attorney, a senior pastor or a fireman, then there is nothing more important in this world that you can do than just that. Embrace that calling as a full-time minister – a servant of others! – and take Christ with you into that setting. Put your heart into connecting with those around you – because God has uniquely equipped you to do that – and be a living testimony to the joy of serving our Living God.

Right now in our army, the foot soldiers are by-and-large sitting back and pushing the officers into the trenches. It's not what they're equipped to do, and not where they belong. And sadly, many of our officers are accepting this impossible responsibility. To use another metaphor, the team is camped out in the locker room while the coaches are on the field, doing their best to compete against a fierce opponent. This is not the way God intended it!

When we finally embrace God's vision of the unified Body of Christ, in which we are all called to full-time ministry regardless of how we make a living, we will overwhelm the enemy, and victory will be near.

--

Complete unity of the mature Body around the world will be the culmination of His original intent for all creation. Just one look around, however, shows we are far from embracing His will in this regard. Drive through some towns and it seems every single block has a building with a steeple on top. We are fragmented and divided – trying to function as a bunch of single-celled organisms instead of one cohesive Body. As long as this is the case, according the Apostle Paul, we have a long way to go before the end comes. He said, "We *will* grow to become in every respect the mature Body of Him who is the head, that is, Christ."[248] This was not Paul's pie-in-the-sky, impossible dream. (Paul got stoned by rocks, not on drugs!) It *will* happen, someday.

Paul knew unity in the Body is at the very core of God's will for mankind, and at the heart of victory. This is why he was so scornful about divisions. Consider these statements he wrote to the brothers and sisters in Corinth: "In the following directives I have no praise for you, for your meetings do more harm than good. In the first place, I hear

---

[248] Ephesians 4:15-16 NIV, *emphasis added*.

that when you come together as a church, there are divisions among you, and to some extent I believe it."[249] And, "I appeal to you, brothers and sisters, in the name of our Lord Jesus Christ, that all of you agree with one another in what you say and that there be no divisions among you, but that you be perfectly united in mind and thought."[250] To the Romans he wrote, "I urge you, brothers and sisters, to watch out for those who cause divisions and put obstacles in your way that are contrary to the teaching you have learned. Keep away from them. For such people are not serving our Lord Christ, but their own appetites. By smooth talk and flattery they deceive the minds of naive people."[251]

The only way we can be "perfectly united in mind and thought" is when we all are united *under the mind of Christ.* I believe the only way we can do that is when we all fix our eyes on God's original intent. His vision of victory – the LOGOS of the Kingdom, the seed we are supposed to plant – will unite us as a mature Body, an unstoppable army.

--

In my experience, it seems many of the various denominations can be known by the parts of Scripture they choose to skip over. On the main, these institutions were founded by great and faithful theologians who were given the tough task of creating, with no contemporary precedent, ways for the Body to function separate from the Dark Ages Catholic system. These guys lived victoriously and are my personal heroes. The problem comes when their modern adherents try to maintain these same, centuries-old ways, seemingly without regard for variations in culture, more

---

[249] 1 Corinthians 11:17-18 NIV
[250] 1 Corinthians 1:10 NIV
[251] Romans 16:17-18 NIV

precise translations, deeper advances in theology, moves of the Holy Spirit, etc. When they do this, they are effectively trying to operate inside a box, and as a result they are forced to skip over any information that doesn't fit in it. For example, try telling the legalists about freedom in Christ (or a tea-totaler that Paul told Timothy to drink wine![252]) Try telling a "faith alone" teacher that "faith without works is dead,"[253] or a works-righteous adherent that we are saved "not by works, so that no man can boast."[254] Try telling a "decision theology" pastor about predestination, or vice-versa. Get an infant-baptism Lutheran in the same room with an age-of-accountability Baptist, and the sparks will fly! Show them Scriptural truths that seem to challenge their revered religious codes, and you'll get anything from blank stares, to hostile words, to charges of blasphemy. Believe me, I know this first hand! They tend to dogmatically defend their belief system and explain away every Bible verse that seems to conflict with it.[255]

Thankfully, God's vision of victory – the Gospel of the Kingdom – is the one key, vital part of Scripture they virtually all seem to skip over. Why do I say thankfully? Because I don't know of any denomination that intentionally

---

[252] 1 Timothy 5:23

[253] James 2:26

[254] Ephesians 2:9

[255] I am in no way anti-organizational or anti-denominational, but I am a realist. Yes, my words here are a bit direct, but I hope you'll see the truth in them. I greatly value and respect the finest traditions of the great Reformers who founded most of our modern denominations. By virtue of our distinct, God-given personality differences, we are each drawn to express our faith differently. Some of us like vanilla, some chocolate. In the same way, some of us are drawn to more structured worship and fellowship, and some are drawn to different flavors. Under the headship of Christ, this is all good. Without the headship of Christ, it is all bad. Growing up into Christ who is the Head is the key.

puts forth the message that we're a bunch of losers,[256] and as a result, I believe that victory is the one message that can unite all Christians for the common cause. It is the highest common denominator of all who follow Jesus: Our identity as His sons and daughters, under the headship of Christ, with a purpose to conquer and destiny rule in eternity.

Without our eyes fixed on God's vision of victory, the Body of Christ today sounds like a symphony orchestra warming up. Each has his own instrument and is playing his own thing. Each warm-up exercise – be it playing scales, blowing random notes or practicing a part of the score – makes sense to the one doing it. *Problem is, the audience has already arrived, and they think this chaotic cacophony is the best we've got.*

Without the vision of victory, the Body of Christ today looks like a basketball team on the floor before a game. Each player has his own ball and is doing his own thing. Some are doing their very best to shoot free throws, some are dribbling the ball, some are doing calisthenics, some are horsing around and some are just resting up. *Problem is, the starting whistle has already blown and the other team is on the floor too – shooting basket after basket and racking up the score – and most of us don't even realize that there's a game on, one that we must win!*

Without God's vision of victory, unity in the Body of Christ is just a nice thing to work towards (so long as it doesn't get in the way of what we *really* want to do). Personal spiritual growth, selfless acts of love, evangelism and discipleship are good things – and some of us are very passionate about

---

[256] While there are theological schools of thought that come to this inevitable conclusion (albeit without outright saying it), these are mainly "winds of teaching" and not fully incorporated into the foundations of the main denominations.

them – but it's mainly out of a sense of obligation, gratitude, to get more personal fulfillment out of our "religion," or to "store up treasures in heaven." I know that's how it always was for me.

Add in God's vision of victory and everything will change! That symphony orchestra will get a score to play from, a Conductor to lead the way – and everyone who is in our presence will be awed by the beautiful music. That basketball team will get in the game, realize there is a goal and an active opponent, follow the Coach's instructions, and the tide will turn. Unity will become urgent and purposeful as our own agendas disappear. Personal spiritual growth, selfless acts of love, evangelism and discipleship will become the very essence of our being; the fulfillment of our victorious identity, purpose and destiny.

When we rise up as an army united by God's original and overarching vision of *His victorious sons and daughters bringing the Kingdom to earth as it is in heaven*, the enemy cannot stand in our way. Victory is certain!

KEY POINTS: God's vision of victory is key to our unity. Victory will only be manifest when we come together as a unified body, each playing our God-given part.

"If a kingdom is divided against itself, that kingdom cannot stand." Mark 3:24 NKJV

Commonplaceness, the surrender to the average, that good which is not bad but still the enemy of the best — that is our besetting danger.

Johann Wolfgang Von Goethe

Chapter 11 – Muslims and Liberals and Atheists, oh my!

"Ok, ok … I hear what you're saying," you may be thinking. "We're designed and destined by God to be winners, to successfully establish His Kingdom on earth as it is in Heaven, and that's great. We have all the power of God at our disposal, blah blah blah. So tell me: *Why does the other side seem to be winning?*"

That's the right question to ask, because if we search for the answer with humble teachability, I believe God will reveal the truth. And while the truth sometimes hurts, if we embrace it, it always brings life, freedom and power.

There is no doubt: If we look at the world to learn our identity, we have every reason to feel like losers. If we look at the world to determine our purpose, our existence seems pretty pointless. If we look at the world to discern our destiny, we have no choice but to expect Christ and His angelic host *must* bring the Kingdom through direct intervention, because it's certainly not coming through our failing efforts. [257] It certainly feels like we are beaten down and completely unable to gain the victory ourselves.

When we look at the Bible and see our true identity as winners, our purpose to bring God's Kingdom to earth, and our destiny to achieve total victory, it simply doesn't seem to line up with the reality in which we live.

Indeed, why *are* they seemingly beating us?

And they do appear to be winning! Islam is reportedly the world's fastest-growing religion, and seems every day to gain ground – not just in the Middle East, Africa and Asia, but in Europe and the US, too.[258] Perverts, pornographers, atheists and abortion activists have achieved unfettered freedom to promote their filth across America, a supposedly "Christian" nation, through the government, the media, and even to our children in public school. And if we try to bring in Christ, we risk the wrath of the powers that be.

Greed dominates in business and self-serving deception in politics. Totalitarianism, hatred, violence and corruption are running rampant throughout the nations of the earth.

In many "free" nations, expressions of Christian faith have been rooted out of the public scene, and in many other parts of the world, Christians are subject to outright persecution and even martyrdom.

Now, I'm familiar with conflicting reports that Christianity is the fastest growing religion on earth. But I'm not talking about whether someone checks "Christian" on a census form, or even sits in a pew on Sunday morning. I'm looking for believers like Jesus described: "And these signs will

---

[257] It is human nature to create mythology to explain things we believe are outside our control.
[258] Foreign Policy Magazine, May 14, 2007

accompany those who believe: In my name they will drive out demons; they will speak in new tongues; they will pick up snakes with their hands; and when they drink deadly poison, it will not hurt them at all; they will place their hands on sick people, and they will get well."[259] By Jesus' standards, there aren't too many Christians around today. *Look around, is the world conformed to the Kingdom of God, or is the body of Christ more conformed to the patterns of this world?* I think any objective observer could conclude that, in most nations, the kingdom of darkness seems to be on the rise, while the Kingdom of God is diminishing. Why?

Let me answer that question with another: In the old fable, why did the tortoise beat the hare?[260]

The hare had all the natural giftedness, but he was prideful and did not focus on the finish line. He was born to occupy the Winner's Circle, *but he did not walk in the reality of that destiny.* He lacked determination! His priority was self-gratification, and so he didn't take the competition seriously. Even though the cost of winning for him would have been relatively small, he was not willing to pay it. He didn't think much of his opponent and assumed winning was a given. Because he didn't run with his identity of winner, he left open the door for the tortoise to do so instead.

The tortoise, on the other hand, was *determined.* He had nothing going for him *except the belief that he could win.* He was disciplined, focused and transfixed on the finish line. He understood that if he did what he believed he could do, it'd all be over soon enough, and he valued the winner's crown over immediate gratification. He had a vision of victory and was willing to pay the price.

---

[259] Mark 16:17-18 NIV
[260] This is precisely why I included the chapter on winning early in this book.

Just like the tortoise, the leaders of Islam believe that victory is *their* destiny. On a widely broadcast television interview, Anjem Choudray, spokesman for the group Islam4UK, said, "We do believe as Muslims the East and the West will be governed by the Sharia. Indeed we believe that one day the flag of Islam will fly over the White House."[261] As a result, they are willing to do whatever it takes to make this happen.

Similarly, followers of then-candidate Barak Obama, the most radical ideologue ever to occupy the US Presidency, seized power under the mantra, "Yes We Can!"

The tortoise had no God-given right to believe he could win; that right was relinquished to him by the hare. Victory belonged to the hare; through his failure to claim it, *he left it for the tortoise to claim.*

The battle between the Kingdom of God and the powers of darkness is a similar matchup. In fact the disparity between the hare and the tortoise is insignificant compared to the difference between the Body of Christ and the forces aligned with satan. Christ is "far above all principality and power and might and dominion, and every name that is named, not only in this age but also in that which is to come."[262] *All things* are under His feet. We are His body, and His feet are part of His body! We, His body, with Him as our head, constitute *"the fullness* of Him who fills all in all."[263] In Christ, walking in our identity and in the power available to us, we are an unstoppable force. *Yes We Can!*

Not only that, but get this: We have an unassailable monopoly on everything that everyone in the history of the world has ever searched for and can't find anywhere else.

---

[261] ABC's "This Week," October 3, 2010.
[262] Ephesians 1:21 (NKJV)
[263] Ephesians 1:23 (NKJV)

When you strip away all the varnish, every human being has a deep, inborn craving for the fruit of the Spirit: true love, deep joy, peace that surpasses all understanding, patience in affliction, a community of kindness, goodness, genuine faithfulness, gentleness and self-control.[264] Behind every pursuit – sex, drugs, rock and roll, money, power, fame, glory … you name it! – is a quest for the contentment only found in a personal relationship with God through Jesus Christ. No other religion or lifestyle offers this, and pursuing any other will only lead one further from the true source.

In the next chapter, I will dig deep into why, with all this going for us, we still seem to be losing. For now, let me just say that currently, as a Body, we are modeling the mindset of the hare. The question in this chapter is, why are *they* winning? The answer is simple: They are filling the vacuum we created by retreating from our identity. We've lost sight of God's original intent for us, His vision of victory, and instead we have aimed for mere survival. *In refusing to claim the victory that is rightfully ours, we are giving the other side that opportunity.* By our failure to manifest Christ's victory, we have given those who oppose us false hope their causes will not only survive, but can in fact conquer the world.

We've abandoned the Winner's Circle that is our birthright, and allowed others to claim it. They seem to be winning because we've let them believe they can! (And because they believe they can, they are willing to pay the price.)

KEY POINTS: The other side is winning because we have allowed them to believe that they *can* win.

---

[264] Galatians 5:22-23 (NIV)

He who heeds discipline shows the way to life, but whoever ignores correction leads others astray.[265]

King Solomon

Chapter 12 - Why on earth are we losing?

Note: Please take this chapter as a chalk talk in the locker room during halftime of a ball game. We are a superior team and yet we're losing, so we're doing something wrong. Here is a wise saying: "If you always do what you've always done, you'll always get what you've always got." Some things have simply got to change, and we can't just point fingers at those who sit under different steeples and blame them. We have to look inward, too. I invoke the example of Peter, Barnabas and the other apostles in Jerusalem when Paul confronted them over the issue of circumcision for Gentiles. Paul admired and looked up to these men, as I deeply respect Christian leaders around the world who are passionately pursuing their call to serve God. Yet the fact remains, we are not anywhere close to conquering the world for the Kingdom of God, even though that is our God-given destiny. I pray we can all agree to listen to the Spirit of God in these matters — and be teachable.

---

[265] Proverbs 10:17 NIV

Edmund Burke famously said, "All that is necessary for the triumph of evil is that good men do nothing." I'd say there are other ways for evil to triumph, and that's when good men do their own things or the wrong things. I know there are countless, passionate, men and women of God all over the world, working as hard as they can, faithfully sacrificing their lives for the cause of Christ.[266] But in spite of this, I don't think many would dispute that the kingdom of darkness sure seems to be advancing, even though God promises victory is ours for the taking. The inescapable conclusion is we must not, as a Body, be engaged in the right things. For all the money and energy we expend, we simply are not employing winning strategies. That goes for me, and it goes for you.

If I were coach of the world championship basketball team and we were losing a game against an inferior opponent, my job would be to analyze what we're doing wrong and steer our team back on track. Saying we're losing because we're doing things wrong is not an insult to anyone. Instead, it is a call for us all to step back and soberly assess what's not working. Not so we can pridefully point fingers, but so we can fix it – and win! If we each are quick to take offense, and defensively cling to our ways, our loss will continue.

In our analysis, we'd probably find the issues include mental, strategic and mechanical problems. On the mental side, a big part of the problem may be that, as a team, we're

---

[266] Those who are led by the Spirit have been advancing the cause of victory all along, whether consciously or not, and definitely have an eternal inheritance waiting for them. It's just like the fact that not every football player with a Super Bowl ring got on the field or touched the ball during the big game. They still played a role on the winning team, even if the coach never ordered them off the bench or even out of the locker room.

simply not playing to win; we may not see the importance of winning this game, we may have been lulled into thinking we're so superior we don't even have to try, or we may have listened to the trash-talk of our opponents and lost confidence in our abilities. Strategically, we may not be passing the ball enough, we could be failing to see and properly respond to the opponent's strategic maneuvering, or any number of things. On the mechanical side, we may simply be shooting badly, not reading from the same playbook, or our star may have his shoes on the wrong feet. There could be many factors at play and the real reason we're losing is probably some combination – thus the need for an honest, humble assessment.

In the past several chapters I've addressed many of the mental and strategic issues we, as a body, are facing. These include:

- We've lost the understanding of God's Big Picture original intent for us – this whole creation exists so God can raise up mature sons and daughters to inherit His eternal Kingdom – and so we are not embracing our victorious identity, purpose and destiny,

- We don't understand the rules of engagement God set in place – we are His agents and so bringing the Kingdom on earth as it is in Heaven is in our hands,

- Many of us don't even realize we're at war, and instead think peace through appeasement is the order of the day,

- We are not operating under the headship of Christ; we're trying to do our own things for Him, instead of allowing Him to do everything through us,

- We don't understand or operate in the power of God, as we have chosen to follow the written Word alone and don't comprehend or accept His personal RHEMA Word,

- We are divisive and divided, and we think that's ok, and

- By acting like the hare in that mythical race against the tortoise, we have allowed the human agents of the forces of darkness to believe that they can win.

This chapter will cover some of the more practical, mechanical issues. I believe Christians are engaged in all kinds of misguided busy-work, wasting resources on frivolities and employing all kinds of foolhardy tactics. Before I go into detail, however, I want you to know two things. First, I understand these issues so well because I am guilty of every single one of them at one time or another. I'm not trying to point out anyone else's mistakes, I'm just asking you to learn from mine. If it comes across that I'm "pointing fingers," I fully realize and accept that four fingers are pointing back at me. I've had to work plenty of planks out of my own eyes[267] and I'm sure I still have a few remaining. Second, please know I am not one to point out problems without offering solutions. In addition to doing my dead-level best to communicate God's vision of victory, which I believe is the primary solution to most of these ills, I also offer a full chapter (Chapter 16 – Endgame) on the most direct, practical, strategic path to delivering final victory.

One more thing... I can recall way too many times I've sat in a pew, listened to a powerful word from the pastor and thought to myself, "Man, I hope that guy over there is

---

[267] Matthew 7:5, Luke 6:42

listening to this one!" God finally slapped me upside the head one day and convicted me of this prideful attitude. *It is my first and foremost responsibility to get myself right with God and fix the issues in my own life.* Concern about whether "that guy over there" is listening should be way, way down on my list of priorities. I hope you'll approach this chapter and the next one with this same attitude. Don't look at the things that criticize the congregation next door and jump, in your heart, to gang up on them. If God had me write it for them, it's their business to receive it, not yours to ram it down their throats. Instead, prayerfully consider how these points may apply to yourself and your own work. This is the heart of humble teachability that God desires; this is how we grow into mature sons and daughters of the King.

What I include here is by no means an exhaustive list. Also, none of these is intended to be a blanket indictment of every single believer or church body, or the Body as a whole. If none of them apply to you or your group, praise God! Still, I encourage you to consider them, if nothing more, as a warning of losing tactics to which humans are naturally drawn. I pray you will allow the Spirit of God, through His RHEMA Word, to "guide you into all the truth"[268] as you pursue this line of inquiry. Consider ... why are we losing? And what am I personally engaged in that may be a losing tactic? Come up with your own list and do your own research.[269] Ok, all that said, here are some practical things I see contributing to why we're currently losing:

We have planted the wrong seed. I'd venture to say most folks in outreach ministry are familiar with the Parable of

---

[268] John 16:13 NIV
[269] Come to ChristianUprising.org to join an online discussion on these issues.

the Sower.[270] It talks about a farmer spreading seed in his field and the four possible outcomes.[271] Some seed falls on hard ground and is eaten by birds, some on rocky soil and springs up quickly then dies, some takes root but is choked out by weeds, and the remaining seed falls on good soil and produces a great return. This parable is found in the books of Matthew, Mark and Luke, and Jesus took great care to fully explain it to His disciples. He was quite intentional, in all three Gospels where it's recorded, to say what the proper seed is. In Mark and Luke it is recorded as LOGOS,[272] which as we know is the original intent, Big Picture vision of God. In Matthew, vital detail is included: He says the seed is the LOGOS of BASILEIA[273] – the message of the Kingdom; the foundational truth of God's royal power, kingship, dominion and rule.

It's the LOGOS of BASILEIA I'm attempting to communicate in this book: It is our destiny and purpose to bring God's Kingdom to earth, and then to rule with Him for eternity. I'd venture to guess that for many readers, this is the first time you're hearing anything like it. Sadly, I've heard this key parable interpreted all sorts of ways.[274] Mainly, for those with a genuine heart for evangelism, they innocently assume the seed is simply the message of salvation, and then they passionately proceed, with the best intentions, to broadcast this incomplete seed as widely as they can.

---

[270] Matthew 13:1-23, Mark 4:1-20 and Luke 8:1-15

[271] When we realize God considers all creation a field for the cultivation of sons, this parable takes on even greater significance – and warrants careful study.

[272] Mark 4:14 and Luke 8:11

[273] Matthew 13:19

[274] Some teachers claim that Jesus here was simply establishing "the principle of sowing and reaping," and then they proceed to say the seed is your money, and the fertile soil is their offering plate. No kidding! I've heard that first hand at a very large, televised church, right before offering time.

A seed contains its own destiny. If I plant an apple seed and the conditions are right, I will grow an apple tree. By and large, we have reached out to lost souls with a message of, "just say this prayer, sit in a pew on Sunday, and then try to live a good life." And so that's what we've tended to grow.[275] I have to ask, how's it working for us?

When we instead sow the seed Jesus said to plant – you are a son of the King, born to conquer the world and destined to rule with Him for eternity – we will inevitably harvest victory! To confirm and clarify His point, Jesus later said, *"This gospel of the Kingdom* will be preached in the whole world as a testimony to all nations, and then the end will come."[276] Today, the gospel of "born again" has been preached in all the nations, and the end hasn't come. That's because Jesus said we must be born again just to see the Kingdom.[277] Christ's Kingdom message – of God's royal power, kingship, dominion and rule – is much more than the teaching that "if you believe in Jesus you'll go to heaven when you die." The LOGOS of BASILEIA, the seed Jesus said we're supposed to plant, contains God-designed DNA necessary for it to grow to cover the earth. And it simply has not been planted to any real extent. Yes, the message of salvation is absolutely true, it is fantastic and life-changing – but it is incomplete seed. When we get the seed right, we will hasten the glorious, victorious end.

We often prohibit the Holy Spirit from doing His job. If you recall the "word" study in Chapter Nine, the written Word is but one of the ways God intends to communicate with us, and by itself it is incomplete. Let me give you an example of

---

[275] Of course, the Spirit of God can and does take people beyond that, but we make it very hard for those believers.

[276] Matthew 24:14 NIV, *emphasis added.*

[277] John 3:3

what I mean. We are commanded to "go and baptize"[278] –
but baptize how? Different denominations interpret this
very differently. Some baptize infants, some after an "age of
accountability." Some do it for brand-new believers, some
after a lengthy class. Some immerse, some sprinkle, some in
tubs, some in rivers, etc., and the words they say when they
do it differ just as much. Each would tell you theirs is the
"right" way. But fact is, Scripture is incomplete on the
subject. It doesn't include specific instructions. In instances
like this, how are we supposed to find the right answer?
Jesus said it quite clearly: "The Holy Spirit, whom the Father
will send in my name, will teach you all things and will
remind you of everything I have said to you."[279] Jesus' point
was this: Filling in the blanks is exclusively the God-
ordained job of the Holy Spirit.

The Bible is an ancient document, written by men who lived
in long-dead cultures. It can't tell you what color carpet to
put in your sanctuary, because they didn't have carpets back
then. But the Holy Spirit, as the messenger of God's RHEMA
Word, is always fresh and relevant. God desires to direct our
paths, in everything we do, all the time. He will even lead
you to pick just the right color carpet He wants for your
congregation! The Bible provides the bones – examples,
underlying principles, historical facts and much more. The
Holy Spirit exists to put meat on those bones so we can
function every day, in every way, in the current will of the
Living God.

The problem comes when we fill the blanks with directions
from any other source. Consider Martin Luther. I believe
wholeheartedly he was led by the Holy Spirit to break away

---

[278] Matthew 28:19
[279] John 14:26 NIV

from Dark Ages Catholic ways and start the Body of Christ down a better path. He lived in a unique time and place. Had he pushed too far, there's no doubt the prince who protected him would have lifted his protection, and the death sentence against Luther would have been carried out. The Holy Spirit guided Luther as far as he could go in that time and place. Fast forward more than four centuries, and guess what? We still have an entire denomination of believers seeking to do things precisely as Luther did in the 1500![280] Even if a Lutheran pastor from a strict branch of the denomination does feel led by the Spirit to apply Scripture differently, his whole peer group, organization structure and paycheck prohibit him breaking away from tradition. Yet the fact remains, it's not Luther's job (or John Calvin's, or anyone else's for that matter) to fill in the blanks for us. It is the Holy Spirit's job. Every time we fill in the blanks with anything else, we've effectively fired the Holy Spirit from His God-given job.

This same pattern is true in virtually every church body, and if we're honest we'll admit it's probably present in our personal lives, too. We fill in the blanks with all kinds of things – patterns of this world, our own understanding, peer pressure, worries, ignorance, etc. And the biggest blank-filler is tradition. We do things a certain way because the one before us did them that way. God intends for the practice of our faith to be organic and always growing, and we have let it fossilize in many ways. This is a dangerous thing! Jesus said, "You have a fine way of setting aside the commands of

---

[280] I'm not singling out the Lutheran denomination for any other reason than it's what I'm most familiar with. I grew up in it – baptized in the ELCA, confirmed Missouri Synod, married in the Wisconsin Synod, held about every church position a layman can hold, and strongly considered going to a Lutheran seminary – so I know a little of what I'm talking about. They're fine people, and I respect them greatly.

God in order to observe your own traditions!"[281] He also said, "If you love me, keep my commands,"[282] so we must know this is a very important matter indeed – because effectively, in Christ's words, traditions can keep us from truly loving Him.

Here's an interesting passage from the book of First John: "As for you, the anointing you received from Him remains in you, and you do not need anyone to teach you. But as His anointing teaches you about all things and as that anointing is real, not counterfeit—just as it has taught you, remain in Him."[283] While of course there is a need for faithful teachers, John is saying we don't need people, organizations or traditions to tell us what to do step-by-step; that's the Holy Spirit's job. He can lead us to do things the way we've always done them or in a bold, new, fresh way. As long as it fits within the bounds of Scripture, we need to have our ears and hearts open to stretch and grow and try new things. Jesus said, "The wind blows where it wishes, and you hear the sound of it, but cannot tell where it comes from and where it goes. So is everyone who is born of the Spirit."[284] We need to learn to function in this Spirit-directed freedom because, "Very truly I tell you, no one can enter the Kingdom of God unless they are born of water and the Spirit."[285]

We seem more concerned with slam dunks and finger spins than winning the game. A good friend coached his son's youth basketball team all the way to a national championship. He did not have much prior coaching

---

[281] Mark 7:9 NIV
[282] John 14:15 NIV
[283] 1 John 2:27 NIV, *emphasis added.*
[284] John 3:8 NIV
[285] John 3:5 NIV

experience but he had wisdom, and that was clearly enough. All he did, he said, was get out the old-school basketball training books and drill the kids in the basics, over and over. They learned to pass, screen, block, dribble, shoot, etc. What they didn't learn, or allow on the team, was any hotshot, human-highlight-reel playing. They mastered the basics, played as a team, practiced diligently ... and emerged as the best in the nation in their league. They laid aside their own egos for the good of the team, and walked away with the biggest trophy. The humble were exalted.

I've talked to other coaches and most say the same thing: It's hard to manage kids today. It seems they watch the highlights on TV, virtually emulate them in video games, and come to the court thinking the sport is nothing but showboating. As a result, the fundamentals of playing as a team – and winning – are lost. Showboating may elicit cheers but it doesn't win games.

I see a lot of this in the ministry world today. It seems many of our leaders want to be superstars. I see pastors' faces on billboards, groups holding large-scale/shallow-impact community events, churches building fancy buildings and ministries fighting for media exposure. It's like everyone watches the old, classic Billy Graham crusades on TV and wants to be just like Billy. What they don't realize is that Graham's organization worked diligently behind the scenes, months in advance, to enlist and equip every willing church within a vast radius, to ensure everyone who came to the crusades was followed up with and had an opportunity for ongoing discipleship. No, the boring basics like that don't seem to matter anymore. Reality is, however, that it's the boring basics of ministry – day-by-day, personal relationships – that will win it for us. Seeking highlights, awards and worldly recognition will never bring victory.

We run from the evidence. I've shown that many of God's most potent promises are only accessible when we go all-in. This means living in the certainty that the Bible is true, and not equivocating one bit. Unfortunately, a huge portion of today's Christians seem squeamish about standing firm on God's written Word as absolute truth. Much of the scientific community seems out to prove there is no God. When new discoveries come to light – in fields like astronomy, evolutionary biology, archaeology or geology – which the scientific community interprets in such a way as to undermine Scripture, many Christians often try to accommodate those scientist's views instead of boldly refuting them. I've heard it taught that "God worked through evolution" – despite the fact this statement blatantly contradicts the Bible. These so-called Christian teachers clearly trust atheist scientists more than they do the Bible, and are more concerned about academic acceptance than they are about God's! When another "missing link" is in the news, and someone brings it up at the office, many times we feel compelled to change the subject; we just "don't want to go there."

It's like many of us have ceded science to the atheists, largely due to our own lingering doubts about the absolute reliability of Scripture.[286] This needs to change. Fact is all creation points to God. Every single scientific discovery that can ever be made can only point to Him, and will never contradict His Word. We need to take a more proactive, aggressive posture. We must actively fight the evolution "thought police" whom we've let take over academia. God is the author of creation, and so those who know Him

---

[286] Like every issue I'm addressing here, this is not a blanket statement. There are many fantastic organizations that actively promote scientific discoveries from a Christian perspective. We need to do more to support them.

personally should naturally be top leaders in the scientific community. We must stop running from the evidence, fully embrace Biblical accuracy and start standing up for the truths we hold dear.

We tolerate and appease evil instead of tearing down and advancing. Every day there seems to be new assaults against God's Kingdom. Some are overt, like removing any public mention of Christmas or the display of "artwork" that denigrates our Savior, and some are covert, like the rapid growth of the pornography industry or the hidden genocide of abortion. Our civilization suffers from a continual erosion of values, and our faith suffers from increasingly brazen, public derision. All the while, it seems we've been conditioned to simply "turn the other cheek."[287] When it comes to flesh and blood, as we model love, grace, mercy and forgiveness, this is great. But we are worse than fools when we apply this to evil. We are hiding our light under a bushel; we are failing to serve as the salt of this world.[288]

Is the advance of evil inevitable? We seem to act like it, even though the opposite is true: The advance of God's Kingdom is what's inevitable, and we absolutely can stop the advance of the kingdom of darkness. Let's get practical here. You don't see things like this happening in the Islamic world, do you? So you see, perversion and the degradation of one's faith *can* be stopped. From the other perspective, if the gay rights movement in America, in less than one generation, can take a sinful behavior that leads to death and make it "mainstream," how much more can we advance "righteousness, peace and joy in the Holy Spirit"?[289] Of

---

[287] Matthew 5:39, Luke 6:29
[288] Matthew 5:13-16
[289] This is how Paul defined the Kingdom of God in Romans 14:17 NIV.

course I don't advocate tactics common among Muslim cultures or gay rights activists – they fight against flesh and blood, using carnal weapons. We can do it God's way and have even deeper results, because our weapons are greater! Just one man standing with God is stronger than any worldly force. When those who call on the name of Christ unify and stand up to the evil advancing in our world today, our economic, cultural and political clout will be an unstoppable force … "and the government will be on His shoulders."[290]

We're not willing to endure the trials necessary for maturity. To affect change in any of the above-mentioned topics – to walk away from popular "altar call"-based ministry and focus on advancing the seemingly less "seeker-friendly" Gospel of the Kingdom, to break away from tradition and imperil your paycheck, to refuse popularity and personal acclaim and instead focus on playing as a team, to stand up for truth against the academic thought police, or to face persecution by actively fighting against public evil – entails significant personal risk. Many of us are quite squeamish about this. While blessings and security are promised in eternity, we operate in a way that reveals we are more concerned about "blessings" and "security" in the here and now. Once again, it comes down to too many of us not being all-in, not fully relying on the truth of Scripture and the headship of Christ. Jesus modeled selfless, personal sacrifice, and told us point-blank, "Blessed are you when people insult you, persecute you and falsely say all kinds of evil against you because of me. Rejoice and be glad, because great is your reward in Heaven."[291] I pray for the day more Christians are seeking permanent reward in Heaven and

---

[290] Isaiah 9:6, *emphasis added*.
[291] Matthew 5:11-12 NIV

eager to take such bold risks for their Savior!

The words we use reveal a lot about where our hearts are. It seems we use the word "need" too much, when we should really use the word "want." Do I really "need" a new car, a bigger TV or a raise? Do we "need" to build another church building? In reality, all I really need is to seek first God's Kingdom and His righteousness. Every other thing is merely a desire. When we say "need," there is an unspoken "so that…" which we rarely speak. For example, I "need" a raise "so that" I can buy more stuff, or often we "need" a bigger building "so that" we can hold a bigger crowd at our Sunday services. I've found it healthy to be honest with myself about the "so thats;" to lay them before the Lord and seek His will on them. If what I'm pursuing is His will, then He promises to take care of the needs! In studying heroes of our faith, many of whom were brutally martyred and yet praised God till the end, it becomes obvious that, when we remain in the will of God, we don't even "need" air to breathe or blood flowing through our veins. When I find myself expressing any "need" beyond staying in the will of God, I am convicted by the fact they could express peace and joy, literally while burning alive at the stake.

In God's Kingdom, personal growth often involves going through tough fires and trials. The Bible repeatedly talks about God refining us as silver,[292] and this is done with a burning furnace. It says we are to "endure hardship as discipline; God is treating you as His children. For what children are not disciplined by their father?"[293] And you should, "Consider it pure joy, my brothers and sisters, whenever you face trials of many kinds, because you know

---

[292] Proverbs 25:4, Proverbs 27:21, Isaiah 1:22, Malachi 3:3
[293] Hebrews 12:7 NIV

that the testing of your faith produces perseverance. Let perseverance finish its work so that you may be mature and complete, not lacking anything."[294] The challenge is we have free will in the matter. We can choose to pursue the wide and easy path,[295] walk away from God's lessons, or respond with resentment and doubt. Jesus wasn't joking when He said, "Small is the gate and narrow the road that leads to life, and only a few find it."[296] When we truly understand God's Big Picture, then we will rejoice in trials and fires, and not run from them, because we know He is fulfilling His purpose in our lives. When the Body wakes up to this, things will start to change.[297]

We give too much credit to the devil. I can't count the number of Christians I've talked to who are afraid of demons. Most believers, it seems, would run the other way if they encountered one face-to-face. Of course these are mighty and fearsome beings, and if you're not walking in complete submission to the headship of Christ you have every reason to be afraid. But a fully-submitted son of the King has nothing to fear. Don't get me wrong: We need to always be on guard, and have a healthy respect for the cunning and influence of the enemy, but that's very different from fear. As Paul wrote to his apprentice Timothy, "God has not given us a spirit of fear, but of power and of love and of a sound mind."[298]

When Jesus was tempted in the wilderness,[299] satan came and offered Him all sorts of riches and power. Based on this,

---

[294] James 1:2-4, NIV
[295] Matthew 7:13-14
[296] Matthew 4:14 NIV
[297] I explore this topic in more depth in *Chapter 14 – The price of victory.*
[298] 2 Timothy 1:7 NKJV
[299] Recorded in both Matthew 4 and Luke 4.

I've heard pastors actually claim satan truly has the ability to deliver on these promises. In effect, they're taking satan's word for it – and last I checked, he's a liar! God did not give satan power over the world. The opposite is true! Jesus said, "All authority in heaven and on earth has been given to me."[300] Satan is referred to sometimes as a "prince," but never anything greater. In contrast, Jesus is the King of Kings! Our position in Christ as sons and daughters of the King, in the power He gives us, grants us absolute authority over the enemy.

Trials and fires are part of the Christian walk, as God is working to grow our faith. Yet all too often we perceive some of God's greatest gifts to be "attacks" of the enemy. I know a fellow who actually kept a tally one day of all the times "the devil attacked" him – like causing a red light in traffic when he was in a hurry. Give me a break! We need to stop giving undue credit to the enemy. It only makes us and those around us needlessly afraid of him. He is a defeated, belly-crawling serpent. He was not put here to beat us up – he's here so the sons and daughters of the King can learn to beat him up and humiliate him on our march to manifest Christ's total victory on earth as it is in Heaven.

We think God is a micromanager. Similar to the way that fellow gave too much credit to the enemy, we often fall into the trap of thinking every single thing that happens is caused by God. If I stub my toe it must have been "God's will." But that's not necessarily true. It is God's will that I grow in maturity, and He established creation as a classroom for that very purpose. There are things in my environment upon which I can stub my toe, and my body is programmed to experience pain when I do. God doesn't will

---

[300] Matthew 28:18 NIV, *emphasis added.*

that I experience that pain; instead, He wills that I learn to watch where I'm walking! There's a big difference.

I think people have good intentions when they try to give God the credit for every little thing. But, to paraphrase the old saying, good intentions can lead us to a very bad place. Because, when we say God is responsible for every little thing, and then bad things happen, that means He's to blame, too. And it paints a very bad picture of our loving Father. Let me make this perfectly clear: God did not cause, will, or desire that the 9/11 terrorists fly those planes into the World Trade Center. He created an environment that allowed it, and afterwards He caused it to work "for the good of those who love him, who have been called according to his purpose,"[301] but those attacks were an act of the terrorists' free will, not God's will!

This misunderstanding of God is an enormous stumbling block for people who refuse to believe in Him because they can't fathom how He could both be love, and also "cause" or "will" such bad things to happen. It's time we grow up and get this. We have free will, God gives *us* dominion over the earth, and we need to start taking responsibility for it. God is not a micromanager. Our lack of maturity in this area has driven people away from Him, and has led us to languish in mediocrity far too long.

We operate as if God stopped working 2000 years ago. Interestingly, many of the same people who think God is a micromanager also believe miracles no longer happen and He no longer speaks directly to us. (I addressed this in depth in Chapter 9 – Firepower.) They seem to picture Him as a distant puppeteer who keeps His face hidden, yet controls our whole existence through invisible strings. How this

---

[301] Romans 8:28 NIV

must grieve His heart! What loving father would want to be perceived this way by his children? Reality is, we have full access to God's supernatural power when we walk in His will, grow in maturity, and operate under Christ's headship.

As a corollary to this false belief, many in the Body of Christ have stopped accepting the gifting of apostles and prophets in modern times. The Bible clearly says otherwise. In his letter to the believers in Ephesus, Paul wrote that God is continually giving some people "to be apostles, some prophets, some evangelists, and some pastors and teachers, for the equipping of the saints for the work of ministry, for the edifying of the body of Christ, till we all come to the unity of the faith and of the knowledge of the Son of God, to a perfect man, to the measure of the stature of the fullness of Christ."[302] And to the Corinthians he wrote that "God has placed in the church first of all apostles, second prophets, third teachers, then miracles, then gifts of healing, of helping, of guidance, and of different kinds of tongues."[303] Yes, there are kooks and impostors, as there have been from the beginning. But for those who deny there are still genuine apostles and prophets in our midst today I must demand: Show me in the Bible where it says this gifting will stop. It doesn't. Rather, it says this gifting is given "TILL we all come to a unity of the faith...." Have we done that yet? Of

---

[302] Ephesians 4:11-13, NKJV, *emphasis added*. The Greek word generally translated as "gave" in verse 11 is DIDOMI, a prolonged form of the word "to give." Assigning it a strictly past tense here reveals the bias of the translators.
[303] 1 Corinthians 12:28 NIV

course not.[304]

God desires that apostles and prophets occupy the top places of leadership in His Kingdom army on earth,[305] and yet we generally deny their existence.[306] No wonder we're fragmented and losing ground.

We accept the lowest standards and have dumbed-down the Word of God. What does it mean to be a Christian? What is our role and responsibility on this earth? Sit through most "altar calls" these days – and heck, sit in every sermon thereafter at way too many churches – and you'll think it's quite easy. "Just say these words, sit in this pew, try to believe what we teach, and you're set. If you're really devout, you can come to our Bible study, listen to the right radio station and put a bumper sticker on your car. See you next Sunday!" Nobody wants to quote Paul's injunction to the Philippians to "work out your salvation with fear and trembling."[307] There's one very popular rock-star pastor today who's proud he never says the word "sin." Observe most youth ministries these days and you'll see the primary focus is on entertaining the kids, and the youth ministers will degrade themselves to no end so they can be "accepted." Discipleship is a class to take and not an overriding lifestyle. Worship is singing a song when the lights are dimmed. Obedience is putting more money in the

---

[304] Most believers seem to think, in a rather knee-jerk fashion, that there were only 12 apostles. Let's do the math. The original 12 included Judas. After his suicide, the others replaced him. That's makes 13. And then, of course, there was Paul: Apostle Number 14. I could go on and say that Baranabas no doubt had the same calling and gifting as Paul, that Paul was clearly mentoring Timothy and several others into apostleship, etc., but there's no need – the 14 I counted prove that the number didn't stop at 12!

[305] 1 Corinthians 12:28

[306] This is a distinct and separate gifting from shepherding (pastors). According to God's precise instructions, pastors are not supposed to run the show.

[307] Philippians 2:12 NIV

plate. The most holy are the ones who can win at Bible trivia – who cares if it's all trivial to them? We seem often to gear our ministries to the lowest common denominator, and not to cultivating the perfect seed of Christ. I'm sorry, I'm not trying to come across as frustrated here, but I guess it's coming out that way. I have been in full-time, front-lines, faith-based discipleship ministry for a decade now and I have to deal with the unhealthy fruit of this approach all the time. To give all the proper disclaimers and gingerly explain it all would take a whole volume, and I don't want to go down that rabbit trail here. If you're offended by what I'm saying, either just forget that you read this paragraph, or better yet, ask the Holy Spirit to confirm to you whether I'm speaking truth.

In spite of our "conventional wisdom," let me tell you what I've found to be true: People today crave high standards, especially our youth.[308] They are drawn to Christ in part because He offers a sharp contrast to the mushy, spineless, meaningless, superficial, entertainment-based world we live in. We need to embrace the high standards to which Christ calls us! Consider His words to the rich young ruler, "Sell everything you have and give to the poor, and you will have treasure in heaven. Then come, follow me."[309] And His firm instructions to the adulteress: "Go and sin no more."[310] That was tough stuff! We need to be bold in drawing distinct lines between death and life, darkness and light, the world and God's Kingdom. We need to be proud, in a God-pleasing way, of the disciplined righteousness in which we walk.

---

[308] As a point of comparison, consider the exceedingly high standards that go along with being a Muslim. And yet they're said to be the fastest growing religion on earth. People crave high standards!
[309] Matthew 19:21, Mark 10:21, Luke 18:22 NIV
[310] John 8:11 NKJV

People are hungry for meat, and yet we are so self-conscious about God that we give them cotton candy instead. We must start eating solid food and feeding it to those who come to us looking for an alternative to the pointless life this world offers. *We need to start calling people out of the fake, and stop trying to fake them out!* We need to heed the rebuke given by the writer of Hebrews:

> We have much to say about this, but it is hard to make it clear to you because you no longer try to understand. In fact, though by this time you ought to be teachers, you need someone to teach you the elementary truths of God's Word all over again. You need milk, not solid food! Anyone who lives on milk, being still an infant, is not acquainted with the teaching about righteousness. But solid food is for the mature, who by constant use have trained themselves to distinguish good from evil.[311]

The Bible clearly states that God's eternal inheritance for mankind is stored up only for those who conquer as Jesus did. Not for those whose only ambition is to "endure," who seek to skip through life down the easy path, who appease evil, or who seek to store up treasures on earth. When we offer Christianity as a watered-down elixir for life's troubles, we are potentially setting people up for a huge disappointment at the end of days, when they enter heaven with no treasures stored up.[312] Jesus didn't sell His followers a bill of

---

[311] Hebrews 5:11-14 NIV
[312] 1 Corinthians 3:12-15

goods about an easy path, and neither should we. [313]

We seem more concerned with growing organizations than people. This is one challenge I faced daily during the decade God used me to build my own ministry.[314] As decision-makers, it is easy to overlook opportunities to build maturity into our staff, and instead focus on expedient actions to enlarge our organizations. Often the course of personal growth makes no sense by the world's standards. For example, I established a firm policy that we would neither recruit nor seek to retain staff in our ministry; instead, we would work to help them find where God wanted them to serve. Many exceptional men applied for positions with our ministry. I know I could have easily offer them a "job" and lured them to join us, and it would have expanded our organizational chart and enlarged our budget. But if it's not perfectly obvious that the Holy Spirit has led them to serve in this positions at this time, who would benefit from it?

Believe it or not, I've helped others start ministries similar to mine because I felt it was more in line with their calling (and I've been criticized for helping our "competition!"). Further, when one of our regional or local leaders would face a difficult decision, I'd usually let him wrestle with it himself. It would have been easier for both of us had I simply stepped in and made the decision. We could have gotten

---

[313] In the big picture, is it really "friendly" to "seekers" to sell them a phony bill of goods? To mark them as a target of the enemy then fail to equip them to fight? To promise them an eternal inheritance but not tell them what it's tied to? I don't think that's "seeker friendly" at all! If they're truly seeking truth, let's lovingly give it to them, so they can distinguish it from the phoniness of the world, and be fully equipped to grow as a son of the King.

[314] I am founder and Chief Outfitter Emeritus of Cross Trail Outfitters, a discipleship-based youth ministry that reaches boys ages 7-20 through the avenues of hunting and fishing. See more at www.TeamCTO.org.

down the road faster, and my own personal "authority" would have grown had I simply issued an order and moved on. For God, however, it's more important that people learn and grow from their life experiences. So I'd set boundaries, share my own experiences and thoughts, pray with them and encourage them to seek additional wise counsel. Then I'd watch them grow through it! I'd tell them all the time, "we are not working to build an organization here, we're working to build mature sons and daughters of God." Organizations are simply by-products of that work!

When leaders take this approach, they are aligned with God's Big Picture will, and the blessings are incredible. We may not build our organizations as big as *we* could, but instead we have organizations that are free from politics and dissention, made up of men and women of the highest caliber who know they are called by God and hungry to grow spiritually, and with exceptional ministry results. I'll take those things over size any day!

There's a leadership principal that says, "You manage what you measure." Too many churches and ministries seem to be all about "the numbers." How many raised their hand for the altar call? How many came on Sunday? How many congregations are affiliated with our program? How much money did we raise? How's our budget growing? When we focus on numbers, we are conformed to the patterns of this world. When we focus on numbers, they ultimately drive our strategies and actions. And in the end, the real work of *building people* and *connecting the Body* suffers. If a leader can quote you his "numbers" at the drop of a hat (as most can), but can't tell you how Frank is doing with that issue with his son-in-law, or identify the areas where Judy needs to grow spiritually and how he's helping her get there, that leader is misguided. My Bible says, "Seek first the Kingdom of God and His righteousness, and all these things shall be added to you."[315] The Kingdom of God is all about people, not organizations or budgets.

No organization or budget is big enough to beat the enemy and deliver victory – only mature sons and daughters of the King fighting as a unified army. We need to be more passionate about God's Kingdom and less about our own. As a Body, we need to focus properly on producing fruit that pleases God – mature spiritual sons and daughters – and let Him handle the rest.

We would rather avoid conflict with each other than do the hard work of building unity. As I mentioned earlier in this chapter, the Bible gives us freedom in different areas – like precisely how to baptize. The job of filling in the blanks rightly belongs to the Holy Spirit, and He often leads us to express the Way uniquely, to serve different segments of our population. Other areas of Scripture are crystal clear and certainly not open for interpretation. There is only one truth. Different flavors are ok, but different fundamental messages are not ok. Unfortunately, in part because of many of the reasons listed above, we either look at other "flavors" of Christianity with suspicion – almost as if they are the enemy – or we turn a blind eye to serious doctrinal differences with an "I'm ok, you're ok" mentality. This chapter is getting long already, so I'm just going to cut to the chase: In light of the fact that our true assignment from God is to build unity founded on His truth, both of these approaches are lazy and counter-productive.

The Bible is clear that diversity of expression is great, but diversity of belief is not. Paul wrote to the believers in

---

[315] Matthew 6:33 NIV

Corinth, "There are different kinds of gifts, but the same Spirit distributes them. There are different kinds of service, but the same Lord. There are different kinds of working, but in all of them and in everyone it is the same God at work."[316] And later, "I am afraid that just as Eve was deceived by the serpent's cunning, your minds may somehow be led astray from your sincere and pure devotion to Christ. For if someone comes to you and preaches a Jesus other than the Jesus we preached, or if you receive a different spirit from the Spirit you received, or a different gospel from the one you accepted, you put up with it easily enough."[317]

The great apostle warned the battle-seasoned brethren in Ephesus to "make every effort to keep the unity of the Spirit through the bond of peace. There is one body and one Spirit, just as you were called to one hope when you were called; one Lord, one faith, one baptism; one God and Father of all, who is over all and through all and in all."[318] And he implored those in Philippi, "Therefore if you have any encouragement from being united with Christ, if any comfort from His love, if any common sharing in the Spirit, if any tenderness and compassion, then make my joy complete by being like-minded, having the same love, being one in spirit and of one mind. Do nothing out of selfish ambition or vain conceit. Rather, in humility value others above yourselves, not looking to your own interests but each of you to the interests of the others."[319]

Notice Paul said, "Make every *effort*...." Keeping "the unity of the Spirit through the bond of peace" is hard work! It is, in fact, part and parcel with the work of building God's

---

[316] 1 Corinthians 12:4-6 NIV
[317] 2 Corinthians 11:3-4 NIV
[318] Ephesians 4:3-6 NIV, *emphasis added.*
[319] Philippians 2:1-4 NIV

Kingdom, and an activity the enemy seeks to derail. It takes time, energy, effort, sacrifice and dedicated attention. Sadly, when we quickly build walls of division, or alternatively, when we so eagerly embrace anyone who has an ichthus (fish) sticker on their car, we are neglecting this vital work. I don't know what's worse, walls of division or false unity. Neither will bring victory. Instead, we need to let the Holy Spirit guide us in the hard work of foundational unity, while respecting various applications and expressions of it. This is the path to establishing God's Kingdom on earth.

We have few true leaders. Democracy is a great form of civil government but a terribly non-biblical way of running a church or ministry. Try as I might, I cannot find one good example of it in the Bible. The five prominent examples I can find of "democratic" decision making – to throw Joseph in the pit,[320] to make the golden calf idol,[321] not to enter the Promised Land the first time,[322] to crucify Jesus[323] and to stone Stephen[324] – don't paint a very good picture of this leadership model. When the original apostles wanted to replace Judas, they specifically did not want to vote on it, so they cast lots.[325] They knew the dangers of politics and preferred seemingly random chance over the "democratic process" in ministry leadership.

I know in our modern culture, stepping back and considering this topic is like a fish studying water – it's hard because it's all around us and it's all we know. There is an alternative, however, the Bible puts forth, and that is leader-

---

[320] Genesis 37:12-36
[321] Exodus 32
[322] Numbers 14:1-35
[323] Matthew 26:57-68
[324] Acts 6:8-15
[325] Acts 1:12-26

driven ministry. Name the great leaders of the Bible. I'll throw out a few: Abraham, Moses, Joshua, David, Jesus, Paul. Not one of these men answered to a committee or board of directors. They received guidance directly from God and led accordingly. And – imagine this – their followers followed them, respectful of the fact their leaders were appointed by God. Yes, they sought wise counsel. Yes, they held themselves accountable (that whole thing about prophets, remember?). But the buck stopped with them.[326]

Christian leaders are supposed to answer to God and not man. My experience with "democratic" organizations is, despite the words they use, the opposite is generally true. Boards and committees vote – and politics is almost always involved, whether they admit it or not – and the "leaders" follow their orders. This gives a false sense of comfort to each one: the boards can blame the "leaders" if things go wrong and take credit when they go right, and vice-versa. Yes, in an organization where the headship of Christ is not recognized, in a culture where the RHEMA of God is not accepted or understood, where God's Big Picture has been lost, I guess democracy is best, because a fully-empowered leader who is misguided is a dangerous thing. But those characteristics should not be embraced by our churches and ministries! In a properly-functioning, submitted Body, God's model of governance is fully leadership-based, and "voting" has no place.[327] We need strong, Godly, Christ-led

---

[326] "What about the elders in the early church?" you may ask. They were *appointed* by the presiding apostle! (Acts 14:23, Titus 1:5, and elsewhere.) Nobody questioned his leadership, or could vote to override his decisions. Maybe this is why we don't accept the reality of apostles in our midst – we'd rather vote than submit to true, Godly, authoritative leadership.

[327] I know this will be shocking to some, and unpopular with others, but please, before you throw it out – or throw stones at me – show me otherwise in the Bible.

leaders to lead us to victory.

--

I know I hit these topics hard and fast. Out of respect for your time, and to remain focused on the subject of victory, I didn't want to go too far down too many rabbit trails. I believe each of these topics is worthy of deep discussion. My goal was not to provoke anyone to anger, but to thought and self-reflection. I hope I've succeeded in this, and that I've provided ample content and footnotes for you to dig into these on your own.

The bottom line is this: The Body of Christ today is doing lots of things wrong, and because of this we are not walking in victory. But this is not God's will, and it's not inevitable. So much more is available to us! Each one of these broken areas is fixable! With proper leadership, accurate teaching, a commitment to unity, and going all-in with God, each of these strongholds will be torn down, and the tide of battle will turn. That is what's inevitable.

KEY POINTS: We are losing because we have not embraced our identity, purpose and destiny as winners, have refused to take God up on His promises, and have been caught up following the patterns of this world.

I find it fascinating that most people plan their
vacations with better care than they do their lives.
Perhaps that is because escape is easier than change.
Jim Rohn

Chapter 13 – Why on earth are we losing? Part Two: The 800 Pound Gorilla

*It is not my purpose in writing this book to single anyone out or to
tear down another person's work. Instead, my purpose is to clearly
and simply communicate God's original intent for mankind, to
help people see and embrace their victorious identity and destiny. I
never intended to include this chapter and I wish I didn't have to.
But as I've shared this message with people around the world, I've
come to realize there is one big, hairy theological block holding
people back from truly embracing their full potential in Christ, and
that is the modern, escapist, "end times" teachings which have
become so prevalent. This stands in such stark contrast to God's
vision of victory, and so completely undermines our true identity,
it simply must be addressed. And since I must address it, I am
compelled by God to address it with all my strength. Please
understand I personally know and deeply respect many men who
hold to this teaching. I do not write this out of anger or malice, and
I intend no disrespect, but fact is the 800 pound gorilla must be
killed if God's people are truly to be set free. To my friends who
have embraced this teaching, all I can say is I pray you are
teachable.*

Just because a teaching is dominant doesn't make it right. I'm sure that's what Christopher Columbus would have told you before 1492 had you challenged his certain belief in a round earth. Standing against dominant dogma can be dangerous – think of the great Inquisition-era saints who were martyred for speaking truth, or the Christians in Holland during WWII who gave their lives to protect Jews. Thank God for brave men and women who have taken the risks – and many times paid the ultimate price – to stand up for unpopular truth against seemingly impossible odds. Were it not for the Reformers, America's Founding Fathers, the great abolitionists, those who stood against the Nazis, or any number of great, historic iconoclasts – like Jesus Himself – the world would indeed be a darker place.

We must always cling to a healthy degree of skepticism of "the powers that be" and never blindly accept a belief system just because it's popular. The great Apostle John wrote, "Dear friends, do not believe every spirit, but test the spirits to see whether they are from God, because many false prophets have gone out into the world."[328] Even if you firmly believe today's popular, "Great Escape" teachings, I encourage you to read this chapter with an open mind. If you consider the facts I present and still cling to your beliefs, then you will have newfound, tested-and-approved confidence in why you believe the way you do. If on the other hand you become convinced, as I have, that today's dominant teaching is wrong, then you have gained the truth. Test the spirits; you have nothing to lose.

God's people are caught up in the greatest war in the history of the universe. In warfare, propaganda and disinformation are common tactics employed by cunning enemies. Tokyo

---

[328] 1 John 4:1 NIV

Rose is a great example. During WWII, the Japanese government aired a radio show across the Pacific that purposefully sounded like an American broadcast. The female announcer, whom American GIs nicknamed Tokyo Rose, would play American music, tell stories and report the news … and then slip in reports of how hopeless the situation was for America, how America was losing the war, how the Japanese were superior and destined to win, etc. It was vital for American military leaders to remind their men this was propaganda; otherwise it may well have demoralized the troops. Solomon wrote, "there is nothing new under the sun."[329] This tactic has been used in warfare since the dawn of time and will be till the end. We must remain vigilant, as our mortal enemy, the devil, is the most cunning deceiver of all. He is a master of propaganda and will work to demoralize our army every chance he gets. The same spirit that animated Tokyo Rose is alive and well in our world today.

When I was a kid I was fed the traditional story of Santa Claus. My family looked forward to his arrival, left out cookies and milk for him and even scanned the night sky for Rudolph's nose before going to bed on Christmas Eve. I guess you could say I believed in him, but what's more accurate is *I went along with* the belief in him because it just seemed like the thing to do and I didn't know any better. Even though I tried to convince my friends of his existence, it never really sat right with me, and I wasn't disappointed when I learned it was all make believe. The modern "end times" mythology was the same way for me, and I wouldn't be surprised if it's the same for you. We've gone along with these teachings because they're popular and no real

---

[329] Ecclesiastes 1:9

alternative is presented these days. Sadly, there's a lot more at stake than a plate of cookies and milk on Christmas Eve.

Modern "end times" teaching tells a simple story, really. It says that someday (probably very soon!) all of the real Christians will be instantly snatched away in a secret second coming they call "the Rapture." Then, the sorry people left on earth will suffer all sorts of maladies in a future "Great Tribulation." During this time, an individual known as "The Antichrist" will rise to supreme world power and do all sorts of bad things. Finally, all the armies of the world will gather somewhere in the Middle East for a final battle. Then, all of a sudden, while we sit back as spectators, Jesus and the angels will return to wipe out the devil and his demons and bring God's Kingdom to earth once and for all.[330]

Christians caught up in today's evangelical, pop-Christianity culture may be shocked that I presented this familiar storyline with such dramatic build-up. "That's all he's talking about?" you may wonder. "That's just the way it is … isn't it?" Truly, it seems to be all that's talked about anymore. It's the overwhelmingly dominant teaching of our culture. It's the theme for a bestselling book series, it's in the movies, it's all over the internet and it's taught from countless pulpits, so it must be true, right? Most don't realize that this teaching hasn't been around very long historically, there is a long list of faithful theologians who vehemently view this as heresy, and an honest analysis shows its biblical underpinnings are shakier than a house of cards built on a wobbly table. Once again, don't take my word for it. The Bible says you can judge a tree by its roots

---

[330] Of course there are more details to it, but the teachers of this doctrine can't seem to agree on most of them. They even passionately debate the timing of it all, but these elements I've related comprise the generally accepted storyline.

and fruits.[331] Accordingly, let's examine both the origins and the impact of this teaching so you can come to your own conclusion. I'll provide ample footnotes so you can do the research for yourself.[332] The truth may surprise you.

--

So where does this "end times" storyline come from? First let's start with the basics. The word "Rapture" doesn't show up in the Bible at all.[333] The words "The Great Tribulation," except for one brief mention in Revelation 7:14, only show up in a section heading added many centuries after the Bible was written. The words "The Antichrist" only show up in brief mentions in the books of 1 and 2 John, and every reference talks about a spirit that was currently active on the planet (nearly 2,000 years ago), and clearly do not apply to an individual person or entity.[334] Do a keyword Search and you'll see for yourself.[335]

---

[331] Romans 11:16, Matthew 7:15-17, Luke 6:43-45

[332] I will do my best to include all I reasonably can in one chapter of one book. There are tons of great resources available to you for additional research. Please, if you are hesitant to accept what I write here, do more research on your own.

[333] I checked ALL TRANSLATIONS under www.BibleStudyTools.com, a great resource with 38 Bible translations in their database. The word does show up four times in the Bible in Basic English version in the books of Psalms and Proverbs, meaning *extreme delight*. With this same meaning, it also shows up once in the Darby Translation in Song of Solomon, and once in the Weymouth New Testament, in Luke. But this is an obscure word in obscure translations, and this meaning has no connection to the way the word is currently used by "end times" teachers.

[334] 1 John 2:18-27 (the section heading in NIV is "Warning Against Antichrists" – note the plurality), 1 John 4:3 (where it says Antichrist is a spirit that is already in the world), and 2 John 1:7 (which says that there are many deceivers who we could call Antichrist). *Nowhere does the Bible point to one great, coming Antichrist.*

[335] By contract, the word BASILEIA (Kingdom, God's royal power, kingship, dominion and rule) is used 154 times in the New Testament, and NIKAO (conquer, carry off the victory) is used 24 times.

The idea of a future Great Tribulation and individual Antichrist do not show up in early church writings, either. In fact, they don't come on the scene till the 1500s, and the "Rapture" idea isn't dreamed up till hundreds of years after that! In light of how widely it's accepted and passionately defended by our fellow Christians, the truth about the roots of this teaching will take your breath away.[336]

In the time leading up to the Reformation, the Roman Catholic Church pretty much ruled Europe, and they ruled it with an iron fist. They fancied themselves as the One True Church, and any teaching or teacher that communicated anything to the contrary was summarily stamped out, often quite brutally. They controlled the relics, writings, educational establishments and all the grand machinery of the "Christian" religion. They sold "indulgences" (basically, tickets to heaven) to generate income for the construction of their cathedrals, and submitted critics to The Inquisition, burning many a good man at the stake for "heresy."

Then in 1517, a theologian named Martin Luther nailed his 95 Theses (or points of debate against the Catholic Church) to the church door in Wittenberg, Germany. This simple act of defiance helped spark the Protestant Reformation (a movement of "protesters" who sought to "reform" Christianity) that burned across Europe and lights our faith to this day. The great Reformers, including Luther, Calvin,

---

[336] In this section on "roots," except as otherwise noted, I lean heavily on the definitive, rigorously-documented work of Steve Wohlberg (*End Times Delusions*, published 2004 by Treasure House, an imprint of Destiny Image Publishers, Inc.). I have read other books and done considerable research to confirm his findings and add to my knowledge, yet I must tip my hat to Wolhberg and give him credit as my primary source. Much of my knowledge of the Reformation and Catholic response to it comes from my many years as an active and passionate Lutheran, as well as countless history books and biographies I've read.

Wycliffe, Tyndale and others, worked diligently to translate the Bible into modern languages, apply it to the daily lives of their countrymen, and in general make Christ accessible to the masses. The people responded. There was a resurgence of faith, a hunger for God's Word ... and a growing disdain for their Inquisition-era Catholic overlords. The Catholic leaders stepped up their book burnings (and people burnings) in an all-out war against the Reformers. It was indeed a time of great tribulation for Christ's followers. The brutal Catholic response led the Reformers to clearly see – and loudly proclaim – that the spirit of Antichrist was alive and well in the Catholic Church of the day.

In the 1,200 or so years since Constantine Romanized the church, this was by far the greatest threat to Rome's iron grip on the reins of power, and the Catholic leaders took it very seriously. They were fighting teachings with fire (literally!) and it wasn't working. So they switched gears, convening the Council of Trent (which ran off and on for 18 years beginning in 1545) to develop Catholic teachings as a countermeasure to the threat of the Reformers. One participant in these proceedings was a Jesuit monk named Francisco Ribera. The Reformers' teaching that the Catholic Church was operating under an Antichrist spirit weighed heavily on Ribera, and he set out to undermine this teaching with a different "interpretation" of Scripture.

Retreating to his home of Salamanca, Spain, Ribera labored for years to develop his teaching, which effectively wove together bits and pieces of the Bible to cunningly deflect attention from his beloved Church, eventually introducing his 500-page theological treatise in about 1590.[337] In it, he originated the school of thought we call the "Futurist" view of the "end times." Ribera's unprecedented teachings included a specific period of "Great Tribulation" and singular Antichrist that were still to come, far in the future. The underpinning of his teaching is based on a novel idea he twisted from a prophesy in the Book of Daniel. Daniel's famous 70 week prophesy paints the story of mankind – past, present and future – with a very broad brush.[338] Christian historians generally agree on how the bulk of this prophesy relates to the past. (The stakes aren't as high with things that are past, so there's not so much debate on that.) They agree the first 69 weeks are chronologically contiguous, each one leading into the next.

Ribera's great leap of interpretation and logic, the string on which his entire treatise hangs, was the idea that Daniel's 70th week was somehow cut off from that chronology and is floating off in space somewhere; that the many centuries between Christ and the "end times" are simply left by God on the prophetic cutting room floor, unaccounted for in the Bible. All of early church history, the rise of Constantine, the Dark Ages Roman Catholic hegemony and their grotesque persecutions and Inquisition, and Reformation – all of these, Ribera claimed – are prophetically meaningless. Why this audacious claim? It's simple. If Daniel's prophesy were taken as a whole, as every other prophecy in the Bible is interpreted, then the great Reformers' claims that the spirit of Antichrist was alive in the Inquisition-era Catholic Church would have a solid Biblical basis! Ribera

---

[337] Ribera's work was entitled *In Sacrum Beati Ioannis Apostoli, & Evangelistiae Apocalypsin Commentarij* (A Sacred Blessed John Apostle, & Evangelist Revelation Commentary).
[338] Daniel 9:20-26

intentionally set out to undermine this very teaching, and the only way he could do that was to sever Daniel's 70th week and stick it at some random time in the future – far away from him or his colleagues who were selling indulgences and burning people at the stake for translating the Bible into modern languages.[339] He must have figured there was nothing anti-Christ about that, I guess!

History shows clearly the modern "end times" view has its tap root in an Inquisition-era Catholic effort to undermine the work of the great Reformers. If you're quick enough to judge a tree by its roots, and are ready to chunk this teaching out the window, feel free to skip to the next section. Even so, the details about how this teaching came to be popular today make a sad but entertaining story – especially the part about the Rapture – so you may as well stick around a bit.

The Jesuit order to which Ribera belonged has a strong tradition of theological activism. They have founded top schools and universities around the world, and are known for being passionate, active and strategic in propagating Catholic teachings and defending their Church. Through his affiliation with this sect, Ribera's teaching was advanced and further developed in the Catholic halls of learning. Even so, it never really had its desired effect of derailing the work of the Reformers ... until about 250 years later.

In the early 1800s, the librarian of the Archbishop of Canterbury, a man named Dr. Samuel Roffey Maitland, discovered and was persuaded by Ribera's writing. In 1826 he published a widely-read book and series of tracts which attacked the Reformation and advanced Ribera's Futurist

---

[339] All the "end times" forecasters of today are simply taking Ribera's bait and scrambling to figure out when Daniel's 70th week will begin. So much for "testing the spirits."

spin.[340] Enter a fellow named John Darby. Considered the father of Dispensationalism, which is the primary theological vehicle of today's "end times" teaching, Darby founded a denomination called the Brethren (popularly called the Plymouth Brethren), and worked tirelessly to advance his school of thought. Influenced by Maitland, he believed "the" all-powerful Antichrist was still coming, along with "a" Great Tribulation. There was just one thing he couldn't grasp, one missing piece of the puzzle: How could a loving God subject His followers to such a terrible thing? Enter Margaret McDonald. Investigative journalist Dave MacPherson did exhaustive research proving this 15-year-old Scottish girl was the first to come up with the idea of a "Great Escape" – while in a trance at a Brethren meeting about the year 1830![341] This idea wound its way to Darby, who eagerly bolted this inventive concept of the "Rapture" on to his new theology, and the rest, as they say, is history.

(An important note for my Dispensationalist friends: I have no beef with the bulk of Darby's theology. He seems to have had a keen insight into the past; he just got it wrong when he tried to predict the future. I don't want to throw the baby out with the bath water, I just want to get the scorpion out of the bathtub. I would submit that my premise of this book fits perfectly within the framework of Dispensationalism; you just need to surgically sever Darby's faulty predictions and replace them with the fact that we now are living in the dispensation of Kingdom Victory – the true, final dispensation of God.)

---

[340] These include *An Enquiry into the Grounds on which the Prophetic Period of Daniel and St. John has been supposed to consist of 1,260 Years* in 1862 and *An Attempt to elucidate the Prophecies concerning Antichrist* in 1830

[341] *The Incredible Cover Up* by Dave MacPherson, published in 1975 by Omega Publications. I am amazed at the first-hand, shoe-leather work he did to exhaustively document this for us. It's a fascinating read!

The trail from Darby to today is quite easy to follow. Darby was a prominent, prolific and persuasive man, quite influential in his day. He visited America six times between 1859-1874, spreading his theological school of thought (including his predictions of the "end times") across the country. A fellow named Cyrus Scofield was persuaded by his teachings. This Kansas attorney and theologian published his most famous work – the Scofield Reference Bible – in 1909, which sold millions of copies. This reference work, still widely used today, includes countless footnotes explaining details of Scripture (which are taken by many readers to be on par with Scripture itself). Woven through these footnotes is – you guessed it – Darby's Dispensationalism, complete with his "end times" view. Ribera's root had finally started to sprout.

Many great American seminaries were founded in the era of Darby and Scofield and influenced by their teachings. Among these is the renowned Dallas Theological Seminary. This highly respectable school has produced some incredible, world-changing men and women of God.[342] Yet woven into its curriculum, along with all the fantastic Bible teaching and ministry training, is Ribera's cunningly devised Futurism. A prominent, successful graduate of this seminary is Hal Lindsey. He's the fellow who took the seeds from Ribera's now fully-grown Futurist theology and cast them to the winds. His 1970 book, *Late Great Planet Earth* – a ripped-from-the-headlines, the-rapture-is-near, everyday-language exposition of Darby's end-times teachings – sold upwards of 30,000,000 copies around the world. Just a couple decades later, built upon the financial success and

---

[342] Prof. John Ofoegbu, my personal friend and mentor, and the founder of Unity for Africa, is a proud graduate of DTS.

popular demand for this kind of book, a couple fellows named Tim LaHaye and Jerry Jenkins published the *Left Behind* book series which, according to Publishers Weekly, is "the most successful Christian-fiction series ever." Spawning movies, a TV series and countless other spin-offs – plus a multitude of "end times" teachers wishing to hitch a ride on their popularity – the success of the *Left Behind* brand has ensured the Futurist view of the "end times" is now the ubiquitous understanding of things to come. Ribera could never have dreamed his life's work would be so successful!

Please hear my heart here: I am not questioning the integrity, intellect or faith of any of our "end times" theologians, and I am not challenging any of their beliefs other than their embrace of Ribera's and Darby's erroneous view of the future. I have many dear friends, whom I look up to as remarkable and faithful men of God, who passionately cling to this teaching. I am actually choked up as I write this, as I do not want to dishonor them or make them feel I disrespect them in any way. I believe they honestly think they are accurately piecing together bits and pieces of Scripture in support of their view of things to come. Here's what I must say, however: In their honest research, they *start* with a belief in today's dominant dogma, and then find evidence to support it. I'm not claiming they do this consciously, but it is at the core. There is zero likelihood that, in a vacuum – without any outside implantation of this teaching into their minds – they could read the Bible and come up with such a fanciful tale on their own.[343] How can I say this? It was never conceived for more than 1500 years after Christ's ascension. It was not imagined

---

[343] In other words, I contend modern "end times" theology can only come about through inductive reasoning, and is impossible to deduce from Scripture alone. And the *original* inducement was an effort to derail the Reformation.

by any of our great Reformers. Were it not for the root planted by Francisco Ribera who desired to undermine the Reformation, then unwittingly cultivated by Darby and others, this theology would never have grown into existence. I'd bet even Francisco Ribera was a man with good intentions; I'm sure he truly believed the Inquisition-era Catholic Church was the One True Church of God and the Reformers were a threat to God's work, and so he honestly set out to prove them wrong. And I'm sure that, 250 years later, Margaret McDonald honestly spoke what she thought she saw in her trance, and Darby honestly thought it was the missing piece to the Futurist puzzle. Just like I know there are many honest scientists who, with the very best intentions, try to fit their latest finding into Darwin's theory of evolution, because it's what they were taught in school. I don't question the integrity of Cyrus Scofield, the Dallas Theological Seminary, Hal Lindsey, Tim LaHaye, or any other modern "end-times" teacher. I have no doubt they are honest, good, faithful men of high integrity and fine moral character. It's just that, on this matter, they are dead wrong, and the consequences are catastrophic.

All I can ultimately say is *consider the roots*. This is, after all, how the enemy works. He is a master propagandist and will stay hidden whenever possible. If the same spirit that animated Tokyo Rose can undermine the morale of God's army today – and thus sap their fighting resolve – then his cause is advanced without ever firing a shot.

--

I would be doing you, and my good friends who embrace and advance modern "end times" teachings, a great disservice if I didn't go into the Bible to address the key verses they reference in support of this theology. They claim the Bible, after all, as the real root of their teachings.

Let me start with probably the most famous one. There's a highly-circulated internet video entitled "Are you ready?" which has logged nearly 8,000,000 views on YouTube. This brief clip shows a congregation sitting in a church service, listening to a pastor preach. He quotes Matthew 24:22, "Watch, therefore, for you don't know the hour your Lord is coming," and then – wham! – most of them disappear, while the ones "left behind" moan and cry in despair.[344] The video ends with a black screen emblazoned with Matthew 24:27, "For as the lightning comes from the east and flashes to the west, so also shall the coming of the Son of Man be." Any Rapturist worth his salt will be able to quote you this part of Matthew. It says, "Then two men will be in the field: one will be taken away and the other left. Two women will be grinding at the mill: one will be taken and the other left."[345] The picture painted here of people suddenly "left behind" is no doubt the basis for the title of that bestselling book series, and seems to fully support the Rapture teaching.[346] There is, however, one key thing missing: In verse 37, just before this, Jesus says the end will be "Just as it was in the days of Noah." He repeats the Noah comparison again in verse 38. Let me ask you, who was suddenly wiped off the earth in the days of Noah? The wicked! Who were left behind? Noah and his family! This fully supports the true "end times"

---

[344] I know people who actually send out links to this video believing that this constitutes evangelism!

[345] Matthew 24: 40-41, NIV

[346] Note this passage says they will be "taken away." It does not say how. I'm sure the folk in Holland in WWII would have similarly described the disappearance of their Jewish neighbors. God promised Noah it would not be another flood. Could it be fire from the sky like for the citizens of Sodom? Will they just drop dead? Will the angels physically round them up and march them somewhere? It doesn't say.

chronology Jesus precisely presented in the Parable of the Wheat and the Tares:[347] "…at the time of harvest I will say to the reapers, 'First gather together the tares (weeds) and bind them in bundles to burn them, but gather the wheat into my barn.'"[348] According to Christ Himself, at the end of time God will first gather and burn the weeds (whom Jesus says are sons and daughters of the evil one), *then* He will gather the mature sons and daughters of the Kingdom into His barn. (Right here, Jesus established precisely the opposite scenario as the *Left Behind* books!) Just as it was in the days of Noah, I pray when the harvest comes, my family and I are among those left behind,[349] because the alternative would mean we were burned with the weeds or drowned in the flood!

The next most prominent verse quoted by Rapturists is 1 Thessalonians 4:16-17: "For the Lord himself will come down from heaven, with a loud command, with the voice of the archangel and with the trumpet call of God, and the dead in Christ will rise first. After that, we who are still alive and are left will be caught up together with them in the clouds to meet the Lord in the air. And so we will be with the Lord forever."[350] Again, on the surface this seems to confirm the "Left Behind" scenario. When you dig into the Greek, however, it is clear this is a faulty interpretation. The Greek word translated here as "caught up" is HARPAZO. This word is used 13 times in the New Testament, in many different ways,[351] and could just as rightly be translated as

---

[347] Matthew 13:24-30

[348] Matthew 13:30 NIV

[349] I explore Christ's Noah comparison in more detail in *Chapter 17 – The end is near … or is it?*

[350] NIV

[351] "catch up" 4, "take by force" 3, "catch away" 2, "pluck" 2, "catch" 1, "pull" 1

"plucked" or "pulled up." This perfectly fits Christ's own "end times" picture that the wicked weeds will be burned up, and only then will the remaining wheat be "pulled up" and brought into the barn, to receive our eternal inheritance. It does say our reunion with Christ will take place in the sky, but it does not talk about the timing of this, or correlate this event in any way to the Matthew 24 verse about people being "taken away." In other words, there's no rational way a "Left Behind"-style Rapture can be deduced from this portion of Scripture.

I've talked to quite a few Rapturists and read a lot about their theology, and as far as I can tell, outside the Book of Revelation, these two sections of Scripture are pretty much all they reference to support their teaching. Not very solid ground if you ask me. Regarding the Book of Revelation, to prevent this chapter from dragging on needlessly, I have included in the appendix a "bonus chapter" entitled *A victorious view of the Book of Revelation*, and if you want to dig into it more I encourage you to read it. Here are the key points:

> • The Apostle John, who wrote the book, was writing about things he saw in the eternal realm. As I mentioned in Chapter Five, linear time was created by God for us to live in. Our entire concept of past, present and future stands in sharp contrast to the "always now" nature of eternity. For an interpreter to assume everything John recorded is going to happen in precise chronological order is an indefensible leap of logic. Many theologians believe the Book of Revelation actually repeats itself, looping back on itself over and over, and that's an equally valid interpretation. Much of the modern "end times" interpretation of the

Revelation is a vain attempt to apply primitive human comprehension to a complex vision of eternity, in that it assumes a strict, chronological order to the events recorded. This is highly debatable, to say the least.

• Similarly, John was shown things in the spirit realm. Many of the pictures he paints are exceptionally abstract, like various unearthly creatures with seemingly magical powers, and vividly dramatic events. Futurist theologians make the unfounded assumption that John's imagery was purely metaphorical, and so they take pains to correlate these creatures and events to specific people and things in the visible realm. Once again, this is an amazing leap of logic. If we could see the spirits around us, I have no doubt we'd witness some fearsome forms and incredible happenings. I believe John's writing was more literal than they give him credit for, and that many of the things he recorded have occurred, and are currently occurring, precisely as he described them – only in the unseen spirit realm.

• One of the most dramatic parts of the Book of Revelation – in fact in the entire Bible – is that Jesus repeats Himself seven times over. I've not found this anywhere else in Scripture. In Chapters 2 and 3, He establishes the fact that every element of God's eternal inheritance is stored up *for those who conquer the world*. Rapturists claim this will never happen, and that instead Christ will have to come back and do it Himself (which would mean the only eternal inheritance is stored up for Jesus alone!).

• Finally, the fact God has made us the earthly
agents of His Kingdom coming is clearly
illustrated in Revelation 19:7, where the angels
rejoice because the Bride of Christ "has made
herself ready." This hardly sound passive to me!

While I'm on this subject of Biblical references used by
Futurists, one other interesting point to make is this: While
they don't admit it, in reality what Futurists are really
looking forward to is Jesus' third coming. Count them. First
He came to live and die and rise again. Second, they believe
He's coming back to rescue us in the Rapture. Then He's
coming back a third time to finish the job. I can't find any
reference to Christ's "third coming" in the Bible, can you?

The modern "end times" view simple can't be deduced from
a reading of the Bible alone; its genesis had to come from
some other source. And this is precisely what history
confirms.

--

My purpose in addressing this head-on is not to debate the
future. Let the ivory tower theologians sit around and do
that if it floats their boats.[352] It is what this modern "end
times" fantasy does to believers today that compels me to
address it, because the practical fruit of Ribera's root is
terribly damaging to our cause of victory. Allow me to
approach it this way: If a completely faithful and trusted
trainer tells his boxer before a big match, "Oh man, you're
going to get the snot beat out of you. But don't worry, before
you're knocked out I'll throw in the towel and get you out of

---

[352] Isaiah said to forget the past (Isaiah 43:18), and Paul said he worked very hard
to just that (Philippians 3:13). Jesus said not to worry about the future
(Matthew 6:34). That only leaves us to be concerned with the here and now!

there…" do you think that fellow will fight his hardest? Of course not. Think about it. The modern American "end times" message tells believers precisely this message, the same kind of storyline Tokyo Rose would have spun. It tells us we are not agents of victory, and that our carrying off the victory is not an option.

Now, a modern "end-times" adherent will tell you that of course they believe in the "victory" of God's Kingdom. But there is one huge, fundamental difference in their idea of victory and the one I see in the Bible: They believe humans are nothing but passive spectators to the Kingdom come. In a nutshell, their teaching says God has a secret clock ticking, and at some point in the future He will start Daniel's 70th week, triggering a series of "end times" events that will ultimately culminate with Him sending Jesus and His angels back to win the final battle and usher in the Kingdom of God.

It simply can't be both ways: We can't be both the agents of victory and at the same time passive spectators to it all. Unfortunately, today's dominant dogma holds that our role in establishing God's Kingdom is entirely passive. The fruit of this view takes various forms. It gives some a license to "live it up" and seek all the "prosperity" they can in the meantime. Some sit and wait for a great escape that could happen at any moment. Some spend a huge amount of time watching the headlines, or engaging in far-out "numerology," to try to predict when all the "end times prophesies" will come about. Some have a bizarre obsession with conspiracy theories about "The Antichrist." Some see mere endurance or survival as their highest goal. Some operate in fear, not wanting to be "caught" doing the wrong thing when Jesus suddenly returns. Most won't take the risks or make the sacrifices necessary to bring victory.

Others sincerely try their hardest to do the work they feel called to do – to get as many souls "saved" as they can and to store up for themselves "treasures in heaven" – but they do all this under the belief that their actions ultimately have no bearing on the cause of victory.

You want to witness something really sad? Try telling a Futurist the antichrist is definitely not going to rule the world, and you are certainly not afraid of him.[353] In my experience, they will go to great lengths to passionately defend their belief in the inevitability of satan's spawn rising to international prominence, and at the same time call you a heretic for embracing the inevitability of God's sons and daughters arising victorious. They'll say our job is to prepare the Body to be persecuted, not to equip it for conquest! Think about this for a moment – whose argument are they really advocating? Until we embrace our identity as winners, and our victorious destiny – and the fact that when we grow up the kingdom of darkness is doomed – we will continue to be "tossed back and forth by the waves, and blown here and there by every wind of teaching and by the cunning and craftiness of men in their deceitful scheming…"[354] [355] and never grow into the unity and maturity Paul wrote about and God so passionately desires for us.

As I wrote the first edition of this book, the American media was all abuzz over a group in Tennessee who had taken out billboards announcing Jesus' return would happen, *for sure this time*, on May 21, 2011. Of course, after May 21 came and went, and the Rapture didn't happen, the cause of Christ

---

[353] If you really want to see something interesting, try telling them you want to be left behind, just like Noah and his family!

[354] Ephesians 4:14 NIV

[355] "Cunning and craftiness of men in their deceitful scheming?" Sure sounds like ol' Ribera to me!

once again was diminished by well-intentioned "end times" kooks. Sadly, it was just another drop in the bucket. The most sensationalistic Futurists are never shy about loudly proclaiming their latest "ripped from the headlines" predictions that never come true. Every week it seems a new world leader emerges who is *for sure* "The Antichrist," and then eventually he fades from view. These ongoing, repeated predictions (and disappointments) do nothing but diminish the credibility of those who represent the true cause of Christ. With "friends" like those Tennessee weirdoes – who have bought the Tokyo Rose of hell's defeatist propaganda hook, line and sinker – who needs enemies?

All things considered, in light of what I have presented as God's original vision for his sons and daughters to grow up and deliver victory, the fruit of Futurist teaching makes my gut ache, and I believe it grieves God even more. The fruit is passive Christians who believe our delivering victory is not an option; it is sons and daughters who are not striving for the Father's definition of maturity or for the eternal inheritance stored up only for those who conquer the world. The three primary elements of winning – knowing the purpose of our pursuit, walking in our identity of winners, and embracing the destiny of our God-given giftedness – are fully gutted from the sons and daughters of God by this teaching. We are simply passive players, at the mercy of a pre-set timeline that includes inevitable events, especially Middle East politics. This keeps us chasing our tails, trying to decipher the meaning of the latest headlines. We are taught to fear the antichrist, the mark of the beast, and all the terrible things that are going to happen during the "Great Tribulation." Truly the fruit of this teaching produces a body of "Christians" that in no way resembles the victorious Body of Christ I read about in the Bible! So, simply doing what the Bible says and judging a tree by its fruits, this teaching is one that, I believe, God desires to cut down and throw into the fire.[356]

--

One of the primary factors one can use as evidence to show Jesus was indeed the Messiah is the fact that an enormous number of details of His life were foretold many years in advance through Old Testament prophesy and "types." There is no Biblical "type" or prophesy pointing to a big rescue or divine intervention in the assignments of God's people, while there are plenty of examples of the coming of the Kingdom as I've presented in this book. Daniel did not get snatched away from the lion's den, he survived it. Shadrach, Meshach and Abednego did not get rescued from the fiery furnace, they walked through it with Christ. Joseph didn't get Raptured out of the pit or prison, he lived through them before ascending to the throne of Egypt. The Israelites weren't miraculously rescued from Goliath, David went down and killed him. Noah wasn't rescued from the flood, he built an ark and rode it out, while the wicked were suddenly removed from the planet! From what I can see, every story in the Bible shows this: Obedient sons and daughters of God conquer every obstacle while the disobedient are swept away.

I can only find one example in the whole Bible that could possibly be twisted to show some kind of "foreshadowing" of some kind of "Rapture:" The rescue of Lot's family before the destruction of Sodom and Gomorrah. And even there, it was Lot's family who were "left behind" and the evil who

---

[356] Matthew 7:19 NIV: "Every tree that does not bear good fruit is cut down and thrown into the fire."

were suddenly wiped away. In light of the overwhelming number of examples foreshadowing our victory, this isn't a great one to build an entire theology upon!

Can you imagine Noah, the last holdout of righteousness and faith in the entire world, viewing his dire circumstances and figuring that, oh well, God will rescue me someday?

Can you imagine Joseph, brutalized by his brothers and imprisoned in Egypt, meditating on his situation and coming to the conclusion his visions of a great destiny must have really been mere daydreams after all?

Can you imagine Job, when his wife told him he should just "curse God and die," agreeing with her?

Can you imagine Moses, after Pharaoh repeatedly refused to free the Israelites, deciding to quit because the God who sent him must not have really meant what He said when He promised freedom for His people?

Can you imagine Joshua, after taking lead of the Israelites in the wilderness, looking across the Jordan River, seeing the races of warrior giants and walled cities, and figuring the Promised Land must really just be a metaphorical promise of Heaven in the afterlife?

Can you imagine David in the cave of Adullam, on the run from Saul, sitting there thinking about his anointed destiny and coming to the conclusion, based on his abject circumstances, that his promised kingship must only be in Heaven?

Can you imagine Elijah, sitting by the brook, lamenting his future and the deplorable state of Israel at the time, deciding there was really no hope, and so he might as well just wait till the Messiah comes to encounter the manifest presence of God?

Where would we be today?

God told Noah to build an ark. After decades of hard labor, Noah finished it – and *then* God wiped out the rest of the world and left Noah behind to repopulate and rule.

Joseph clung to his faith through incredible hardship and emerged victorious from the pit to the prison to the palace.

In the midst of incalculable hardship, Job boldly declared, "I know my redeemer lives," and indeed, everything that was taken from him was restored, many times over, *in this life.*

Moses pushed through rejection and, following step-by-step instruction from the Lord, led the people out of captivity.

Joshua walked on faith, and so was used by God to conquer the Promised Land in the here and now and establish a foreshadowing of God's Kingdom on earth.

David was a man after God's own heart – a heart of victory! – and continued to trust Him even in his darkest days, when everything he hoped for seemed impossible, and so was ultimately led to occupy the throne of God's Kingdom on earth.

And Elijah pressed in on God, found His presence, was encouraged and revitalized in his work … and was used by God to raise the banner of the Kingdom for all to see.

These Old Testament types and countless more – along with example upon example from the New Testament – all point to the same conclusion: God's sons and daughters emerge victorious, in the here and now, when we latch on to His promises and continue to live by faith, regardless of seemingly insurmountable worldly circumstances.

Yes, the Body of Christ is in a sorry state of affairs today. It is easy to feel like Noah, Joseph, Job, Moses, Joshua, David or

Elijah on their darkest days, and there are many reasons to feel that way. But the worst thing we can do is try to explain away God's promises as impossible in the here and now. The worst thing we can do is resign to the assumption we cannot win, those promises must be for the next life, we are powerless and must wait on God to do it for us as we sit passively by. The worst thing we can do is slice and dice Scripture to torture out an escapist theology that supports our deep-seated hopelessness!

This is the worst thing we can do, yet this is the fruit of today's "end times" mythology! Thank God Noah, Joshua, David, Elijah and the other heroes of the Bible weren't sitting around waiting for a "Rapture," believing the promises of God were only for the afterlife! They knew God works through His sons and daughters to accomplish His goals, and through their simple obedience God would fully deliver on His promises to them.

The Bible says, "Just as it was in the days of Noah, so shall the coming of the Son of Man be." Noah had a building project: the ark. So do we: the Kingdom. When he was done, the flood came and washed the wicked away. When we are done, the wicked will be similarly washed away. He was left to rule and reign, and so will we. This is the Gospel of the Kingdom that Jesus came to proclaim.

--

There is quite a bit of rock-solid research and academic writings out there that shine a bright light on the origins of today's "end times" teaching and completely obliterate it. What I haven't seen, until now, is a clear and bold statement of the alternative. Many scholars know that the Rapture, etc., are not accurate teachings, but they don't teach God's vision of victory in its place. That is in part the purpose of this book. Simply put, the Body of Christ won't languish here till we're rescued; we're going to successfully advance the Kingdom until Christ returns to celebrate the victory with His risen-up Bride. You don't have to be a seminary-trained, academic theologian to cobble this truth together from random bits and pieces of Scripture. It's clear as crystal! (Maybe you have to be a seminary-trained, academic theologian to miss it!)

Modern "end times" teaching is an interpretation based on, at best, very sketchy biblical evidence – just like Darwin's theory of evolution is an interpretation of sketchy scientific evidence. Belief in it requires faith in the interpreters more than faith in God. I believe the view I've presented, of God's intent for his sons and daughters to deliver victory, is not "an interpretation" at all but instead the only accurate reading of the sum total of Scripture – starting with God's stated purpose for creation and His instructions to Adam, including all Old Testament types and prophesies, reflecting Christ's words and work, embracing the writings of Paul and the other early apostles, and concluding with our total victory (and inheritance) in the Book of Revelation. However, if you do believe this is simply a choice between two competing "interpretations," consider this: First, both can't be true. Either God intends the sons and daughters He is raising to be agents of victory, or mere spectators. Second, I acknowledge quite clearly in this book that Scripture is incomplete; there are gaps that must be filled in. The job of filling these gaps belongs one hundred percent to the Holy Spirit. If you believe Francisco Ribera was led by the Holy Spirit, and if the Spirit affirms to you that the roots and fruits of today's "end times" teaching is pleasing to God, then by all means, embrace that teaching. Enjoy waiting for "the Rapture." I, for one, am doing all the Lord directs me to do in bringing His Kingdom on earth as it is in heaven, and I look forward to being "left behind" to rule with Christ after the wicked are washed away, "just as it was in the days of Noah."

Let me just leave you with this question: Which of us will be better off if we're wrong? Would you rather be "caught" operating under the headship of Christ and in His power, working to achieve total victory for the Kingdom of God ... or operating under the belief the antichrist will rise and there's nothing we can do about it?

KEY POINTS: Modern teachings of the "end times" are blocking our path to victory. They rob us of our identity, distract us from our destiny, keep us tied up in knots, and make us look like kooks to those we are called to reach.

"So the men Moses had sent to explore the land, who returned and made the whole community grumble against him by spreading a bad report about it – these men who were responsible for spreading the bad report about the land were struck down and died of a plague before the LORD. Of the men who went to explore the land, only Joshua son of Nun and Caleb son of Jephunneh survived."
(Numbers 14:36-38 NIV)

No one who puts his hand to the plow and looks back
is fit for service in the Kingdom of God.
Jesus Christ[357]

Chapter 14 - The price of victory

As the Body of Christ rises up in unity and spiritual
authority in our endgame drive to bring God's Kingdom to
earth, it will be like kicking the proverbial hornets' nest. The
devil will be "filled with fury, because he knows that his
time is short."[358] When God's sons and daughters finally rise
up and push towards victory – driving satan further and
further into a corner, cutting him off from hearts and minds
to control – his demon force will be increasingly
concentrated into influencing an ever smaller throng. These
sons and daughters of the enemy, as Jesus called them, will
exert demonic power to an unprecedented extreme. This will
be the enemy's last stand in the final, decisive battle in the
greatest war in the history of the universe. Never doubt for a
moment the sons and daughters of God will endure extreme
hardship, probably worse than anything that has come

---

[357] Luke 9:62 NIV
[358] Revelation 12:13 NIV

before.[359] Jesus warned us about this:

> Nation will rise against nation, and kingdom
> against kingdom. There will be famines and
> earthquakes in various places. All these are the
> beginning of birth pains. You will be handed over
> to be persecuted and put to death, and you will be
> hated by all nations because of me. At that time
> many will turn away from the faith and will
> betray and hate each other, and many false
> prophets will appear and deceive many people.
> Because of the increase of wickedness, the love of
> most will grow cold, but the one who stands firm
> to the end will be saved. *And this gospel of the
> kingdom will be preached in the whole world as a
> testimony to all nations, and then the end will come.*[360]

According to church history, every single one of Jesus'
original apostles was martyred for the faith (except John,
who was boiled alive but lived to tell about it). Jesus, the
firstborn of many brothers, endured the punishment of the
cross. They counted the cost, they had a choice, and they
weren't fools.

*Jesus knew even He had to go through suffering and death so He
could grow the character necessary to rule with God for eternity.*
Hebrews 5:7-9 says, "During the days of Jesus' life on earth,
He offered up prayers and petitions with loud cries and

---

[359] Two more Greek words of note here. The one we translate as "tribulation" is
THLIPSIS, which means "pressing together." When you're seeking to unify the
Body and press out the impurities, then pressing together is good, right? Also,
the word "apocalypse" – Greek APOKALUPSIS – means revelation, unveiling or
manifestation. Isn't this the spirit Paul prayed for the Ephesians to have? Aren't
we all eagerly awaiting the unveiling of Christ's Bride? Like tribulation, the
apocalypse, too, is indeed a good thing when you understand God's Big Picture!
[360] Matthew 24:7-14 NIV, emphasis added. Note what will be preached in every
nation – God's BASILEIA.

tears to the one who could save Him from death, and He was heard because of His reverent submission. Although He was a son, *He learned obedience from what He suffered* and, *once made perfect,* He became the source of eternal salvation for all who obey Him."[361]

Those who look at biblical prophecies that paint a picture of extreme trials and tribulations, and interpret them as a doom-and-gloom future for the Body of Christ – seeing Christians as helpless victims of it all – are missing a huge point: We have a choice! *We* are the agents of God who will trigger this tribulation! Yes, the battle will be bloody. Yes, it may cost us everything, including our earthly lives. And yes, it will be worth it, because *"He who NIKAO (conquers, carries off the victory) will inherit all things."*[362]

There is a chance your narrow path of obedience may lead to great wealth and worldly recognition. The Body certainly needs faithful vessels on earth for God to work through to fund its advancement and raise its profile. But your God-ordained path may instead lead to a vast desert wilderness with no earthly way to feed those who rely on you, a poor widow's home during a dire famine with barely enough flour for one day, a lion's den or a fiery furnace with no logical means of escape, a Philippian dungeon awaiting executing, tied to a stake and surrounded by flames, or even nailed to a cross. Wherever your trail leads, regardless of the world's perception, *it is the only place you'll find the promised peace and joy of the Lord.* It is not my job to choose my destiny, God already chose it for me: a glorious, victorious, eternal inheritance, surpassing anything I can scrape together on my own here on earth. It is my job to walk into it, along the path

---

[361] NIV, *emphasis added.*
[362] Revelation 21:7 NKJV, with original Greek replacement

of His choosing.

If tribulation scares you, realize this: When we face hardships, God is training us in authority and power. At the same time, satan is throwing everything he has at us because we are now a threat. Which one of those do you want to avoid? Being trained by God, or being a threat to the enemy? You can opt out any time you want.

--

In firmly establishing the fact NIKAO means *to conquer, to carry off the victory* and that "endure" is a terrible, meaning-sapping interpretation of the word, in no way am I intending to diminish the vital importance of the word "endure" in Scripture. Endurance is vital to our lives on earth as sons and daughters of the King. We will face terrible trials and fires. These come part and parcel with growing in spiritual maturity and gaining victory over the kingdom of darkness. Without endurance we will be wiped out.

I've studied the lives and deaths of many Christian martyrs. Every one I've studied knew going into it his course of action could cost his life, and this was a price he was willing to pay. God gives us a choice. We can *choose* to continue to be "tossed to and fro and carried about with every wind of doctrine, by the trickery of men, in the cunning craftiness of deceitful plotting,"[363] as we have, for the most part, since the church was Romanized by Constantine. Or we can count the cost and willfully *choose* to endure the tribulation necessary to "come to the unity of the faith and of the knowledge of the Son of God, to a perfect man, to the measure of the stature of the fullness of Christ."[364]

---

[363] Ephesians 4:14 NKJV
[364] Ephesians 4:13 NKJV

Endurance of tribulation is one of the main ways we grow into maturity as sons and daughters of God, as He prepares us for our eternal inheritance. Jesus said, "Whoever finds his life will lose it, and whoever loses his life for my sake will find it." He repeated similar words five times in Matthew, Mark and Luke.[365] Christ didn't teach that a Christian's life is about making the most of the here and now; He taught and modeled that *it is about bringing the Kingdom in the here and now* – often through incredible trials and affliction – so that we can be made ready for our best life in the world to come. Tribulation is not punishment, it's strength training.

I could quote many Bible verses to establish this point, but let me just reference two: "Endure hardship as discipline; God is treating you as sons. For what son is not disciplined by his father? If you are not disciplined (and everyone undergoes discipline), then you are illegitimate children and not true sons."[366] And, "Consider it pure joy, my brothers and sisters, whenever you face trials of many kinds, because you know that the testing of your faith produces perseverance. Let perseverance finish its work so that you may be mature and complete, not lacking anything."[367]

Paul spoke with particular authority on this subject. Not many people in history have endured more than Paul for the sake of the Kingdom and lived to write about it. He wrote to the brothers in Corinth:

> I have worked much harder, been in prison more
> frequently, been flogged more severely, and been
> exposed to death again and again. Five times I

---

[365] This is Matthew 10:39. Also in Matthew 16:25, Mark 8:35, Luke 9:24, Luke 17:33 (NIV)
[366] Hebrews 12:7-8 NIV
[367] James 1:2-4 NIV

received from the Jews the forty lashes minus one.
Three times I was beaten with rods, once I was
pelted with stones, three times I was shipwrecked,
I spent a night and a day in the open sea, I have
been constantly on the move. I have been in
danger from rivers, in danger from bandits, in
danger from my fellow Jews, in danger from
Gentiles; in danger in the city, in danger in the
country, in danger at sea; and in danger from false
believers. I have labored and toiled and have often
gone without sleep; I have known hunger and
thirst and have often gone without food; I have
been cold and naked."[368]

I have seen in my mind's eye an image of Paul as he
shuffled, in chains, into his eventual audience with Caesar.[369]
What a sight he must have been! Think of his back. One lash
leaves a scar. From the literally hundreds of marks from
Roman rods and Jewish lashes, Paul's back must have been
an inch-thick mass of scar tissue, which no doubt greatly
restricted his arm movement and caused him to walk with
an extreme hunch. Then there'd be the disfigurement from
broken bones and facial fractures caused by being stoned
(till his attackers thought he was dead) and other beatings.
His skin must have been crusty, cracked and calloused from
all the extreme exposure. No matter how much he dressed
up and prepared himself, standing before Caesar he must
have appeared like a mangled junkyard tomcat that had
been through a wringer. But oh, the glimmer in his eyes! He
was not a man defeated! All through his troubles, he knew
he could have quit any time, returned to Tarsus and lived a
prosperous life as a highly-educated tentmaker. But no, Paul

---

[368] 2 Corinthians 11:23-27 NIV
[369] Not recorded in the Bible but chronicled in early church history.

knew the reason for his hope – *His God-given identity, purpose and destiny* – and quitting was never a viable option in his heart. In that same letter to the Corinthians he wrote, "Our *light affliction,* which is but for a moment, is working for us a far more exceeding and eternal weight of glory."[370] He *tackled* the hardships, *embraced* the trials and tribulations, because he knew every step, every breath, every word of obedience *inflicted even more damage on the enemy.* Paul was a mighty warrior! He jumped off the landing craft, fought his way through enemy fire, and helped start the Body of Christ up the path toward ultimate victory. Poor pompous, pampered Caesar was no match for that old, decrepit, abused, physically-broken prisoner in chains!

A major paradigm shift is needed today, because the idea of counting the cost – willful self-sacrifice, going all-in, deferring gratification till the next life – is not particularly popular today, either in the pew or the pulpit.

--

Some of today's "end times" teaching, as far as it is based on the Bible, is perfectly accurate: There *will* be terrible affliction as the enemy puts up his goal-line defense. There certainly are plenty of Biblical prophesies yet to be fulfilled. Where modern "end times" teaching is inaccurate is that *it casts God's children as passive victims of these activities.* This couldn't be further from the truth.

The movie "Ike"[371] contains a sub-plot in which General Eisenhower (played by Tom Selleck) has to count the cost. His forecasters predicted the cost of lives rather accurately, if not even more severely than it ended up being, for a

---

[370] 2 Corinthians 4:17 NKJV, emphasis added. "Light affliction" indeed!
[371] "Ike: Countdown to D-Day," 2004, A&E Television Networks

particular action that was vital to the overall effort. This action was going to cost buckets of American blood, and so you could say Ike had a revelation of great sacrifice, suffering and death to come. But he ordered the action anyway. Why? *Because he knew we were the masters of our destiny.* The tribulation of D-Day wasn't something to be feared, it was something to be faced, even *embraced.* The tides didn't blow us into Normandy – we willingly sped there on landing crafts! We knew the price and paid it *on purpose,* because we had our eyes fixed on the finish line. The men who died on those French beaches weren't victims, they were part of a victorious, conquering army. When you're facing a brutal, entrenched enemy, winning doesn't come cheap.

Warfare requires great tribulation, regardless of the purpose it is fought. But the purpose it is fought makes a huge difference in the way the required tribulation is engaged, embraced and endured – and ultimately determines the outcome of the war. I am going to use two examples from America's history of warfare to illustrate the point.

The first example is the American Revolutionary War. This was one of the toughest wars for Americans in terms of human cost. With the relatively primitive weapons and medicine of the day, the long-term effects of injuries marred a generation of men. Americans died by guns, cannons and bayonets; they were burned alive and frozen to death. It was a brutal war.

The British were seasoned, professional soldiers who possessed superior firepower. The Americans were volunteers who came from all backgrounds, including farmers, bakers, merchants, silversmiths and clergy. They were loosely organized, minimally trained, and their weapons were mainly brought from home. Indeed, for much of the war, victory seemed nearly impossible.

Please pause for a moment, go back to the previous paragraph and look at what I just wrote, because in those facts is a key and dramatic point: *A rag-tag, unprofessional, poorly-armed militia fought against a full-time, battle-hardened, highly-trained standing army, endured unimaginable tribulation, and NIKAOed.*

How? Because they had a *purpose*. They believed their leaders who said victory would be costly but was inevitable. More than that, *they won because they shared a vision of victory.* They were fighting to throw off an oppressive regime and establish freedom and righteousness in the land, for their children and generations to come. Because of this, they considered every hardship, every sacrifice – even death itself – to be a worthwhile investment. This sentiment was best exemplified by American soldier Nathan Hale, whose last words before being hanged by the British were, *"I regret that I have but one life to give for my country."*

Tribulation goes part in parcel with victory. The determination factor in winning speaks to just that: Victory goes to the one who best keeps his head, remains fixed on victory, continues pressing forward and endures the tribulation of conflict. *The victory-hearted warrior considers it pure joy when he faces the trials of battle, because he knows he is growing stronger, and that his suffering is an investment that will ultimately result in a glorious, purposeful victory.* Nathan Hale and the other American heroes knew what they were fighting for and believed deep inside their sacrifices were worth it.

Even today the heroes of the Revolutionary War are lionized in American culture. From the Washington Monument –

which dominates the skyline of the nation's capital – to the smallest details on the currency, Americans still pay tribute to these brave men, in appreciation for the victory they gained.

Contrast this with the American experience in the Vietnam War. The monument to this war is a black gash in the ground, like an open wound in the nation's collective consciousness. As a culture, Americans have finally come to pay rightful respect to the men who endured that conflict, but it is mainly out of sympathy for their great suffering and obedient service. America is proud of her soldiers but ashamed of that war.

The American military was a superior fighting force. The difference in technology, training, funds and firepower was nearly incalculable. Victory should have been a walk in the park. So why is the Vietnam War considered a dark chapter in American History? Because there was no meaningful point to it!

Men were drafted against their will, thrown into a terrible environment and ordered to endure hardship, injury and death – all for no clear purpose whatsoever. Americans were not fighting for victory. They were fighting to "contain" the enemy (whatever that means), not conquer him. Winning was never an option. The Americans would pay a high human price to take a hill, then retreat, and then fight to take it again. The enemy was allowed to torment and torture America's fighting men, and there was little they were allowed to do about it. Their greatest hope was that some far-off decision maker would end the war and pull them out of there, the timing of which would be based on nothing they could affect or understand. (Now go back and read this paragraph again. It sounds a lot like our plight as portrayed by modern "end times" teachings, doesn't it?)

The American blood spilled in Vietnam was not an investment towards any great future; it was a pointless waste. The American military did not grow stronger by the trials in that war; it was weakened nearly to the breaking point. The war turned the American public sour towards warfare – even the righteous variety – and nearly ripped the nation apart at the seams. America is still suffering from the results of that terrible tribulation.

Are you beginning to see the distinction here? There is tribulation that leads to victory, and there is pointless tribulation.

The God we serve, the God of love, does not draft His sons and daughters to pointless, Vietnam War-type tribulation. Instead, the tribulation we face is purposeful; it is the price of ultimate victory and the training for our glorious destiny.

Listen again to the words of the Apostle Paul, who endured unimaginable tribulation during his own tough assignment in advancing God's Kingdom: "I consider that our present sufferings are not worth comparing with the glory that will be revealed in us. For the creation waits in eager expectation for the children of God to be revealed."[372]

If the Body of Christ understood this today, we would be preparing for tribulation by passionately working for unity, focusing on spiritual growth, edifying each other and loudly proclaiming God's vision of victory and our destiny as *more than conquerors*. Instead, today we have too many Christians preparing for the "Great Tribulation" by building isolated bunkers, storing up survival supplies, preaching a message

---

[372] Romans 8:18-19 NKJV

of fear, grabbing all they can in the meantime, and hoping we'll soon be "Raptured."

As Paul said, we need to grow up! We have a superior Commander in Chief, the most powerful weapon in the universe at our disposal, divine promises of full provision of every necessary resource, and the best army God Himself could engineer. *All that is lacking today is the vision of victory.* Praise God, I feel that's about to change! This spark will light a fire that will burn the kingdom of darkness off the face of the earth! A Christian uprising is coming!

--

Several years ago, as the American military was preparing to launch into the conflict that would topple Iraqi dictator Saddam Hussein, American troops were staging on the Kuwaiti border, ready to assault. Drums of war were beating loudly in America, and while it seemed like "all systems go," there was still an extended period of delay. The world was holding its breath.

I remember watching a TV news reporter interview a soldier who was soon to march into front-line combat. It was hot and dry, there was constant threat of attack and nobody knew for sure what kind of resistance they'd be up against. Would the Iraqis use weapons of mass destruction? How tough was Iraq's Republican Guard? No doubt there was a lot of uncertainty and many reasons for soldiers to get cold feet. Even in the best case scenario it'd still be extremely tough and many US soldiers would die. In the midst of this setting, the reporter asked this soldier if he'd like to go home. I'll never forget his reply: "Yes, ma'am, I'd like to go home. But I know that the only way home is through Bagdad, so I'm eager to get it on."

If the Body of Christ today would grasp the maturity of this comment, and how precisely it aligns with our own situation, it would change everything. Yes, we're facing tribulation. Yes, even in the best case there are tough challenges and terrible battles ahead. *But the only way home to our eternal inheritance is through our establishment of God's Kingdom on earth.* Instead of being afraid of the enemy and the tribulation to come, we should, like this young solder, be eager to get it on!

--

It is important never to overlook the full manhood of Christ. It was His *faith* that gave Him the willingness to face death on the cross as an act of obedience to the Father. And it was this *obedience*, even unto death, that allowed the Father to pour His resurrection power through Him. Had Jesus faced the cross unwillingly, as a passive victim, His death would not have led to our salvation. He had a choice and He chose obedience, fully knowing the cost. *And because He faced the cross as a victor and not a passive victim,* He delivered victory over death, hell and the devil. It is up to us now to walk in His footsteps.

There is no promise we will face anything less than Christ did as we bring the victory of God's Kingdom to earth.

Remember the tools of satan. He controls men through puppet strings. Fear of tribulation – of pain, death, losing riches, being unpopular, etc. – is one of the most powerful strings he has. Today this string is tied to many parts of the Body of Christ, and our "end times" theologians are unwittingly complicit in helping him tangle it around us. We must cut that string!

Kingdom victory will be close at hand when the Body of

Christ has the faith and maturity to rise up as one and say, "I don't care what it costs! The worst 'end times' prophesy, the worst the enemy can dish out – bring it on! We are willing, Lord, to allow you to train us up as victorious sons and daughters, whatever that looks like, whatever the price. We are all in!"

KEY POINTS: When the Body of Christ finally rises up and moves to establish God's Kingdom on earth, and the enemy makes his last stand, the conflict will be brutal and costly. We must view this in light of eternity. God is raising up warring sons and daughters, not wimps.

"If our soldiers are not overburdened with money, it is not because they have a distaste for riches; if their lives are not unduly long, it is not because they are disinclined to longevity." (Sun Tzu, The Art of War)

"The Kingdom of Heaven is like treasure hidden in a field. When a man found it, he hid it again, and then in his joy went and sold all he had and bought that field. Again, the Kingdom of Heaven is like a merchant looking for fine pearls. When he found one of great value, he went away and sold everything he had and bought it." (Matthew 13:44-46, NIV)

"I have told you these things, so that in me you may have peace. In this world you will have trouble. But take heart! I have NIKAOed the world." (John 16:33, NIV with Greek insertion)

It's not good enough that we do our best; sometimes we have to do what is required.

Winston Churchill

Chapter 15 - Endgame

Let's get super-practical for a bit. Here we have a big job to do, and the things we've been doing for generations just aren't working. The world is a big place – upwards of six billion souls – and right now the people who are truly all-in for God seem but a small fraction. Already we spend countless hundreds of billions of dollars building fancy buildings, broadcasting around the clock on numerous television and radio networks, cranking out thousands of full-time clergy per year, distributing millions of books, filling stadium after stadium for rallies and concerts, and on and on and on ... *and we're not really getting anywhere*. The world's governments, media and cultures are increasingly hostile to us and our long-established church bodies are shrinking, all while false faiths and philosophies grow. If we're going to win, we've got to take things to a much higher level, but how? How much more money can we raise and spend? How many more can we recruit to volunteer, or harder still, to go to seminary and commit to a career in ministry? Despite all the promises of God and occasional glimmers of hope, sometimes it all seems hopeless. It sure would be a lot easier to just wash our hands of the whole mess and resign to believing in a Great Escape!

We have been doing *our* best *for* God, and it's not working too well. We've employed the best strategies, tools and conventional wisdom *the world* has to offer, *and we're failing*.

We need to wake up and realize *the world's best strategies, tools and wisdom are insignificant compared to God's!* Where the world has led us to go wide, *God wants us to go deep*. We've focused on quantity of members, whereas God wants us to focus on *quality of relationships*. We've worked to broadcast the seeds, but God wants us instead *to cultivate each seed with care and attention*. We've built buildings instead of *disciples* and programs instead of *people*.

It's as if we've focused on the first half of the Great Commission and ignored the rest:

> And Jesus came and spoke to them saying, "All authority in heaven and on earth has been given to me. Therefore go and make disciples of all nations, baptizing them in the name of the Father and of the Son and of the Holy Spirit ...." (That's the easy part; now here's the rest:) "... and *teaching them to obey everything I have commanded* you."[373]

The Gospel of Mark's version is even more dramatic:

> He said to them, "Go into all the world and preach the gospel to all creation. Whoever believes and is baptized will be saved, but whoever does not believe will be condemned...." (Now part two:) *"And these signs will accompany those who believe: In my name they will drive out demons; they will speak in new tongues; they will pick up snakes with their hands; and when they drink deadly poison, it will not hurt them at all; they will place their hands on sick people,*

---

[373] Matthew 28:18-20 NIV,(parenthetical information) and *emphasis added*.

and they will get well."[374]

The early Church knew what Jesus meant, and embraced it. Here's what's recorded about their first outreach effort after His ascension:

> With many other words he (Peter) warned them; and he pleaded with them, "Save yourselves from this corrupt generation." Those who accepted his message were baptized, and about three thousand were added to their number that day.

> (And how were those 3,000 expected to live?...) They devoted themselves to the apostles' teaching and to fellowship, to the breaking of bread and to prayer. Everyone was filled with awe at the many wonders and signs performed by the apostles. All the believers were together and had everything in common. They sold property and possessions to give to anyone who had need. Every day they continued to meet together in the temple courts. They broke bread in their homes and ate together with glad and sincere hearts, praising God and enjoying the favor of all the people. And the Lord added to their number daily those who were being saved.[375]

Conventional wisdom is this: When we focus on just the first parts of these verses – the geography and numbers – then it *may* be possible, given enough marketing funds and time, for us to someday "sell" Christ to the entire world. But when you add in the rest, it doesn't make sense! I mean, here we are stretching things as far as we can, trying to make

---

[374] Mark 16:15-18 NIV, *emphasis added*. These being the signs of those who believe, how many believers do *you* know?

[375] Acts 2:40-47 NIV, (parenthetic information) and *emphasis added*.

"Christianity" as appealing as possible to the masses, and still not gaining ground … and *God wants us to raise the bar so high that few of even the most devout of us can reach it?* And *this* is how He expects us to conquer the world? Like I said, a Great Escape is sounding pretty good about now!

Hold on to your hat, because I'm about to show you something that will blow your mind. The Bible says "The foolishness of God is wiser than human wisdom, and the weakness of God is stronger than human strength."[376] On the surface, God's strategies seem counter-productive. I was trying to explain this a while back to a potential donor – that is, why my ministry focuses 100 percent on personal discipleship instead of mass-market outreach – and was having a hard time communicating it. This man just couldn't see how a group like ours that reaches narrow and deep was a good investment of his funds, compared to others that "reach" significantly more people, albeit with a significantly shallower approach.[377] Frustrated by my inability to relate to him what I knew in my gut, I turned to God in prayer. God's three word RHEMA answer to me was so simple, and yet it changed my life (and ultimately inspired this book). He said this: "Run the numbers."

I did, and here they are:[378]

Scenario One, based on our focus on fulfilling just the first half of the Great Commission: 1) Say I start a ministry today that leads 1,000 people per year to make a "decision" for Christ. I'm talking real, honest-to-goodness coming to the front of the church after a straight-up altar call. That's 20

---

[376] 1 Corinthians 1:25 NIV

[377] This book is dedicated to this fellow.

[378] To see the underlying formulas, and more information about this strategy, log into www.5 for3to1.com.

new people every Sunday (not counting my two-week vacation). Few of even the biggest megachurches can claim numbers like that. 2) Say my retention rate is 25 percent. That means out of 100 people who answer the call, 25 of them really take to it and grow to somewhat fulfill the second half of the Great Commission. Mind you, this number would beat today's average evangelism retention rate *five times over*.[379] 3) Say I can do all this for just $100,000 per year – an unheard of, low rate. And finally, 4) Say I get this so completely figured out that I can duplicate this ministry far and wide, and eventually I set up 100,000 identical ministries around the world, each with identical results. It'd take a gigantic world map to fit that many thumbtacks to mark all these locations!

Sounds pretty incredible, right? It's a paradigm many in ministry today would fantasize about, if only they would dare let their minds wander so far into the impossible. If all the Body of Christ today, working together, pulled out all the stops and did everything just right, I still doubt we could ever hit these variables ... 100,000 outposts around the world, each delivering 1,000 legitimate "conversions" per year, with a 25% retention rate, for just $100,000 per outpost. For a moment let's assume our wildest dreams come true and we accomplish this. Here's the big question: How long till we reach every man, woman and child on earth?

Gosh, if we could achieve that level of results it'd have to be no time, right?

Wrong. At this rate, *if the population of the earth were to stop growing*, it would take us 280 years to reach the planet, at a cost of $2,800,000,000,000.00! Add in the average rate of

---

[379] Patrick McIntyre, *The Graham Formula: Why Most Decisions for Christ Are Ineffective*, White Harvest Publishing, 2006.

population growth, and *there are nearly three times as many people born each year than we could ever reach.*[380] We could never get results this spectacular, and even if we did, *it is a sure-fire recipe for losing,* and an unconscionable waste of manpower and funds. *Yet this is the paradigm under which virtually every single church and ministry on earth seems to be operating!* It may be a great way to build your own kingdom, but it's no way to build God's.

What are we to do? Allow me to present...

Scenario Two, based on fulfilling the entirety of the Great Commission (aka, building people and the Body instead of organizations and buildings): 1) Say I walk away from every man-made structure, program and pre-packaged "ministry," and instead simply live my life in a way that reflects Christ. 2) Say that in doing this, over the course of time, just five people are drawn to the fruit of the Spirit they see in my life and ask me the reason for my peace, joy and contentment. 3) Say I pour my heart into these five people for three years, leading them to a real relationship with God through Christ and discipling them into a strong level of spiritual maturity. 4) Say that after these three years, the six of us go out and do likewise, and this continues to roll forward.

Not very glamorous, is it? No flash and dazzle. No building projects. No bright lights, broadcasts, billboards or big budgets. No fame. Just a simple life dedicated to Christ, and a commitment to personal discipleship as He modeled it.

Now here's my question: If just *one person* in the entire world feels called to this and commits to this thankless path, how

---

[380] With these variables, we'd be "reaching" 25 million souls per year, while the net population grows by more than 72 million. At this rate, we can't even keep up with the interest, much less pay down the balance!

long do you think till the Great Commission (both parts of it) will be fulfilled?

Don't think it's even worth running the numbers? Think again. *It would take less than 39 years!* This not only factors in population growth, it actually puts us about 2 billion people beyond our goal of reaching every man, woman and child on the face of the earth.[381] With a total cost of zero dollars!

This should come as no surprise, when you consider this is precisely what Jesus and the early churched modeled for us. They knew the power of discipleship! Jesus didn't build buildings, launch sophisticated "outreach" campaigns, or seek to establish a formal organizational structure. Instead, He spent the bulk of His three years in ministry personally guiding His 12 apostles to spiritual maturity, and in fact most of His attention was focused on His closest three – Peter, James and John. Similarly, Paul would go into just one or two communities in a vast region, raise up a handful of believers straight out of abject paganism, focus his time on discipling them, then move on. His letters weren't written to an organization or as tracts for mass distribution – they were for his spiritual sons and daughters, to help them grow into mature sons and daughters of the King. He didn't cast seeds far and wide like some kind of Gospel Johnny Appleseed; instead, he carefully planted and cultivated the precious seed of the Kingdom.

Let me say it again in case you missed it: Through our currently dominant "numbers-based" model for ministry, even in a "perfect world," *victory is impossible.* No wonder the concept of Kingdom victory has never crossed the minds of most Christians! And since it's a losing strategy and an

---

[381] Under this model, the precise number of people having been discipled in 39 years would be 8,272,328,125 – way more than the population of the planet.

incalculable waste of resources, why continue it one day longer, or throw another dollar at it?[382] The real "numbers" show that if we return to the method of ministry modeled by Jesus, Paul and the early church – that is, authentic, personal discipleship – we can bring the victory in less than one generation!

Think about it: You... yes YOU, the one reading this book right now ... *you have within you the power of God to bring total victory over the world in one generation.* It could start with YOU.

If the Body of Christ would wake up, stop conforming to the patterns of this world,[383] stop seeking to indulge our senses,[384] stop leaning on our own understanding,[385] stop worrying about what other people think about us, and instead start seeking first God's Kingdom and His righteousness,[386] *victory will be ours, in our lifetime!* We can choose to be the Last Generation!

KEY POINTS: Our current strategies will never lead to victory. By returning to the strategy of Biblically-based, Christ-modeled discipleship, we can deliver victory over the planet in less than one generation.

"We proclaim Him, admonishing and teaching everyone with all wisdom, so that we may present everyone *perfect in Christ. To this end I labor, struggling with all His energy, which so powerfully works in me." (Colossians 1:28-19, NIV, emphasis added.)*

---

[382] I don't think this pleases God, to put it mildly. Consider Proverbs 26:11 NKJV: "As a dog returns to his own vomit, so a fool repeats his folly."

[383] Romans 12:2

[384] Colossians 2:23

[385] Proverbs 3:5-6

[386] Matthew 6:33

It is fatal to enter any war without the will to win it.
General Douglas MacArthur

Chapter 16 - Can we really do this?

I've endeavored to show in this book that we have not only
the mandate of God to deliver victory over the kingdom of
darkness, but also the authority, power, team and
everything else we need to get the job done. Our victory is
promised, prophesied, and our entire eternal inheritance is
tied to it. It all sounds good on paper, but let's get real here:
Do I really think – in this day and age, considering all that's
stacked against us and the culture we live in – that the Body
of Christ can really do this? You bet I do. I've not only seen
the fire of victory burning in Nigeria, I've experienced it
right here in America, among the segment of the population
folks would likely say are the toughest of all to reach:
teenage boys.

Let me tell you a story. It was near the end of one of our
sessions of summer camp and the whole group was
gathered for dinner. We'd had an incredible week with these
12 teenage boys. It was fun, adventurous and exhausting.
But most of all it was powerful. Each of these boys met God
in a deeply personal way, for the first time, and He had
radically transformed their lives. They had come with deep
issues of anger, doubt, fear, guilt, self-loathing, religiosity,

pornography, pride, disrespect, insecurity, hate and more. They had carried wounds of betrayal, disappointment, lies, broken homes, abuse, and even sexual molestation. But now, when I looked at them, I could see 12 young men who stood tall, who smiled and had a glimmer in their eyes, who really got it. They had come to know Christ personally, and their lives, families and futures would never be the same.

As I was sitting there looking at the boys and reflecting on the week, God told me something very simple and powerful, but it didn't really hit me at first. What He said was simply, "These boys are average."

Like I said, on the surface it wasn't earthshaking. But as I have unpacked it, it has taken on a huge meaning, re-energized my passion for His work, and renewed my hope for the world. God's RHEMA words are like that – multifaceted and folded up tight.

It was true, these boys were average by every measure. That's not to say anything negative about any one of them. But they came from average circumstances, and faced average issues: broken homes, drugs, problems with school, girls and parents. Issues of lust and pornography. The few who were involved in a congregational setting were average as well – involved in the youth group, knew all the Sunday School answers, etc., but didn't truly know the Lord. None of them really stood out in any big way.

They were a melting pot, too. Out of the 12, there were boys from multiple races and a range of economic backgrounds, family situations, academic standing, intelligence, athletic ability, etc. So not only each boy was average, but the group as a whole was average. They could have been a dozen kids plucked from anywhere and thrown together for a week.

When I say they were average, I know a lot of people, on first reaction, almost take that as an insult. That's because we don't think much of the current crop of young people. We seem to think this generation is already lost, wasted, gone.

The boys were average, but for a week we showed them above average love, attention and respect. We took time to earn their trust, to build real relationships and to be living testimonies to them to the reality of the Living God. We took time to move beyond curriculums and programmatic interaction, and just be real with them, listen to them, hear their hearts, help them dig deep and find God in their own way, the way He was personally calling to them.

It really wasn't rocket science. We just spoke the truth. *And they were dramatically changed.* One of the nights around the campfire, when the Spirit of the Lord seemed to drop on a boy like a ball of fire from the sky and he truly *got it*, God showed me a vision of the earth in space shifting on its trajectory, and He said to me, "The future of the world will never be the same, because this one boy got it." I don't know if that boy will someday be president, or even prominent. But he will be a God-honoring man, husband and father – and this alone will ripple through the world in untold ways.

You know what God was saying when He told me these boys were average? He was saying if we get any 12 youth, boys or girls, from anywhere in the world, and give them the same love and attention, that they will get it too, just like these! The same could be said for grownups, too. In our fake, superficial, programmatic world, they are all hungry for truth, for real relationships … for the Living God!

In saying, "these boys are average," I felt that God was giving encouragement to my ministry team for obediently embracing the things He's shown us to do. He was confirming the fact that authentic, relationship-based discipleship really works! As we walk in step-by-step obedience as led by the Spirit, He will use us to raise up mature sons and daughters of the Kingdom. This revelation gives me passion and determination to teach others to do things the same way. That's what discipleship is all about.

But wait, there's more! God's Word is multifaceted, and by calling those boys average, I believe He was saying something even more profound, something that gives me even more hope: This current generation has more potential to take the Gospel of the Kingdom to every tribe and nation than any other generation in the history of the world.

And I'm not talking about the technology – internet, TV, etc. Yes those are unprecedented, powerful tools the Lord has prepared for them to use. But I'm talking about the kids themselves. They are ripe!

Everybody writes them off. Do a little research on "Generation Z" and here's what all the researchers say:

- They are "jaded ... skeptical ... cynical."
- They question everything and make up their own mind.
- They are not trapped by formality or tradition.
- They are independent, not afraid to stand up and speak their mind.
- They are "rebellious and obnoxious."
- They are street smart. "7 is the new 17."
- They are more socially minded and tend to worry about things.
- They have anxiety about performance because

so much of their lives is geared around testing.

For folks in the marketing business this is reason to be distressed. Kids these days have seen it all and done it all, and they're a hard sell. They have heard every sales pitch and attempt at manipulation known to man. They have been shoehorned into factory-style school systems and cookie-cutter programs. They grew up as infants watching infomercials called "children's television." They get bombarded with ads, spam, texts, product placement and celebrity endorsements. Many parents view them as a distraction, push them into daycare and drug them up with ADD meds to keep them in line.

And you know what? They're sick of it! They're sick of fake! They've tried everything the world has to offer and they know that it's not what they really want!

What the devil intends for evil, God uses for good.[387] Satan has thrown everything he's got at them. Through it all, God has only turned up the strength of the vacuum He built into their hearts. He has trained them like no other generation before: They can pick something up, look at it, see that it doesn't fit the hole in their heart, discard it and move on. They're relentlessly searching.

Better still, they're free from the constraints of "religion." Where their parents may have found some comfort in man-made religiosity, which is a thin stand-in for a real-relationship with Jesus, that's not good enough for these kids. They've thrown that away, too, and they want more!

Their whole lives and the whole world around them are fake and they know it. They're desperately searching for something real, something fulfilling, that can truly satisfy

---

[387] Genesis 50:19-20

that hole in their heart. They may not have put their finger on it yet, but they're desperately craving a real relationship with the Living God.

It doesn't take much! Just spend some real, quality time with them. Don't try to force them into some man-made religious system that, when you get down to it, is just about as fake as everything else out there.[388] Just love them and be real. Model a Christ-centered life. Gently guide them as they start to venture deep into their hearts, deep into Him. And Bingo! When they draw near to God, He draws near to them![389] They taste and see that He is good[390] and they want more of Him – all they can get! You'll be shocked, as they'll go deeper than you can imagine, right out of the gate. Free from the constraints of traditionalism, there's nothing holding them back from truly having a real, back-and-forth-communication, personal, intimate, living and active relationship with God through Jesus Christ. It's real and they know it – and they don't care what anyone else thinks or says or does.

It gets even better. Look at how fast Facebook, Twitter, YouTube and all those have taken off. When these kids find something that they're passionate about, they recruit their friends. The same is true with the Kingdom of God. These boys become some of the most powerful and effective witnesses you've ever seen! I've seen lost teenage boys become powerful online evangelists in a short time.

Yes, those boys were average; average representations of the youth of this generation. And I believe the Lord will use

---

[388] To those practitioners of entertainment-based youth ministry, please, for God's sake, work to get them out of the fake, and stop trying to fake them out!
[389] James 4:8
[390] Psalm 34:8

these stones that everyone has rejected to become building blocks in the construction of His Kingdom.[391] He is going to use them to spark an uprising across the face of the earth that is unprecedented in human history.

I've read the end of The Book and *we win*. The Lord can use this generation, like none before in history, to deliver final victory. We can be the Last Generation. The iron is hot. Let's strike it with all we've got!

KEY POINTS: Yes, we really can do this!

"Is not this the kind of fasting I have chosen: to loose the chains of injustice and untie the cords of the yoke, to set the oppressed free and break every yoke? Is it not to share your food with the hungry and to provide the poor wanderer with shelter— when you see the naked, to clothe him, and not to turn away from your own flesh and blood? Then your light will break forth like the dawn, and your healing will quickly appear; then your righteousness will go before you, and the glory of the LORD will be your rear guard. Then you will call, and the LORD will answer; you will cry for help, and He will say: Here am I. If you do away with the yoke of oppression, with the pointing finger and malicious talk, and if you spend yourselves in behalf of the hungry and satisfy the needs of the oppressed, then your light will rise in the darkness, and your night will become like the noonday. The LORD will guide you always; He will satisfy your needs in a sun-scorched land and will strengthen your frame. You will be like a well-watered garden, like a spring whose waters never fail." (Isaiah 58: 6-11, NIV)

---

[391] Psalm 118:22

The permanent temptation of life is to confuse dreams with reality.

James A. Michener

CHAPTER 17: The end is near ... or is it?

With "end times" forecasts so popular these days, I want to make clear this book is not an attempt to predict the future. I don't claim to have a crystal ball. Instead, I am endeavoring to spell out what I see as the Biblical truths of God's original intent, including the prerequisites He's established – that we must achieve – before the end comes.

To me, what's more important than knowing the future is that we know our correct identity, posture, rights, abilities, responsibilities and job description *in the here and now*. We need a clear handle on what God wants us to be doing *today*, and what we have available from Him to do it. Last I checked, we're not supposed to worry about tomorrow anyway.[392] If you're frustrated that what I'm presenting here upsets your favorite flavor of "end times" chronology, please realize that is not my intent. You are free to believe whatever future timetable you can honestly justify with

---

[392] Matthew 6:34

Scripture.[393] What I *do* intend to upset is the belief that we're passive observers to it all, like cosmic plankton in some current we cannot control, because that belief robs from us the very things we need to know: our correct identity, posture, rights, abilities, responsibilities and job description.

There are many people today who believe "the end is near" and could come any time now. Whether they believe we will be snatched away at any moment in the "Rapture," or just "the world will end" in one way or another, this belief is misguided and, ultimately, harmful to the individual and the Body.

I'd sure like to be able to believe that our escape is imminent. Life in this world isn't easy, and it'd be fantastic to wash our hands of the whole mess, sit back and watch as Jesus comes and cleans house. If the end *is* near today, considering the current, fragmented, dysfunctional state of the Body of Christ, then the message of the Kingdom I present here is all wrong, and our only job as a Christian is just to keep our nose clean, enjoy it while we can, and endure till Christ's return. To be honest with you, on one level I find that a lot more appealing than having any responsibility in the matter. But try as I might, I just can't find any basis for this popular thinking in the Bible. As much freedom as God gives us, as much power as He puts in our hands, one thing we are *not* free to do is re-write Scripture to fit our own desires or traditions. As much as it pains me to say it, in light of the current condition of Christianity today, the end is *not* near; it

---

[393] There are plenty of Biblical prophesies of to come that are perfectly valid when properly interpreted. Yes we have free will, and God has put the timeline for victory in our hands, but at the same time He sees the end from the beginning, and knows what we will choose before we've chosen it. This doesn't negate our free will; it's just one of the mind-bending aspects of eternity.

could *not* come at any moment. We still have a lot of work to do, and the end won't come until we're done!

Don't get me wrong. The Bible is clear when the end *does* come, it will be all of a sudden,[394] and nobody can predict the day or the hour it will happen.[395] I believe this wholeheartedly. It's just not going to happen anytime soon. How do I know? The long answer is this entire book. The short answer is this: Jesus said that the coming of the end will be "just as it was in the days of Noah."[396] He could have picked countless other examples. Yet it's not "just as it was in the days of Sodom and Gomorrah,"[397] or anything else. It's Noah. And Jesus wasn't into giving shallow or random examples. If we really want to understand the "end times," we should give more weight to the story of Noah than to newspaper headlines.

Consider this: When *did* the flood come in Noah's day? Was there a secret alarm clock ticking in Heaven, and when it went off God sent the rain? Absolutely not. Instead, Noah had a building project to accomplish, with designs, guidance and miraculous provision given by God. When Noah finished, God gave him a one-week heads up, He personally sealed them in the ark, and only *then* did He release the floodwaters.[398] Let me ask you, do you think if Noah had taken a two-week vacation sometime in the building process, he and his family would have died in the flood? (He had free will, remember.) Was he the luckiest man in history

---

[394] Matthew 24:27, and other verses
[395] Matthew 24:36 and Mark 13:32
[396] Matthew 24:37 and Luke 17:26
[397] Honest dispensationalists would admit their teaching is best summarized by this Biblical story – good guys rescued, bad guys wiped out. The whole Noah reference is one they typically skip over or minimize.
[398] The story of the flood is recounted in Genesis 6-7.

– that after so many decades of labor, he happened to finally finish the ark in the nick of time, just before the flood came? If Noah's completion of the ark had nothing to do with the timing of the flood, this is the inescapable conclusion. But we must admit otherwise. God gave Noah a building project, and did not intervene after that, other than to guide, encourage, and empower Noah's hands. Then, *after Noah finished*, God sent the flood.

Noah certainly worked passionately at his God-given project – out of love and obedience. There's no way anyone can reasonably argue Noah lived in fear, or labored out of panic, from a belief that "the flood is near" any time prior to completion of the ark. Noah knew God's original intent – that God would save the world through him and his labor – and one cannot fathom the thought ever crossed his mind the flood would take him by surprise when the hull was still half-done.

Yes, after the ark was finished, the end came in an instant and it took almost everyone (all except Noah's family) by surprise. Nobody knew the day or the hour because Noah had free will, and it was based entirely on his completion of the ark. *Jesus said the end of our age will come in precisely this same way.*

Because of this fact, I, too, endeavor to labor out of love and obedience, certain the end is nowhere near. Like Noah, we are given a building project – the Kingdom – and all the tools we need to accomplish the task. Like Noah, God desires to populate His eternal Kingdom with obedient, mature sons and daughters, and everyone else will, sadly, be snatched away in an instant. There are plenty of pictures He gives us in the Bible so we can know when the time is close – that is, when the Kingdom is becoming manifest on earth as it is in Heaven. In the Book of Revelation, the angels rejoice because "the Bride has *made herself* ready."[399] In Ephesians, Paul said God is giving us gifts "*until* we all reach unity in the faith and in the knowledge of the Son of God and become mature, attaining to the whole measure of the fullness of Christ."[400] These things will be easy to see. Have they happened yet? Has the Body of Christ manifest His fullness on earth? Have we grown "to become in every respect the mature body of Him who is the Head"?[401] Are we, as a Body, truly ready to marry Him? Have we conquered the world for Christ? Nobody I know would honestly make these claims. Until we do – as long as we are like "infants, tossed back and forth by the waves, and blown here and there by every wind of teaching and by the cunning and craftiness of people in their deceitful scheming"[402] – then we still have quite a bit of growing to do before the end comes.

There is no secret alarm clock hidden under God's throne. The wheat determines the harvest time; it's not arbitrarily set in advance by the farmer. The end won't come at a random time. It is in our hands, graciously put there by a wise and loving Father.[403] The longer we deny this, and the more of us who believe "the end is near" – even though everything the Bible says God's mature sons and daughters will accomplish before then is still miserably unfinished – the further off final victory really is.

---

[399] Revelation 19:7

[400] Ephesians 4:13 NIV, emphasis added

[401] Ephesians 4:15 NIV

[402] Ephesians 4:14 NIV

[403] Of course, as His sits above time, He sees the end and knows when it will come. This is the mystery of the concept of eternity, and does not contradict this statement in any way.

I think God said "no one knows the day or the hour" because He does not want us wasting our time trying to figure it out. Where's the fruit in that? Had one of Noah's sons stopped building the ark, and instead focused his time on trying to predict when the flood would come, Noah would have rightly kicked him in the pants – "stop looking up at the clouds, get off your rear end and help us build this darn thing!" This is just like the angels said at the ascension, as Christ's disciples stood there gazing up: "Men of Galilee, why do you stand there looking at the sky?"[404] Christ had just given them the Great Commission, and here they were with their heads in the clouds. I pray angels today will visit our end-times forecasters and tell them the same thing: "Come on guys, get your heads out of the clouds – we've got work to do!".

--

I had a long conversation the other day with an intelligent, educated and devout Catholic fellow. He's always believed "the world could end at any moment," and finds this an odd source of comfort. He doesn't seem to care so much about predictions of when or how the end will come; instead, he actually *likes* not knowing. He said when he's tempted to do something bad, this belief helps keep him straight because, effectively, he doesn't want to get caught with his hand in the cookie jar. He also said he uses this as outreach of sorts to help set other people straight. It's like a cosmic game of musical chairs – the tune could end at any moment and you don't want to get caught without a chair. He would hear nothing to the contrary.

To me, this reveals a fundamental lack of understanding of salvation, repentance and God's judgment. I can relate.

---

[404] Acts 1:11, NIV

When I was a kid I thought if I died after sinning and before asking for forgiveness, I would go to hell. This simply isn't the case. Fact is, "If anyone is in Christ, he is a new creation."[405] Those who are all-in for Christ live in a *state* of grace.

Also, as I wrote in a previous chapter, when you're on God's path, you find everything everyone has ever truly desired: The fruit of the Spirit – "love, joy, peace, patience, kindness, goodness, faithfulness, gentleness, self-control."[406] One who lives a life full of this fruit knows it cannot be found anywhere else. As a result, temptation doesn't hold the weight it once did, and we certainly don't need the fear of a sudden judgment to keep us on track. Obedience is its own reward, and the loss of peace and joy when we stray is more than enough deterrent to keep us on the narrow path.

I understand this fellow's rationale. But that's the problem with it: It's *rationale*. I understand it because I used to try to make "rational" sense of God's Word, too. I felt I had to rationalize, justify and "make sense" of things in the Bible before I could embrace them. For example, "the Bible says not to commit adultery ... *and that makes sense* because of sexually transmitted diseases, the cultural benefits of monogamy, the strength of two-parent households, the emotional attachment of intimacy, blah blah blah." This kind of thinking is, I believe, what God considers "leaning on our own understanding" – and when we do this, we block Him from delivering on His promise of directing our path.[407] Eventually I came to realize that rationalizing God's Word is dangerous, because the enemy can take that train of thought

---

[405] 2 Corinthians 5:7
[406] Galatians 5:22-23 NASB
[407] Proverbs 3:5-6

and lead it straight to explaining away miracles, justifying the rejection of portions of Scripture, and ultimately questioning the deity of Christ. I can tell you this: When I finally went all-in and started taking the Word of God at face value – when I let God be God, and stopped trying to do His job – my whole life changed for the better, and my relationship with Him launched into levels I never thought possible.

Sure, it "makes sense" to think God is a distant judge, seeing who He can trip up in some cosmic game of musical chairs. No doubt, when we don't walk in the manifest fruit of the Spirit in our personal lives, this belief may give us a mental crutch to avoid temptation. But that's not what it's about. God says, "If you love me, keep my commandments,"[408] and that He doesn't give us a spirit of fear.[409] So as much as this fear-based, "the end-is-near" motivation may work for you, I'm sorry, but it's simply wrong, from every possible angle. If you are hesitant to let go of this theological crutch, let me encourage you – the truth will set you free.[410] Our God is a loving Father seeking to raise up mature sons and daughters to inherit His Kingdom. Walk in *this* truth and you won't need a crutch ever again!

--

There's one other issue that often comes up regarding predictions of the end. Folks often ask me, *what comes next? What will things look like after Christ's return?* The answer is easy: I don't know, but I know it will be good![411]

---

[408] John 14:15 NKJV
[409] 2 Timothy 1:7
[410] John 8:32 NIV
[411] Sure there are some things we know, about a "new Heaven and new earth," etc., but not many details are given to us, and to be honest, they really don't make much difference to me in the here and now. We've got a job to do!

Is Heaven for us going to be somewhere else, or will there be a "new heaven and new earth"[412] right here on this planet? What exactly will we be ruling over? Are there cosmic struggles beyond our frame of reference, or will we be living it up in the lap of eternal luxury?

This is sort of like Noah's wife asking him, "What comes after the flood? Where will the ark land? What will the world look like after the waters recede? What will we eat?"

I can just imagine Noah patiently replying, "I don't know, Honey. I'm just building an ark, and I'm trusting God with the rest."

What will Heaven look like? Where will it be? Exactly what treasures are we storing up there, and how will it be different for those who don't store up any?

I don't know. I'm just seeking first the Kingdom, and I'm trusting God with the rest!

--

So when is the end coming? Is it another 2,000 years away? I don't think so. Once the Body of Christ catches on to God's original intent and the role He created for us, learns how to walk under His headship, and rises up in our true identity as sons and daughters of the King of Kings, the devil can't stand long.

Once it dawns on the sons and daughters of God that the self-proclaimed "emperor" of this age is wearing no clothes – that satan and his demons are powerless in the face of mature, submitted, obedient Christ followers ... Once we abandon the old, losing tactics we stubbornly cling to out of

---

[412] 2 Peter 3:13, Revelation 21:1

religious traditionalism and the patterns of this world ...
Once we go all-in, to a man ... then the end will be near
indeed!

Jesus made it crystal clear: "Watch out that no one deceives
you. For many will come in my name, claiming, 'I am the
Messiah,' and will deceive many. You will hear of wars and
rumors of wars, but see to it that you are not alarmed. Such
things must happen, but the end is still to come. Nation will
rise against nation, and kingdom against kingdom. There
will be famines and earthquakes in various places. All these
are the beginning of birth pains."[413]

And so how will we know when it's near? Here's what Jesus
concluded: *"This gospel of the Kingdom[414] will be preached in
the whole world as a testimony to all nations, and then the
end will come."*[415]

I've shown that, starting with just one person, we can
conquer the world through discipleship in less than 39 years.
Now imagine it starts with 1000 ... 10,000 ... 100,000 ... 1
million ... or the 1 billion-plus people who claim to follow
Christ. We will indeed gain victory "like a bolt of lightning
from the east to the west!"[416]

**KEY POINTS: As long as the status quo of Christendom remains,
the end is nowhere near. When we get our act together, it will
come quickly.**

---

[413] Matthew 24:4-8 NIV
[414] Remember that the word for Kingdom is BASILEIA and means "royal power,
kingship, dominion and rule." This is a far greater Gospel than simply the
salvation message.
[415] Matthew 24:14 NIV (emphasis added)
[416] Matthew 24:27

Your beliefs become your thoughts. Your thoughts
become your words. Your words become your actions.
Your actions become your habits. Your habits become
your values. Your values become your destiny.

Mahatma Gandhi

Chapter 18 - The big question: What happens when the Body of Christ catches this vision?

I have endeavored to clearly and concisely present to you
what I believe is the overriding vision and purpose of God
as communicated throughout Scripture, and to minimize
unnecessary rabbit trails and stepped-on toes. This is no
Frankenstein theology, with a piece from here and another
from there. I'm not asking you to "just trust me" or make
any great theological leaps. Instead, I have included more
than 400 footnotes, so you can check all my references and
do the research for yourself.

And here is the long-lost vision of God that I have
endeavored to communicate: God created creation for one
purpose, to raise up sons and daughters with whom to share
His Kingdom for eternity. Everything we experience as we
live in creation is designed for this purpose. He cast His
utterly defeated and defanged enemy here for this purpose,
too: So we may grow stronger by fighting, beating and
humiliating him. God has planted the seeds of His "sons of

the Kingdom"[417] in this environment so that we may develop all the traits necessary to rule and reign with Him for eternity. This incubating ground is in fact so fertile that, the Bible says, even Jesus grew in wisdom and stature,[418] learned obedience and was made perfect[419] by His experiences here.

There is one very clear measurement, one goal we must accomplish, that God is using to determine when His sons and daughters have reached the maturity necessary to inherit His Kingdom. This one thing is so vital that Jesus said seven times in a row in the Book of Revelation that every portion of God's eternal inheritance is stored up for those who do this.[420] Later in that book He again made it crystal clear: He who does this one thing "will inherit all things."[421] Scripture also says seven times that Jesus is seated in Heaven waiting *until* this happens, and Paul said that God is giving gifts to men *until* it does. When this, God's original intent, is accomplished, it will usher in the end of creation as we know it, and God's sons and daughters who participate in this will inherit His eternal Kingdom.

What is God waiting for? What is the culmination of our purpose on earth, and will trigger the end of time? The Greek word is NIKAO, and it means "to conquer, to carry off the victory." And what is it we are to conquer? John, the writer of Revelation, made it clear: "Whoever is born of God NIKAOs the world."[422] Our God-given assignment on earth, if we choose to accept it, boils down to one thing, and one thing only: To bring God's Kingdom – His *royal power,*

---

[417] Matthew 13:38
[418] Luke 2:53
[419] Hebrews 5:8-9
[420] Revelation Chapters 2-3
[421] Revelation 21:7
[422] 1 John 5:4

dominion, kingship and rule – to earth as it is in Heaven. In doing so, we will make Jesus' enemies His footstool, and the Body of Christ will grow to the full stature of Christ on earth. We will once again walk in the everyday manifestation of God's power on earth, as the early church did in the book of Acts.

At the very beginning of creation, God gave this mandate to Adam: "Go and establish dominion." In talking to the heavenly host regarding His newly created race of men He said, "Let them rule." Adam forfeited this rightful place to the enemy. Jesus came to institute a spiritual regime change, and He opened the door for each of us to access the Father's presence, power and provision the same way He did. The keys to the Kingdom are now in our hands.

The only way to fully access the gifts of God and ultimately walk in victory is by personally going all-in, and then coming together as a Body, in unity, under the divine guidance and authority of God. When we are fully submitted to Christ as our Head, Satan cannot stand. He was not put on earth to beat us up, he was put here for us to beat him up – for our training and for his humiliation and punishment. We are not stuck in a war we cannot win; we are in a war we cannot lose.

The enemy is formidable and ruthless. He will defeat us at every step when we rely on our own senses and understanding. He wins when he can diminish our vision; that is, when he can cause us to question our identity as sons and daughters of the King, our purpose to conquer, and our victorious destiny. We give him footholds when we pursue earthly gain, give credence to tradition over God's living Word, and when we let petty differences and "offenses" divide the Body. Satan's dread is the inevitable unveiling of the unified, mature, victorious Bride of Christ; this is his one concern and the one thing he is fighting against.

Jesus is sitting at the right hand of the Father, waiting until we bring total victory. He will not get tired of waiting and violate His original plan! He will not jump in and do it for us simply because we haven't grown up and "got it" yet! God is patiently raising up sons and daughters to inherit His Kingdom, and Jesus will not return to rescue losers – He will return to rule with winners. The world as we know it will end when we as a Bride "make ourselves ready" for our eternal marriage to Christ; when we rise up as a Body and finally cross the finish line. The world will not end before then, or in any way other than victory for the Kingdom of God. "No one knows the day or the hour" this will happen *because this task was given to us, and we have free will.*

There is a prominent teaching that has taken root in the Body today that sucks away our identity as victorious sons and daughters and stands 100 percent in opposition to God's original intent for creation. This teaching is the modern, popular theology of the "end times" – including a specific period of "great tribulation" to come, the rising of a world-controlling "Antichrist," and the rescue of God's helpless people in a sudden "rapture." It is not deduced from Scripture, was not taught by the early church or the great Reformers, and was not conceived until the late 1500s. This teaching originated as a strategic effort by the Inquisition-era Catholic Council of Trent to develop a theological spin to undermine the Reformation. The adherents of this teaching vary greatly in their application of this theology, yet they all agree on one thing: *God's people will never deliver victory.* Instead, they believe Christ Himself, together with an army of angels, will return to do so; we will be but passive observers as Christ brings God's Kingdom to earth. As God continues to work all things toward the inevitable victory of His sons and daughters, it is certain the days of this false teaching are numbered, as He leads us to throw off the shackles of this deception and once again embrace our victorious destiny.

This book has demonstrated the mathematical fact that the primary way we, as a Body, have been approaching our work *for* God, victory is impossible. On the other hand, just one person under the headship of Christ, starting alone and without earthly resources – who follows the divine blueprint of authentic discipleship – can be used by God to carry off total victory over the planet in less than one generation. Each and every son and daughter of God carries the seed of global victory.

Noah *could have* refused to build the ark, and God would have raised up another man, and another, until He got His ark built. The first generation of Israelites, after leaving Egypt, *could have* chosen to cross the Jordan River and conquer the Promised Land, but they refused. The second generation *could have* turned around like the first … and God would have raised up another generation, and another, until He finally got His people where He wanted them. In the same way, God is calling our generation to rise up and make the sacrifices and embrace the obedience necessary to finally bring His Kingdom to earth as it is in Heaven. We can choose to be the Last Generation!

As I've traveled presenting this message, I've found it simply clicks with people, from all walks of life and all different "church" backgrounds. Not only that, I've found it to be the most powerful way to lead the lost to Christ. (Hardly surprising if you remember the seed we're supposed to plant is the *word of the Kingdom*, not just the

Good News of salvation, which is just a small part of it. We are designed by God to want to be part of a winning team!) I believe it is the message that ultimately will unify the Body of Christ, as it transcends generational, cultural and denominational differences.

My question for you is this, and I pray that you take time to dwell on it:

What will happen when all who claim Christ latch onto the Gospel of the Kingdom – God's original intent, His vision of victory for mankind ... when we embrace the fact that victory is possible in one generation, and our personal actions in obedience to His will have a direct impact on this outcome ... when we determine that *we* are the generation who will "cross the Jordan" into the promised Kingdom ... when we pull out all the stops, go all-in, and just go for it?

(I, for one, won't be buying any green bananas.)

KEY POINTS: When the body of Christ once again embraces God's vision and plans for His Kingdom, it will dramatically shift our paradigms and set us on the path to final victory.

What is essential in war is victory, not prolonged operations.

Sun Tzu – The Art of War

Chapter 19 – Marching Orders

If you've stuck with me through this book, I feel as if right now, at this point, we have come to the banks of a spiritual Jordan River, and together we are looking over at the land before us, our promised future in the Lord.

Right now *our Promised Land* is populated with scary giants, hostile clans, powerful warlords and formidable strongholds. Right now we are living like fugitives in a hostile wilderness – while *they* are dug in, battle-hardened, and dead set on keeping their territory.

My deepest prayer is that the message in this book calls to you like the voice of Joshua: "The land we passed through and explored is exceedingly good. If the LORD is pleased with us, He will lead us into that land, a land flowing with milk and honey, and will give it to us. Only do not rebel against the LORD. And do not be afraid of the people of the land, because we will swallow them up. Their protection is gone, but the LORD is with us. Do not be afraid of them."[423]

Yes, I am outnumbered by leaders, many more popular than I, who are equally emphatic: "We can't attack those people;

---

[423] Numbers 14:7-9 NIV

they are stronger than we are. The land we explored devours those living in it. All the people we saw there are of great size…. We seemed like grasshoppers in our own eyes, and we looked the same to them."[424][425]

My dear friends, God has given us the freedom of choice. And right now the choice is yours. Will you follow those fearful ones who would lead you to remain in the wilderness, or even back to captivity? Or will you cross over with the company of God's victorious sons and daughters, so that together we may walk in the power of God, carry off the victory over the world, and claim the inheritance He has set aside for the conquerors? Will you latch on to God's original intent, take Him up on His promises, follow Christ's example, seize this mandate, and help NIKAO the world?

If this generation does not embrace our identity, purpose and destiny in Christ, then God will raise up another. That is certain. If we chicken out like the first generation of Israelites who faced the Jordan, we will all surely die without fulfilling our God-given destiny – and He will lead a future generation to this same point, to make this same decision, and *they* will be the ones to fulfill His original intent.

Someday, the Body of Christ will choose to rise up as the Last Generation and cross over to victory. So I must cry out: Why *not* us? Why *not* now?

The line in the sand is clear: Either the Bible *is* the Word of God, Jesus *is* who He claimed to be, and His promises *are* true. Or not. If it *is* true, there is no disputing the fact that in Him *we are more than conquerors, victory is our destiny, our*

---

[424] Numbers 13:31-33
[425] I hate to say it, but it seems that many of our leaders, instead of counting the cost and leading us to conquer the promised land of milk and honey, would rather just stay in the wilderness and continue milking the sheep!

inheritance is stored up for those who NIKAO the world, and
*Jesus is seated in heavenly places waiting for His enemies to be
made His footstool.*

And so we each must decide: Will I go through the motions,
do it my way, wait to be rescued, and simply trust God with
my death? Or will I put my money where my mouth is, trust
Jesus with *my life*, take Him up on His promises – *and help
carry off the victory?*

Just as the Promised Land was to the Israelites, *this whole
world is ours for the taking!* When we are obedient to God, no
giants, no warlords, no walled strongholds – nothing the
enemy can throw at us – *nothing can stand in our way!*

--

Near the beginning of this book, I included the text of the
opening speech from the movie Patton. It is a fantastic
expression of the heart a winner, a real man who embraced
his victorious identity, purpose and destiny. With a few
minor changes, I believe this is the ideal sermon for right
now. *God, I pray for church leaders with the boldness to preach
like this, and for sons and daughters of the King to arise who will
be gripped by this mandate:*

> Now, I want you to remember that no man but
> Jesus ever won a war by dying for his cause, and
> He rose again! Instead, he won it by making the
> other poor dumb bastard die for his cause. Men,
> all this stuff you've heard about Christians not
> wanting to fight, wanting to stay out of the war, is
> a lot of horse dung.
>
> Christians traditionally love to fight. All real
> Christians love the sting of battle. When you were
> kids, you all admired hard-working Noah, young

David with his slingshot, mighty Sampson, brave Daniel facing a den of lions. Christians love a winner and will not tolerate a loser. Christians play to win all the time. I wouldn't give a hoot in hell for a man who lost and laughed. That's why Christians have never lost and will never lose a war. Because the very thought of losing is hateful to sons and daughters of the Living God.

Now, the Church is a team. It lives, eats, sleeps, fights as a team. Our divisiveness today is a bunch of crap. The bilious bastards who wrote that stuff about individuality for Sojourners Magazine don't know anything more about real battle than they do about fornicating.

We have the finest food and equipment, the best Spirit and the best men in the world. You know, by God I actually pity those poor demons we're going up against. By God, I do. We're not just going to resist the bastards, we're going to drag them under the feet of our glorious King. We're going to cast out those lousy demon bastards by the bushel.

Now, some of you folks, I know, are wondering whether or not you'll chicken out when you face fires and trials. Don't worry about it. I can assure you that you will all do your duty. Our battle is not against flesh and blood. Satan and his demons are the enemy. Wade into them. Spill *their* blood. Shoot *them* in the belly. When you see kids hooked on drugs, smut on television, families falling apart, and babies aborted by the millions, *you'll know what to do.*

Now there's another thing I want you to remember. I don't want to get any messages saying that we are holding our position or building another building. We're not holding anything this world has to offer. Let the unbelievers do that. We are advancing constantly and we're not interested in holding onto anything except the enemy. We're going to hold onto him by the nose and we're going to kick him in the ass. We're going to kick the hell out of him all the time and we're gonna go through him like crap through a goose.

There's one thing that you men will be able to say when you get back home to eternity. And you may thank God for it. Three hundred years from now when you're sitting on the throne of God with your grandson on your knee and he asks you what did you do in the great war to bring the Kingdom of God to earth, you won't have to say, "Well, I sat on a pew every Sunday for 52 years."

Alright now, you sons-of-God, you know how I feel. Oh, and I will be proud to lead you wonderful guys into battle – anytime, anywhere.

That's all.[426]

KEY POINTS: Like the Israelites on the banks of the Jordan, you are now confronted with two divergent views of our identity and destiny. Will you choose to conquer, or merely endure?

---

[426] Based on the opening scene from the movie *Patton*, produced in 1970 by Frank McCarthy, screenplay by Francis Ford Coppola and Edmund H. North.

Proclaim this among the nations: Prepare for war!
Rouse the warriors!
Let all the fighting men draw near and attack.
Beat your plowshares into swords
and your pruning hooks into spears.
Let the weakling say,
"I am strong!"
Come quickly, all you nations from every side,
and assemble there.
Bring down your warriors, LORD!
"Let the nations be roused;
let them advance into the Valley of Jehoshaphat,
for there I will sit
to judge all the nations on every side.
Swing the sickle,
for the harvest is ripe.
Come, trample the grapes,
for the winepress is full
and the vats overflow—
so great is their wickedness!"
Multitudes, multitudes
in the valley of decision!
For the day of the LORD is near
in the valley of decision.
(Joel 3:9-14, NIV)

What is my identity?

In Christ, I am an offspring of the Creator of the Universe, with full access to His presence and power. God sees me as His innocent child.

What is my purpose?

My purpose on this earth is, like Jesus, to grow in wisdom, stature and obedience, as I am being made perfect by my Father. To accomplish this, He has given me a specific place in the Body of Christ, and the job of advancing His Kingdom (royal power, kingship, dominion and rule) to every tribe and nation.

What is my destiny?

My destiny is victory on this earth, and ultimately to inherit His Kingdom in eternity, where I will sit on the throne with Jesus.

SUMMARY OF CHAPTER KEY POINTS

The Bible calls followers of Jesus Christ to conquer the world.

Winning requires 1) Knowing the objective of the competition at hand, 2) Having natural giftedness for the endeavor (akin to a sense of destiny), and 3) Being determined (embracing the identity of Winner).

God's objective is to establish His Kingdom on earth as it is in Heaven – which is one hundred percent. Christ came for this purpose, not to rescue people from earth.

God is waiting for His sons and daughters to embrace their true identity and rise up in their purpose to establish His dominion over the earth. This mandate was given to Adam, re-established by Christ, reinforced in the Revelation, and continually repeated throughout Scripture. He has chosen to do this through us so that in the process, we may develop the character and maturity necessary to rule with Him for eternity.

God has constrained Himself (and our enemy) to working through people. There is no neutral ground – we are either working for God or against Him. The choice is ours, and it's a hard one.

When the Kingdom of God is fully manifest on earth as it is in Heaven, there will be no more room for the enemy. All of God's children will live in a community of absolute love, peace and joy as modeled by the early church in Acts. God's miraculous power will be an integral part of our daily lives. Jesus Christ will be exalted as the King of all nations.

The Bible says the LORD is a warrior, and we are made in His image. We must learn to focus our inborn aggression towards our real enemy, the devil, and not our fellow man.

While it is our calling to establish the Kingdom of God on the earth, God is by no means a passive observer. On the contrary, He promises to give us step-by-step instructions and everything else we need to do the job. Victory will come only when we allow Him to call the shots and live a life of full submission to His will.

The most powerful force in the universe is the living Word of God. It is freely available to us. Things we do in our own strength are meaningless.

Victory will only be possible when we come together as a unified body, each playing our God-given part. God's vision of victory is key to our unity.

The other side is winning because we have allowed them to believe that they *can* win.

We are losing because we have not embraced our identity, purpose and destiny as winners, have refused to take God up on His promises, and have been caught up following the patterns of this world.

Modern teachings of the "end times" are blocking our path to victory. They rob us of our identity, distract us from our destiny, keep us tied up in knots, and make us look like kooks to those we are called to reach.

When the Body of Christ finally rises up and moves to establish God's Kingdom on earth, and the enemy makes his last stand, the conflict will be brutal and costly. We must view this in light of eternity. God is raising up warring sons and daughters, not wimps.

Our current strategies will never lead to victory. By returning to the strategy of Biblically-based, Christ-modeled discipleship, we can deliver victory over the planet in less than one generation.

Yes, we really can do this!

As long as the status quo of Christendom remains, the end is nowhere near. When we get our act together, it will come quickly.

When the body of Christ once again embraces God's vision and plans for His Kingdom, it will dramatically shift our paradigms and set us on the path to final victory.

Like the Israelites on the banks of the Jordan, you are now confronted with two divergent views of our identity and destiny. Will you choose to conquer, or merely endure?

AFTERWARD

Picture yourself sitting in the optometrist's chair getting a new prescription for corrective lenses. The doctor is flipping lenses back and forth in front of your eyes. "Which is clearer," he asks, "A or B ... A or B?" You must choose which one you will view the world through from now on. The difference between the two lenses couldn't be more profound. It's decision time, and the consequences of your choice will affect the rest of your life.

As you read this, the battle for your mind is raging. Two conflicting views of Scripture have been clearly established; one by me in this book, the other by the pop theology of today. One paints the picture of God's sons and daughters growing into maturity and unity until, under Christ's headship, they usher in God's Kingdom on earth as it is in Heaven. The other says that a hidden alarm clock is ticking in Heaven, and someday God will send Jesus and His angels to finish the job while His powerless sons and daughters sit by as passive spectators.

There is no middle ground: Both of these views can't be right. There is a line in the sand.

Through which prism will you choose to view God, the Bible, and your own identity, purpose and destiny? The one embraced, modeled and proclaimed by the first apostles and the early church, or the one cunningly contrived by Francisco Ribera in in the 1500s and amended by 15-year-old Margaret McDonald in 1830? The one that brings a unifying, comprehensive, overarching clarity to Scripture, or the one that is hammered together by taking snippets of verses from here and there, with a bunch of conjecture thrown in? The one that proclaims the inevitable supremacy of the Body of Christ, or the one built on belief in the inevitable supremacy of an Antichrist? The one that gives hope, passion, purpose and empowerment to Christ followers, or the one that tells them of their powerlessness in the last days?

Two boxers are in the ring. One knows he's a champion, imbued with all the strength and skill necessary to knockout the opponent, and that his victory is certain no matter how hard the opponent fights. The other just knows he's going to get clobbered, and his goal is simply to stay on his feet and make a good show till his manager decides to throw in the towel. Which identity do you believe Christ intends for you? Which identity do you choose to embrace?

Which does the enemy fear most: You choosing to believe in your Christ-given power over him, or you choosing to hunker down in the face of his might? You choosing to forcefully and confidently engage him in battle, or you choosing merely to "endure" his attacks? You seeking total victory over the kingdom of darkness, or you waiting for the "Rapture" to come any day now?

I know men who argue passionately and aggressively to defend their belief in the coming Antichrist and his inevitable reign of terror – and then in the next breath call me a heretic for believing the Body of Christ is destined for victory. Think about that. I am a heretic for seeing the message of victory and supremacy of Christ that is prevalent in scripture from Genesis to Revelation, while they are righteous for proclaiming the helplessness of the church and the right of "The Antichrist" to rule the world. That's what it comes down to. Now, whose side do you choose to take in this argument?

Indeed, what is your choice? Will you join those of us who

are fighting to manifest Christ's victory, or will you resign yourself to mere endurance till the end?

Remember: You will stand before God on the last day and give an account for your decision. Choose wisely.

APPENDIX I – A victorious view of the Book of Revelation

When presenting God's vision of victory, I am occasionally asked, "What about the Book of Revelation?" That's a fair and fine question, because the majority of "end times" teaching is supposedly based on this book. I answer this way: God's Word never contradicts itself. Everything I read in Revelation confirms the vision of a victorious Bride of Christ establishing God's Kingdom on earth.

Sadly, for too many generations, too many prognosticators and would-be prophets have looked into John's highly impressionistic portrait as if they were Nostradamus peering into his infamous pot of boiling oil, using the great apostle's writings to justify all sorts of kooky theories and crystal-ball-type fortunes. Equally sad, for too many generations, too many Christians have been all too eager to buy into these fantastic theories. If today's "end times" headline interpreters were stock pickers, they'd have gone broke years ago, or been thrown in jail with Bernie Madoff.

Mainly, these "end times" oracles engage in what I call "hindsight prophesy." That is, they look at an event that is already happening, then all of a sudden find it prophesied in the Revelation (or some obscure Old Testament prophetic text). The L.A. freeways? Of course, can't you see? That's what John was talking about here! The European Union? Didn't you know? The Bible predicted that 2,000 years ago! Just recently I saw a prominent TV preacher tell his enthralled audience the alliance between Russia and Iran to build a nuclear reactor was prophesied in the Bible. I'm not kidding! (If only he'd been decent enough to share this insight *before it happened*, maybe we could have done something about it!)

It seems every new development on the world scene, especially in the Middle East, was predicted, clear as mud, in Scripture, and we must continue to fund our favorite "hindsight prophet" to ensure he keeps us up-to-date on the latest developments. Without him we never could make sense of world events! When you realize what's happening, it's like reading the daily horoscope in your newspaper – they make all sorts of new predictions every day, yet no one ever seems to go back and check their track records. Folks just keep buying into them, regardless. I know just in the past 30 years since I've been aware of such things, every enemy of the US has supposedly played the role of Biblical bogeyman – from the Soviet Union, to Communist China, to al Qaida, to Iran, and now back to Russia, with countless stops in between. Remember when Mikhail Gorbachev's birthmark was the mark of the beast? Remember when one "hindsight prophet" said Ronald Reagan was the antichrist because the letters of his name, R-o-n-a-l-d W-i-l-s-o-n R-e-a-g-a-n, equaled 666? Most recently, many have said Barak Obama is the antichrist. Or is it Osama bin Laden? Or ... the leader of the European Union? Like the weather here in Texas, if you don't like today's interpretation of the Revelation, just wait a few days and it'll change. It ties us up in knots. Sadly, these professional "hindsight prophets" just move from headline to headline; their hindsight never applies to their own track record, and they never apologize for continually being wrong.

It is human nature to want to make sense of things. We develop theories and theologies that allow us to put things that are out of our comprehension into a pretty little box called our worldview. The people who can do this to our satisfaction are exalted. Darwin is a prime example. Many people want to believe there is no God. Yet when they look at creation, they see Him all around. Darwin gives them a neat package called "evolution" to explain it all. Every piece of evidence they see, they force into that box, and everything that doesn't fit, they ignore or attack. This same human compulsion gave us the rich tapestry of Greek mythology. Lightening? That's Zeus, of course! Our modern "hindsight prophets" operate in the same mode in their attempts to fit current events into the popular "Left Behind" theology. I am not picking on them; it is simply human nature – human nature for them to supply it, human nature for many to demand it. Those who have mastered the art of this current-events theological alchemy have always been able to achieve popularity and riches – from ancient oracles to modern evolutionary biologists, to American "end-times" teachers. It's human nature.

And like every other element of human nature, the enemy uses this against the Body of Christ. George Orwell wrote in the classic book 1984, "To keep a population in line, wage a perpetual war against a vague enemy." This is precisely what these "hindsight prophets" accomplish. They keep the Christian population in line – *in line for the enemy*. Sun Tzu said in The Art of War, "All warfare is based on deception. Hence, when we are able to attack, we must seem unable; when using our forces, we must appear inactive; when we are near, we must make the enemy believe we are far away; when far away, we must make him believe we are near." We can't fight something we can't understand, and since only these exalted, insightful "prophets" can properly make sense of world events, we'd better just sit down, shut up, listen to them, and keep sending our money. Unfortunately, all we're really buying with our money is more time for the enemy to enjoy a reprieve before entering eternal torment.

The Bible warns us about this. Jesus said: "Watch out that no one deceives you. For many will come in my name, claiming, 'I am the Christ,' and will deceive many. You will hear of wars and rumors of wars, but see to it that you are not alarmed. Such things must happen, but the end is still to come. Nation will rise against nation, and kingdom against kingdom. There will be famines and earthquakes in various places. All these are the beginning of birth pains.

"At that time if anyone says to you, 'Look, here is the Christ!' or, 'There he is!' do not believe it. For false Christs and false prophets will appear and perform great signs and miracles to deceive even the elect—if that were possible. See, I have told you ahead of time. So if anyone tells you, 'There he is, out in the desert,' do not go out; or, 'Here he is, in the inner rooms,' do not believe it."[427]

Thankfully God, through the Apostle Paul (who had a true gift of "foresight" prophecy!) promised us that we'd eventually have victory over these forces. In Ephesians, he says that once the Body of Christ unites in victory, "Then we will no longer be infants, tossed back and forth by the waves, and blown here and there by every wind of teaching and by the cunning and craftiness of men in their deceitful scheming."[428] I pray that the Body of Christ reclaims His vision of our victorious identity and destiny, so we can finally grow past this season of being blown around!

So no, I don't buy into the Nostradamus-type, ripped-from-the-headlines gobbledygook that today passes as legitimate interpretation of the Book of Revelation. I choose to view that book through the prism of the entirety of Scripture, which tells us that the Body of Christ will rise up and deliver victory. Remove that lens and you *do* need some imaginative

---

[427] Matthew 24:4-8, 23-26
[428] Ephesians 4:14 NIV

theology to make sense of it all. Thank God that with this lens it's not hard to decipher. Here are a few key points to understanding the Book of Revelation. Get these down, and you'll be able to debunk most of the pop-prophesy junk that's out there:

Despite too many Christians being conditioned to fear the Apocalypse, fact is this is something to look forward to. Apocalypse means "Unveiling" in Greek – as in the unveiling of the Bride of Christ. In light of a victorious church, the only one who needs to fear this is the enemy!

In the Spirit, John was taken into the throne room of God and shown many remarkable things. It is vital to understand he was taken into the realm of the eternal, which stands apart from the time/space continuum. Time/space was created by God for us to live in, for the fulfillment of His divine purposes. He is not bound by it! The view that eternity is "a long, long time" is primitive. Instead, as we understand it today, eternity is the absence of time. Everything is current in eternity. This mind-bending reality is evident in Paul's statement to Timothy that "grace was given us in Christ Jesus before the beginning of time."[429] Understanding this, it is dangerously naïve to attempt to put the things recorded in the Revelation in any kind of rigorous chronological order. In God's realm, it's always now – past, present and future is all the same for Him. Since writing is linear, John had to take the things he saw and write them down in some order, but there is no logical reason to assume

---

[429] 2 Timothy 1:9 NIV

they are sequenced on a linear timeline.[430]

In his vision, John was shown things that are invisible to our flesh eyes; he was seeing the invisible, spirit realm. Many of the activities in the Revelation occur in this realm. Much of the book itself is addressed *to angels and not to men*. (Each of the seven letters in Chapters Two and Three is addressed "To the Angel of the church in...") I have no doubt John painted as clear a picture of what he saw as any man in the First Century could have done. I believe his descriptions are more literal than even the most fanatical Revelation interpreter would like to admit – meaning, the dragon may well be just that: a demonic being that looked to John like a dragon, *and not a metaphor for some human bogeyman*. The occurrences so vividly described may well be raging right now in the heavenlies and we just can't see them. Every "end times" teacher I've ever heard takes every word in the Revelation to be merely a metaphorical description of an occurrence in the natural realm. This is a huge, unsubstantiated and indefensible leap of logic. It is inductive reasoning at its finest.[431]

In the letters to the angels of the seven churches, concluding each of the letters Jesus makes a stunning promise "to him who NIKAO (conquers, carries off the victory)...." This is

---

[430] For example, if you look at the infamous Four Horsemen of the Apocalypse found in Revelation 6, you can easily deduce that these are not sequential but concurrent. The white horse represents political power, the red horse war, the black horse commerce, and the pale horse death. There is no doubt at all that all four of these forces are all at work in the world at the same time, and have been from the beginning. For an interpreter to attempt to say these are chronologically separated, and able to be identified with a specific person or earthly power, is in my opinion akin to theological malpractice.

[431] Inductive reasoning starts with a conclusion – in this case, Ribera's Futurism – and then looks for "evidence" to support it.

one of the most repeated phrases in all of Scripture and a key part of the Revelation. Christ repeats these words over and over to drive the point home: This Book is all about God's people delivering victory. Quite a bit else in the Revelation may be up for interpretation but this point is indisputable.

If you read the book thoroughly, you'll find corresponding to virtually every description of some kind of torment or tribulation, it clearly states that God's people will be taken care of. He will not turn His back on us, ever! This is another consistent element that is not open for interpretation.[432]

There is no doubt that our final push to bring the Kingdom of God to earth will be met with the fiercest resistance in the history of the universe. As the forces of darkness make their last stand, it will make the cliffs of Normandy and beaches of Iwo Jima look like a walk in the park. Imagine if Gen. Eisenhower's chaplain had seen a vivid, impressionistic revelation of D-Day, and communicated it to him. If the chaplain were a modern "end times" teacher, no doubt he'd have moaned and wailed about how unmercifully the Allies were pinned down on the beach, how we were massacred so badly the ocean turned to blood (he may have even found it "prophesied" in the Book of Revelation!). Had Ike listened to his doom-and-gloom fear-mongering, we may well be speaking German right now! Yes, D-Day was bloody and brutal. Yes, it was a tribulation. Yet *we chose* to attack. *We initiated it and faced it willingly as victors – not helplessly as*

---

[432] In addition to all the promised rewards for the victorious in Chapters 2 and 3, check out these verses in Revelation: 5:9-10, 7:14-17, 11:15, 11:18, 12:10-12, 13:8-10, 14:6-7, 14:12-16, 15:3-4, 17:8, 17:14, 18:4-8, 18:20, 19:6-10, 20:4, and pretty much all of Chapters 21-22. God's people have nothing to fear! Don't give any credence to the popular doom and gloom prophecies – victory is our identity and destiny, throughout the entire Bible.

victims! We prevailed, *and we set the nations free.* The Revelation is a book of victory, from beginning to end, in full harmony with the victorious message of the rest of Scripture. I would not have wanted to be Hitler on D-Day, nor would I want to be satan during any coming tribulation – because the victory of the sons and daughters of God is certain. We are more than conquerors!

"The agency of man" is clearly spelled out in the Revelation. We are not like cosmic plankton, blown around by every current in the spirit realm. In the first part of Chapter Eight, John describes how the prayers of the saints on earth are taken up to God in a golden censer. The angel then takes that vessel, fills it with fire from the altar and hurls it back down to earth.[433] This paints a beautifully clear picture of the power of prayer – we offer it up to God, and He returns it to earth full of His power. In Rev. 19:15, it says Jesus strikes down the enemy with the "sharp sword" that comes out of His mouth. As we know, the Sword of the Spirit, according to the Apostle Paul, is the RHEMA of God.[434] Indeed, it does come out of Christ's mouth – *as He directs our path to advance His Kingdom.* Additionally, in Rev 19:7, it says that when we achieve victory, "Let us rejoice and be glad and give him glory! For the wedding of the Lamb has come, and *his bride has made herself ready.*" Of course, the bride here is the Church ... and her *"making herself ready"* hardly sounds like we are passive players in this whole thing.

In conclusion, an honest and credible interpretation of the Book of Revelation fully advances the message of Kingdom victory, and has no legitimate pegs for today's "end times"

---

[433] Revelation 8:3-5
[434] Ephesians 6:17. RHEMA is the personal, relationship Word of God, clearly distinguished from GRAPHOS, which is the word for Scripture.

teachers to hang their theological hats on. Because John was taken to the eternal/spiritual realm, and because there is no claim otherwise, it is impossible for an honest interpreter to successfully argue that everything in the Revelation is able to be tracked chronologically, or will be directly tied to anything in the natural/visible realm. The only crystal clear points in the book are: 1) that the followers of Christ will eventually conquer/carry off the victory, 2) "the agency of man" – meaning God is constraining Himself to work through mankind to accomplish His objectives, 3) God never turns His back on His people – they are always protected, and 4) we win in the end – we have a victorious destiny!

APPENDIX II: Late great hymns of victory

These hymns were popular with previous generations, before modern "end times" teachings took hold. How far we've fallen! Read them and I believe you'll see what I mean. I long for a day when Christians once again join their voices in these verses of victory.

Stand Up, Stand Up for Jesus – *George Duffield, Jr., 1818-1888*

Stand up, stand up for Jesus,
ye soldiers of the cross;
lift high his royal banner,
it must not suffer loss.
From victory unto victory
his army shall he lead,
till every foe is vanquished,
and Christ is Lord indeed.

Stand up, stand up for Jesus,
the trumpet call obey;
forth to the mighty conflict,
in this his glorious day.
Ye that are brave now serve him
against unnumbered foes;
let courage rise with danger,
and strength to strength oppose.

Stand up, stand up for Jesus,
stand in his strength alone;
the arm of flesh will fail you,
ye dare not trust your own.
Put on the gospel armor,
each piece put on with prayer;
where duty calls or danger,
be never wanting there.

Stand up, stand up for Jesus,
the strife will not be long;
this day the noise of battle,
the next the victor's song.
To those who vanquish evil
a crown of life shall be;
they with the King of Glory
shall reign eternally.

Am I a Soldier of the Cross – *Isaac Watts, 1674-1748*

Am I a soldier of the cross,
a follower of the Lamb,
and shall I fear to own his cause,
or blush to speak his name?

Must I be carried to the skies
on flowery beds of ease,
while others fought to win the prize,
and sailed through bloody seas?

Are there no foes for me to face?
Must I not stem the flood?
Is this vile world a friend to grace,
to help me on to God?

Sure I must fight, if I would reign;
increase my courage, Lord.
I'll bear the toil, endure the pain,
supported by thy word.

Thy saints in all this glorious war
shall conquer though they die;
they see the triumph from afar,
by faith they bring it nigh.

When that illustrious day shall rise,
and all thy armies shine
in robes of victory through the skies,
the glory shall be thine.

Rise Up, O Men of God – *William P. Merrill, 1867-1954*

Rise up, O men of God!
Have done with lesser things.
Give heart and mind and soul and strength
to serve the King of kings.

Rise up, O men of God!
The kingdom tarries long.
Bring in the day of brotherhood
and end the night of wrong.

Rise up, O men of God!
The church for you doth wait,
her strength unequal to her task;
rise up, and make her great!

Lift high the cross of Christ!
Tread where his feet have trod.
As brothers of the Son of Man,
rise up, O men of God!

Onward Christian Soldiers – *Sabine Baring-Gould, 1834-1924*

Onward, Christian soldiers, marching as to war,
With the cross of Jesus going on before.
Christ, the royal Master, leads against the foe;
Forward into battle see His banners go!

At the sign of triumph Satan's host doth flee;
On then, Christian soldiers, on to victory!
Hell's foundations quiver at the shout of praise;
Brothers lift your voices, loud your anthems raise.

Like a mighty army moves the church of God;
Brothers, we are treading where the saints have trod.
We are not divided, all one body we,
One in hope and doctrine, one in charity.

What the saints established that I hold for true.
What the saints believ-ed, that I believe too.
Long as earth endureth, men the faith will hold,
Kingdoms, nations, empires, in destruction rolled.

Crowns and thrones may perish, kingdoms rise and wane,
But the church of Jesus constant will remain.
Gates of hell can never gainst that church prevail;
We have Christ's own promise, and that cannot fail.

Onward then, ye people, join our happy throng,
Blend with ours your voices in the triumph song.
Glory, laud and honor unto Christ the King,
This through countless ages men and angels sing.

GLOSSARY OF GREEK WORDS, in order of first appearance

Abridged definitions, taken from Thayer and Smith King James Version Greek Lexicon (unless otherwise noted), as found at www.BibleStudyTools.com.

NIKAO (nik-ah'-o) *Strong's number 3528*: To conquer; to carry off the victory, come off victorious.
Usage in the KJV: overcome 24, conquer 2, prevail 1, get the victory 1

BASILEIA (bas-il-i'-ah) *Strong's number 932*: Royal power, kingship, dominion, rule. A kingdom, the territory subject to the rule of a king.
Usage in KJV: kingdom (of God) 71, kingdom (of heaven) 32, kingdom (general or evil) 20, (Thy or Thine) kingdom 6, His kingdom 6, the kingdom 5, (My) kingdom 4, miscellaneous 18

HUIOS (hwee-os') *Strong's number 5207*: A son; in a wider sense, a descendant, one of the posterity of any one.
Usage in KJV: son(s) 85, Son of Man + (444)&version=kjv 87 {TDNT 8:400, 1210}, Son of God + (2316) 49, child(ren) 49, Son 42, his Son + (848) 21, Son of David + (1138) 15 {TDNT 8:478, 1210}, my beloved Son + (27) + 3350 7, thy Son + (4575) 5, only begotten Son + (3339) 3, his (David's) son + (846) 3, firstborn son + (4316) 2, miscellaneous 14

EXOUSIA* (ex-oo-see'-ah) *Strong's number 1849*: Privilege, i.e. (subjectively) force, capacity, competency, freedom, or (objectively) mastery (concretely, magistrate, superhuman, potentate, token of control), delegated influence: authority, jurisdiction, liberty, power, right, strength.
Usage in KJV: authorities 7, authority 65, charge 1, control 1, domain 2, dominion 1, jurisdiction 1, liberty 1, power 11, powers 1, right 11

DUNAMIS (doo'-nam-is) *Strong's number 1411*: Strength power, ability; the power and influence which belong to riches and

wealth; power and resources arising from numbers; power consisting in or resting upon armies, forces, hosts.
Usage in KJV: power 77, mighty work 11, strength 7, miracle 7, might 4, virtue 3, mighty 2, miscellaneous 9

OURANOS (oo-ran-os') *Strongs number 3772*: The vaulted expanse of the sky with all things visible in it the universe, the world; the aerial heavens or sky, the region where the clouds and the tempests gather, and where thunder and lightning are produced; the sidereal or starry heavens; the region above the sidereal heavens, the seat of order of things eternal and consummately perfect where God dwells and other heavenly beings.
Usage in KJV: heaven 268, air 10, sky 5, heavenly + (1537)

EKKLESIA (ek-klay-see'-ah) *Strong's number 1577*: A gathering of citizens called out from their homes into some public place, an assembly; an assembly of the people convened at the public place of the council for the purpose of deliberating.
Usage in KJV: church 115, assembly 3

LOGOS (log'-os) *Strong's number 3056*: A word, uttered by a living voice, embodies a conception or idea;
what someone has said; decree, mandate or order; reason, the mental faculty of thinking, meditating, reasoning, calculating.
Usage in KJV: word 218, saying 50, account 8, speech 8, Word (Christ) 7, thing 5, not translated 2, miscellaneous 32

GRAPHE (graf-ay') *Strong's number 1124*: A writing, thing written; the Scripture, used to denote either the book itself, or its contents; a certain portion or section of the Holy Scripture.
Usage in KJV: scripture 51

RHEMA (hray'-mah) Strong's number 4487: That which is or has been uttered by the living voice, thing spoken, word; any sound produced by the voice and having definite meaning; speech, discourse; what one has said; a series of words joined together into a sentence (a declaration of one's mind made in words); an utterance.

Usage in KJV: word 56, saying 9, thing 3, no thing + (3756)&version=kjv 1, not translated 1

KOINONIA (koy-nohn-ee'-ah) *Strong's number 2842*: Fellowship, association, community, communion, joint participation, intercourse; the share which one has in anything, participation; intercourse, fellowship, intimacy.

Usage in KJV: fellowship 12, communion 4, communication 1, distribution 1, contribution 1, to communicate 1

DIAKONIA* (dee-ak-on-ee'-ah) *Strong's number 1248*: Waiting at table.

Usage in KJV: ministries 1, ministry 19, mission 1, preparations 1, relief 1, serve 1, service 7, serving 2, support 1.

HARPAZO (har-pad'-zo) *Strong's number 726*: To seize, carry off by force; to seize on, claim for one's self eagerly; to snatch out or away.

Usage in KJV: catch up 4, take by force 3, catch away 2, pluck 2, catch 1, pull 1

THLIPSIS (thlip'-sis) *Strong's number 2347*: A pressing, pressing together, pressure.

Usage in KJV: tribulation 21, affliction 17, trouble 3, anguish 1, persecution 1, burdened 1, to be afflicted + (1519)&version=kjv 1

APOKALUPSIS (ap-ok-al'-oop-sis) *Strong's number 602*: A disclosure of truth, instruction concerning things before unknown; manifestation, appearance.

Usage in the KJV: revelation 12, be revealed 2, to lighten + (1519)&version=kjv 1, manifestation 1, coming 1, appearing 1

*Definition taken directly from Strong's Concordance, not from Thayer and Smith.

Get the UPRISING Group Study Guide
Visit www.ChristianUprising.org

Were you moved by this book? Want to share it?

Take a look at our Group Study Edition. This version includes the complete book plus a 12-week group study curriculum, integrated into one simple package.

Available resources include a Leader's Guide, videos for each section, promotional tools, online community and more.

This is perfect for church and ministry leadership teams, home group/small group studies, Sunday Schools, youth ministries, business roundtables – really, any group who meets together and seeks to experience more of God's power and love in their lives.

The message of UPRISING is the message of revival. Cultivate it in your group, and then watch what God will do!

From author Mike Arnold:

> "Over the years, we found that virtually every pastor or ministry leader who read UPRISING wanted to share the message, and so they'd turn around and buy a dozen or more copies to give away. Problem is, when you give away books, they usually sit on desks collecting dust! That's why we developed the Group Study Edition. Instead of handing someone a book, now you can invite them to join you in reading and discussing it. If you think the book is powerful, wait till you read it together with your small group. The impact you'll experience is simply amazing!"

About the author

Mike Arnold is a missionary, entrepreneur and adventurer. He's stared down a charging hippo in Tanzania, and caught giant squid in the Sea of Cortez and a crocodile in the Amazon. Seriously!

He once stood on the spot where William "Braveheart" Wallace was executed. He traveled by dugout canoe and slept in grass huts in the Mosquito Coast jungle to preach the gospel to natives who had never seen an outsider. And he sipped a soda in the lounge where Princess Diana had her last drink.

When he was 28, Mike founded a broadcast television network that was called "the most sophisticated television production facility in the world." Over the years, Mike has spent quality time with presidents, governors, billionaires and CEOs.

Mike's passion is helping people reach their full potential in Christ, as they see and latch onto God's amazing (and long-lost) vision for mankind, and their own special place in it. He's reached the lost everywhere from grade schools and college campuses to Third World prisons, orphanages, villages and a Nigerian leper colony. He built from scratch a coast-to-coast youth discipleship ministry and has baptized hundreds. One year he baptized 14 high school boys and girls in a horse trough.

Mike has an MBA from the University of Texas at San Antonio. He's led international leadership conferences, spoken in countless churches, and has spent many hours on live TV and radio. He's produced network TV shows, and is a producer of the most award-winning Christian film in history.

A country boy at heart, he lives on a small ranch in Texas with his wife and kids, where they raise chickens and horses, cure their own bacon, and make their own mustang grape wine.

Mike is available for select speaking and consulting engagements.

Contact Mike through www.MikeArnoldMinistries.org.

www.ingramcontent.com/pod-product-compliance
Lightning Source LLC
Chambersburg PA
CBHW071950040426
42447CB00009B/1299